MARGINALITY AND DIFFERENCE IN EDUCATION AND BEYOND

MARGINALITY AND DIFFERENCE IN EDUCATION AND BEYOND

edited by Michael Reiss, Renée DePalma and Elizabeth Atkinson

Trentham Books

Stoke on Trent, UK and Sterling, USA

Trentham Books Limited
Westview House   22883 Quicksilver Drive
734 London Road   Sterling
Oakhill   VA 20166-2012
Stoke on Trent   USA
Staffordshire
England ST4 5NP

First published 2007

British Library Cataloguing-in-Publication Data
A catalogue record for this book is available from the
British Library

ISBN: 978-1-85856-412-8

Designed and typeset by Trentham Print Design Ltd, Chester and
printed in Great Britain by Hobbs the Printers Ltd, Hampshire.

Contents

Introduction

Michael Reiss, Renée DePalma
and Elizabeth Atkinson

nterrogation of marginality and difference has never been more central to an understanding of education and its reform than it is at present. This collection of writing focuses on these issues and arises from a seminar series entitled *Discourses of Difference Within and Beyond Education*, co-hosted by the University of Sunderland and the Institute of Education, University of London in 2004 and 2005. We are grateful to all those who participated in the seminar series and to those who kindly agreed to rework their material for this volume. They have enabled us to produce a book with three key themes:

- current policy and practice in education and educational research

- educational imperialism and its legacy

- cultures and sub-cultures within and beyond educational contexts

In Part One, *Educational policy and practice: internal colonisations*, the opening chapter by John Storey identifies the contribution cultural studies can make to an understanding of educational and social processes, focusing particularly on the importance of understanding the production and circulation of meaning within educational and social policy and practice. This focus on meaning at the macro level is followed by Elizabeth Atkinson's presentation of a range of voices expressing meanings at the micro level, which are all too often silenced or unheard in the contexts within which the policies which shape educational experience are formed. Atkinson's focus on the personal is complemented by David Gough who argues for the value of a large scale systematic review of educational research findings as a means of democratising the educational process and giving voice to those whose voices are not otherwise heard.

Maddalena Taras explores prevailing metaphors of assessment to demonstrate both the dominance of one pattern of ideas and the close links between formative and summative assessment. Michael Reiss also focuses on metaphors, this time in the context of science education, with a particular emphasis on the language and imagery employed within sex and reproduction education and their implications for notions of gender identity. In the final chapter in Part One Carrie Paechter also looks at gender identity, exploring artificial binaries between masculinity and femininity and their consequences for practices of equality.

Each of the above chapters explores what might be described as the internal colonisation of education by a certain set of hegemonic ideas and practices which the authors in this book set out collectively to resist. However the focus of the book turns in Part Two, *Educational imperialism and its legacy*, to external imperialism within education. Ruby Greene interrogates the inappropriateness of westernised sex education as a means of HIV/AIDS prevention in the Caribbean where powerful messages conveyed through popular culture such as Calypso perpetuate established patterns of multiple sexual partnerships and transactional sex. Jennifer Lavia's focus is also on the Caribbean, this time exploring the stranglehold of western academic practice both over approaches to educational research and her chosen research focus: educational policy and practice in the immediate post-colonial era.

Lavia's struggle to find a channel for the voice of the marginalised and colonised is echoed by Renée DePalma who explores the difficulties of addressing diversity issues with monocultural groups of trainee teachers and the added difficulties when such groups occasionally include just one representative of the Other. In the final chapter in this section, Ahmad Nazari explores the ideology inherent within textbooks for Iranian high school students learning English as a foreign language, both in terms of the representation of non-negotiable, ready made meanings which carry implicit messages about what constitutes valid educational practice and in the representation of specific classed and gendered identities which are not open to negotiation within the use and interpretation of the texts.

In *Part Three, Culture and subculture within and beyond education*, notions of space, place and identity are interwoven with linguistic, symbolic and material cultural markers. Takako Takano compares notions of land held by rural residents of an Inuit community and communities in rural Scotland, focusing in particular on notions of respect and their diverse symbolic interpretations. In contrast, Stephen Dobson focuses on urban living and on the need for an urban pedagogy that takes a deep account of the particularities of urban experience. In the penultimate chapter Deborah Youdell analyses pupil sub-cultures and their classed and gendered constructions of identity in a London secondary school, drawing on analyses of markers such as dress, language, musical preference and group labelling. Finally, Stephen Ball interrogates the class markers which can divide middle-class sub-groups within London, exploring the ways in which these class fractions isolate and insert themselves and their children differently into education and other aspects of the social fabric.

While the contexts of these analyses are diverse, the three themes bind the contributions together into a whole which offers important insights into educational processes in specific social and cultural contexts and suggests lessons to be learnt for all involved in education.

PART ONE:
Educational policy and practice: internal colonisation

1

Culture and hegemony

John Storey

The focus of this chapter is culture, power and difference from the perspective of cultural studies. My intention is to strip cultural studies to some of its basic assumptions and in so doing to attempt to link its project to the themes of this book.

Cultural studies works with an inclusive definition of culture. Rather than study only what Matthew Arnold (2006, p6) famously called 'the best which has been thought and said', cultural studies (at least in theory) is committed to examining what Raymond Williams refers to as 'all forms of signification' (1984, p210). This is a rejection of the Arnoldian and Leavisite mapping of the cultural field (see Storey, 2006a). The Leavisites, influenced by Arnold's idea of culture, divided the cultural field into minority culture and mass civilisation (see Leavis, 2006).

According to Arnoldian/Leavisite mapping, culture belongs to a minority; it involves the values and standards of great art and more importantly the ability to appreciate the standards and values of great art. Mass civilisation, on the other hand, is the commercial entertainment of the supposedly uneducated masses. Whereas culture demands serious consideration, the texts and practices of mass civilisation require only a fleeting sociological glance, which is just long enough to condemn the culture of the so-called masses.

Against the Leavisite division of the cultural field into the minority culture of an elite and the mass civilisation of the masses, Williams (2006, p32) proposed what he called the social definition of culture, in which culture is a description of a particular way of life, which expresses certain meanings and values not only in art and learning but also in institutions and ordinary behaviour. The analysis of culture, from such a definition, is the clarification of the meanings and values implicit in a particular way of life. Such analysis will include ... analysis of elements in the way of life that to followers of the other definitions are not 'culture' at all: ... the characteristic forms through which members of the society communicate. (originally published in 1961)

This definition is crucial to the development of cultural studies for two reasons. First, it broadens the definition of culture. Instead of culture being defined only as a series of elite cultural texts and practices such as ballet, opera, the novel, poetry, it can be redefined to include pop music, television, cinema, advertising, and going on holiday, for example. Second, and perhaps more importantly, Williams's definition links culture to meanings. The importance of a particular way of life is that it 'expresses certain meanings and values'. In addition, cultural analysis from the perspective of this definition of culture 'is the clarification of the meanings and values implicit in a particular way of life'. The emphasis in discussions of this passage is always on a particular way of life, but in my view, the idea of cultures as networks of meanings, that is culture as a 'realised signifying system' (Williams, 1981, p209), makes a far more significant contribution to British cultural studies. Moreover, culture as a realised signifying system is not reducible to a particular way of life, but it is fundamental to the shaping and holding together of *all ways of life*.

This is not to reduce everything to culture as a realised signifying system but to insist that culture defined in this way should be seen 'as essentially involved in all forms of social activity' (p13). As Williams explains, 'the social organisation of culture, as a realised signifying system, is embedded in a whole range of activities, relations and institutions, of which some are manifestly 'cultural'' (p209). Cultural analysis from the perspective of this definition of culture, 'is the clarification of the meanings and values implicit in a particular way of life'. While there is more to life than signifying systems, 'it would ... be wrong to suppose that we can ever usefully discuss a social system without including, as a central part of its practice, its signifying systems, on which, as a system, it fundamentally depends' (p207). In other words, signification is fundamental to all human activities. Nevertheless, while culture as a realised signifying system is 'deeply present' (p209) in all social activities, it remains the case that 'other quite different human needs and actions are substantially and irreducibly present' (*ibid*). In certain social activities signification becomes dissolved into what he calls 'other needs and actions' (*ibid*). By building on this cultural studies defines culture as the production, circulation, and consumption of meanings. As Stuart Hall (1997, p2) explains,

> Culture ... is not so much a set of *things* – novels and paintings or TV programmes and comics – as a process, a set of *practices*. Primarily, culture is concerned with the production and exchange of meanings – the 'giving and taking of meaning' – between the members of a society or group.

According to this definition, cultures do not so much consist of, say, books, but are the shifting networks of signification in which books are made to exist as meaningful objects. For example, if I pass a business card to someone in China, the polite way to do it is with two hands. If I pass it with one hand I may cause offence. This is clearly a matter of culture. However, the 'culture' is not so much in the gesture, but in the meaning of the gesture. In other words, there is nothing essentially polite about using two hands, but using two hands has been made to signify politeness. Nevertheless, signification has become embodied in a material practice, which can produce material effects.

To share a culture, according to this preliminary definition, is to interpret the world, make it meaningful and experience it as meaningful in recognisably similar ways. So-called culture shock happens when we encounter a radically different network of meanings, when our 'natural' or 'common sense' is confronted by someone else's 'natural' or 'common sense'. However, cultures are never simply shifting networks of shared meanings. On the contrary, cultures are always both shared and contested networks of meanings. Culture is where we share and contest meanings of ourselves, of each other and of the social worlds in which we live.

Cultural studies draws two conclusions from this way of thinking about culture. First, although the world exists in all its enabling and constraining materiality outside culture, it is only in culture that the world can be *made to mean*. This is to posit a distinction between the real and reality. Culture constructs the realities it appears only to describe. Signification has a performative effect; it helps to construct the realities it appears only to describe. Ernesto Laclau and Chantal Mouffe (1979, 2001, 2006) have had a significant influence on cultural studies in Britain, especially through their impact on the work of Stuart Hall. They use the word discourse in much the same way as I am using the word culture. According to Laclau and Mouffe (2006),

> If I kick a spherical object in the street or if I kick a ball in a football match, the *physical* fact is the same, but *its meaning* is different. The object is a football only to the extent that it establishes a system of relations with other objects, and these relations are not given by the mere referential materiality of the objects, but are, rather, socially constructed. This systematic set of relations is what we call discourse. (p159)

Whereas cultural studies tends to call these systematic relations culture, both positions share the view that to stress the discursive or the cultural is not to deny the materiality of the real. Again, according to Laclau and Mouffe,

> the discursive character of an object does not, by any means, imply putting its *existence* into question. The fact that a football is only a football as long as it is integrated within a system of socially constructed rules does not mean that it ceases to be a physical object. (*ibid*)

In other words, objects exist independently of their discursive or cultural articulation but it is only within discourse or culture that they can exist as meaningful objects in meaningful relations. As Williams (1979) makes clear, 'the natural world exists whether anyone signifies it or not' (p67). But the natural or the material world only ever exists for us layered in signification.

The second conclusion that cultural studies draws from this way of thinking about culture is the inevitability of a struggle over meaning. Because different meanings can be ascribed to the same 'text', meaning-making is always a potential site of struggle and negotiation. For example, masculinity has real material conditions of existence ('biological') but there are different ways of representing masculinity in culture ('being masculine'). Although masculinity might appear to some to be fixed by its biological conditions of existence (for a discussion of the problems with this assumption, see Butler, 1999), what it means, and the struggle over what it *means*, always takes place *in* culture. This is not simply a question of semantic difference, of interpreting the world differently, it is about relations of culture and power, about who can claim the power and authority to define social reality – to *make the world mean* in particular ways. The making of meaning is always entangled in what Valentin Volosinov (1973) would call the politics of 'multi-accentuality'. Rather than being inscribed with a single meaning, a text can be articulated with different 'accents'. It can be *made to mean* different things in different contexts with different effects of power. For example, as the Four Tops (1992) sing,

Now it's the same old song
But with a different meaning since you've been gone

'It's the same old song' tells the story of how a song that once signified a loving relationship has come to signify only pain and regret. Nothing about the materiality of the song has changed – it's the same old song. But what has changed is the context in which the song is heard and made meaningful – with a different meaning since you've been gone. A text is not the issuing source of meaning but a site where the articulation of meaning, variable meaning(s), can be produced in specific contexts. Too often cultural critics confuse the difference between meaning and materiality, confusing a text's specific materiality (words on the page) with its meaning (how a reader makes sense of the words on the page); that is, how the words can be 'performed', using a range of different 'accents'. We implicitly recognise this whenever we refer to a feminist reading, a marxist reading, a queer reading, or a post-colonial reading. In each instance, the intertextuality of the text is confronted by the intertextuality of the reader. One text is read in the light of other texts. In this way, the 'symbolic work' of consumption is never a simple repetition of the semiotic certainties of the lecture theatre and seminar room.

Cultural studies has always been interested in the consumption practices of everyday life. Inevitably, this takes it beyond an interest in the *meaning* of a 'text'; meaning as something 'essential', inscribed and guaranteed. Rather, the focus is on the range of meanings that a 'text' makes possible; its 'social' meanings, how it is appropriated and used in the consumption practices of everyday life. This point is often missed in critiques of ethnography. Cultural studies ethnography is not a means to verify the 'true' meaning or meanings of a 'text'. Ethnographic investigation is undertaken as a means to discover the meanings people make, the meanings which circulate and become embedded in the lived cultures of people's everyday lives. Rather than engage in a fruitless quest for the true meaning of something, cultural studies fixes its critical gaze on how particular meanings acquire their authority and power. For example, over the last four years I have been doing research on opera (Storey, 2002, 2003b, 2006c): my critical focus has not been on opera as a body of texts and practices; rather, I have focused on opera as a shifting network of meanings (the culture of opera), on how at certain times and in certain spaces opera is 'popular culture', while at other times and in other spaces it is 'high culture'. Opera's changing meaning and status is a question of culture and power.

Culture and power is the primary object of study in cultural studies. As Stuart Hall (1997, p4) explains,

> Meanings [i.e. cultures] ... regulate and organize our conduct and practices – they help to set the rules, norms and conventions by which social life is ordered and governed. They are ... therefore, what those who wish to govern and regulate the conduct and ideas of others seek to structure and shape.

Meanings have a material existence in that they help to organise practice and establish norms of behaviour. What I have said about masculinity and about the passing of business cards in China are both examples of where signification organises practice. But, as Hall indicates, those with power often seek to regulate the impact of meanings on practice. Dominant ways of making the world meaningful, produced by those with the power to make their meanings circulate in the world, can generate the hegemonic truths that may come to assume an authority over the ways in which we see, think, communicate, and act in the world. They become the 'common sense' (Gramsci, 1971) that organises our actions.

How I think about the relations between culture and power is informed primarily by the work of Antonio Gramsci, in particular his concept of hegemony. Hegemony is first and foremost a political concept used to describe processes of power in which a dominant group does not merely *rule by force* but *leads by consent*: it exerts 'intellectual and moral leadership' (Gramsci, 2006, p85). Hegemony involves a specific kind of consensus, one in which a social group presents its own *particular* interests as the *general* interests of the society as a whole: it turns the particular into the general. Hegemony works by the transformation of potential antagonism into simple difference. As Ernesto Laclau (1979, pp161-2) explains, it works by the

> partial absorption and neutralisation of those ideological contents through which resistance to ... domination ... is expressed. The characteristic method of securing this objective is to eliminate antagonism and transform it into a simple difference.

This works in part through the circulation of meanings which reinforce dominance and subordination by seeking to fix the meaning of social relations. As Williams (1977) explains,

> It [hegemony] is a lived system of meanings and values – constitutive and constituting – which as they are experienced as practices appear as reciprocally confirming. It thus constitutes a sense of reality for most people .... It is ... in the strongest sense a 'culture' [understood as a realised signifying system], but a culture which has also to be seen as the lived dominance and subordination of particular classes. (p110)

Hegemony works in part by transforming potential antagonism into simple difference. Difference is important because it is central to the making of meanings (or the making of cultures). For example, we define black in relation to white, male in relation to female. These terms do not have a fixed or essential meaning; it is the difference between them which signifies. These differences are rarely ever neutral: they exist in relations of power, one in a position of dominance over the other. For example, the term writer exists in relation to female writer, black writer, gay writer and working-class writer. The absent other in all these constructions is the hegemonic figure of the male, white, heterosexual, middle-class writer. This is the 'normal' against which the others are defined; each is situated in a relation of difference, a relation of culture and power, with this unmarked other.

The cultural studies focus on consumption is often linked to work on identities (Storey, 1999). The example of a writer demonstrates how identities are always entangled in relations of difference. But there is difference within difference: class is divided by gender, sexuality and ethnicity; ethnicity is divided by gender, class and sexuality; sexuality is divided by gender, class and ethnicity; gender is divided by class, sexuality and ethnicity. A working-class man, a gay man, a black man are only starting points in terms of identity formation: they will mean different things in different contexts. These identities are not self-contained; as with any identity, they are always caught up in relations of difference and sameness. Some differences may appear to be given by nature but they are only ever constructed as meaningful in culture, in relations of culture and power.

In many ways, actual differences are not really the issue, what matters is how differences are made meaningful. If we think of the possibility of equality between men and women as a question of establishing sameness, which in the world in which we live would probably mean that women must become like men, we will never achieve equality because men and women cannot be the same. If, however, we think of equality in terms of difference, starting from the assumption that men and women are different, the issue is not difference as such but how this difference is made meaningful. It is often argued that women are not as physically strong as men, and we know that some men are less physically strong than others. What matters here is not physical strength as such but what differences in physical strength are made to mean. Clearly, physical strength does not issue its own meanings, it has to be made to signify. So women and men may be different but what is significant is what this difference is made to mean. With regard to men and women, it is a question of culture, not biology. In these and other ways meanings (i.e. cultures) limit possibilities: they can regulate practice and justify subordination. It is not the difference which matters; what matters, is how the difference in made meaningful.

Hegemony involves the attempt to saturate the social with meanings which support the prevailing structures of power. In a hegemonic situation subordinate groups appear to actively support and subscribe to values, ideals and objectives which *incorporate* them into the prevailing structures of power. Hegemony, as Williams observes, 'does not just passively exist as a form of dominance. It has continually to be renewed, recreated, defended and modified. It is also continually resisted, limited, altered, challenged' (p112). Therefore, although hegemony is characterised by high levels of consensus, it is never without conflict; there is always *resistance*. For hegemony to remain successful, conflict and resistance must always be channelled and contained – re-articulated in the interests of the dominant (Laclau, 1979; Hall, 1996 and Storey, 2006b).

The introduction of the concept of hegemony into cultural studies in Britain in the 1970s brought about a re-thinking of culture (Hall, 1996). It did this in two ways. First, it brought about a re-thinking of the concept of culture, which involved bringing two dominant ways of thinking about culture into active relationship: those which stress structure and those which stress agency. To see culture as a structure is to envisage it as something imposed by the culture industries. Culture, according to this argument, is something provided for profit and ideological manipulation which establishes subject positions and imposes meanings. This way of seeing culture can be found in the work of the Frankfurt School, in political economy, and in some versions of structuralism and post-structuralism (Storey, 2003a). To see culture as a means of agency is to understand it as emerging from below, say, an authentic working-class culture (or any other subordinate culture). This is culture as expression, the voice of the people. Examples of this way of thinking about culture can be found in the work of culturalism, some versions of social history (history from below), and some versions of postmodern theory (Storey, 2006a).

According to cultural studies informed by Gramsci's theory of hegemony, culture is neither an authentic working-class culture (or any other subordinate culture), nor a culture imposed by the culture industries but a 'compromise equilibrium' between the two (Gramsci, 2006, p86). That is, a contradictory mix of forces from both below and above, both commercial and authentic, marked by 'resistance and incorporation, involving both structure and agency.

The introduction of Gramsci's theory of hegemony into cultural studies also brought about a re-thinking of the politics of culture. According to Gramsci, culture is a key site for the production and reproduction of hegemony: the continual winning of consent to relations of domination and subordination. The world is made up of societies divided unequally in terms of, for example ethnicity, race, gender, disability, generation, sexuality and social class. Cultural studies argues that culture, especially culture which is popular, is one of the principal sites where these divisions are established and contested. Cultures are arenas of struggle and negotiation between the interests of dominant groups and those of subordinate groups.

Hegemony is a complex and contradictory process, it is not the same as injecting people with false consciousness. This is not to deny power but to insist that a politics in which 'ordinary' people are seen as mute and passive victims of processes they can never hope to understand is a politics which can exist without causing too much trouble to the prevailing structures of power. Therefore cultural studies insists that we will not understand the relations between culture and power, entangled as we are in the complex processes of everyday life by fixing our critical gaze on everyday life and seeing only structure and imposition, manipulation and false consciousness. In every decade in the history of cultural studies, the point has been repeatedly made, learned in part from Marx (1977), that we make culture and we are made by culture; there is agency and there is structure. It is never enough to celebrate agency, nor is it enough to simply detail the structure(s) of power. We must always keep in mind the dialogical play between structure and agency, production and consumption, incorporation and resistance. We can witness this critical dialogue at work in queer, ethnic and feminist cultural politics where forms of production and ways of consumption actively seek to counter the circulation of meanings which deny them a voice in so-called mainstream culture.

If events do not have natural or intrinsic meanings but can be made to mean in a variety of ways, what is the process by which events acquire dominant meanings; how are they repeatedly made to signify in a particular way? As Hall (2006) makes clear,

> The signification of events is part of what has to be struggled over, for it is the means by which collective social understandings are created – and thus the means by which consent for particular outcomes can be effectively mobilized. (p137)

As Hall also points out, the media are the dominant means of social signification in modern societies. As a signifying institution the media continually give support and legitimacy to a whole series of values, procedures and assumptions which operate in the interests of powerful sections of society. It is not that descriptions and explanations are necessarily distorted and biased; rather, it is more that the media tend to accept the prevailing structures of power as natural and inevitable. The UK is characterised by a massive concentration of economic and social power. To assume that this is a natural or inevitable state of affairs is to support the prevailing structures of power, to lend to them legitimacy and authority.

However, the hegemony that the media help to constitute and sustain is not the articulation of the narrow interests of the powerful; rather they defend the social structure in which these interests are free to develop and expand. Hegemony builds a consensus around capitalism, not around particular capitalists. Of course capitalism is rarely ever actually named as capitalism: it is always re-configured in the language of 'common sense' as 'the economy'. The media do not distort social reality, they are the main mechanism by which it is produced and reproduced. Similarly, the media do not simply reflect or express an already established consensus, but produce consensus around existing structures of power, a consensus that always already favours certain powerful groups. The media do this not necessarily by intention or bias but by the articulation of what Gramsci (1971) calls common sense, the 'compromise equilibrium' of the currently acceptable. Therefore, while we might be cynical or disbelieving about this or that aspect of news reporting, there is little doubt that the media have both enormous social authority and unprecedented social presence. For example, when something important happens we still turn on the television or the radio or read a newspaper to find out *exactly* what has happened.

Media ideology, therefore, is never just a matter of statements but of the assumptions that underpin statements. The normative power of 'common sense' is as much in the enabling and constraining structure, as it is in the utterance. Immigration, legal and illegal, has once again become a hotly debated topic in the British media. The embeddedness of these assumptions is revealed by the fact that Hall (2006) draws attention to more or less the same 'common sense' in an article first published in 1982. Underpinning the debate, current and historical, are certain assumptions, a certain 'common sense' about numbers. If immigration is assumed to be a question of numbers in which racial tension is seen as a direct result of there being too many immigrants and not as a consequence of white racism, it would not matter how radical a position is because the position will be constantly undermined in the media by the organising logic of the numbers game. To argue outside the logic of the numbers game is to risk presenting an argument that seems hopelessly outside 'common sense' and therefore not relevant to the issues under discussion. Such an argument will continually be told to stick to the point. But by sticking to the point, in another small way, hegemony is reproduced. The British media's working assumptions about the supposed 'problem' of immigration, how it frames and encourages the debate, has the effect of side-stepping racism and blaming the victims for the racism they have to endure.

Stonewall, the gay and lesbian campaigning organisation, recently published a report in on the way in which BBC television represents gay life and gay people (Cowan and Valentine, 2006). The report is partly based on a study of 168 hours of primetime BBC television programming (7pm to 10pm). The report draws three conclusions, each of which is another example of the media's articulation of 'common sense'. First, the report identifies massive under-representation of gay life and gay people: 'During 168 hours of programmes, gay lives were represented positively for just six minutes' (2006:6). Second, when gay people and gay lives are represented, 'Gay lives are five times more likely to be portrayed in negative terms than positive ones' (6). Third, gay people are almost always reduced to their sexuality. They are never allowed to be simply this or that character; invariably, they have to be this or that gay character. If a taxi driver is gay, he or she is a gay taxi driver; if a taxi driver is heterosexual, he or she is just a taxi driver. The dominant is thus produced and reproduced by its apparent invisibility.

There are many competing and alternative accounts of the meaning of social reality. However, in terms of the reach and quantity of the media's output and the social authority it carries, its power far exceeds that of all other possible voices. It is this that defines the media as the dominant institution for the circulation of meaning and the production and reproduction of hegemonic common sense.

References

Arnold, Matthew (2006) Culture and Anarchy. In John Storey (ed) *Cultural Theory and Popular Culture*, third edition. London: Pearson, pp6-11

Butler, Judith (1999) *Gender Trouble*, 10th anniversary edition. London: Routledge

Cowan, Katherine and Valentine, Gill (2006) *Tuned Out: The BBC's Portrayal of Lesbian and Gay People*. London: Stonewall (www.stonewall.org.uk)

Four Tops (1992) *The Four Tops – Motown Greatest Hits*. Motown Record Company

Gramsci, Antonio (1971) *Selections from Prison Notebooks*. London: Lawrence and Wishart

Gramsci, Antonio (2006) Hegemony, intellectuals, and the state. In John Storey (ed), *Cultural Theory and Popular Culture: A Reader*, third edition. London: Pearson, pp85-91

Hall, Stuart (1996) Cultural studies: two paradigms. In John Storey (ed), *What is Cultural Studies: A Reader*. London: Arnold, pp31-48

Hall, Stuart (1997) Introduction. In Stuart Hall (ed), *Representation*. London: Sage, pp1-11

Hall, Stuart (2006) The rediscovery of ideology: return of the repressed in media studies. In John Storey (ed), *Cultural Theory and Popular Culture: A Reader*, third edition. London: Pearson, pp124-155

Laclau, Ernesto (1979) *Politics and Ideology in Marxist Theory*. London: Verso

Laclau, Ernesto and Mouffe, Chantal (2001) *Hegemony and Socialist Strategy*, second edition. London: Verso

Laclau, Ernesto and Mouffe, Chantal (2006) Marxism without apologies. In John Storey (ed) *Cultural Theory and Popular Culture: A Reader*, third edition. London: Pearson, pp156-85

Leavis, FR (2006) Mass civilisation and minority culture. In John Storey (ed), *Cultural Theory and Popular Culture: A Reader*, third edition. London: Pearson, pp12-19

Marx, Karl (1977) *The Eighteenth Brumaire of Louis Bonaparte*. Moscow: Progress Press

Storey, John (1999) *Cultural Consumption and Everyday Life*. London: Arnold

Storey, John (2002). Expecting Rain: opera as popular culture. In Jim Collins (ed), *High-Pop*. Oxford: Blackwell, pp32-55

Storey, John (2003a) *Inventing Popular Culture*. Oxford: Blackwell

Storey, John (2003b) The social life of opera. In *European Journal of Cultural Studies,* 6:1, 5-35.

Storey, John (2006a) *Cultural Theory and Popular Culture*, fourth edition. Pearson: London

Storey, John (2006b) Rockin' Hegemony: West Coast rock and Amerika's War in Vietnam. In John Storey (ed), *Cultural Theory and Popular Culture: A Reader*, third edition. London: Pearson, pp100-110

Storey, John (2006c) Inventing opera as art in nineteenth-century Manchester. In *International Journal of Cultural Studies*, 9:4

Volosinov, VN (1973) *Marxism and the Philosophy of Language*. Seminar Press: New York

Williams, Raymond (1965) *The Long Revolution*, Harmondsworth: Pelican

Williams, Raymond (1977) *Marxism and Literature*. Verso: London

Williams, Raymond (1979) *Politics and Letters: Interviews with New Left Review*. London: Verso

Williams, Raymond (1980) Base and Superstructure in Marxist Cultural Theory. In *Problems in Materialism and Culture*. London: Verso, pp31-49

Williams, Raymond (1981) *Culture*. Fontana: London

Williams, Raymond (1984) *Crisis in English Studies. In Writing in Society*, London: Verso, pp192-211

Williams, Raymond (2006) The analysis of culture. In John Storey (ed), *Cultural Theory and Popular Culture: A Reader*, third edition. London: Pearson, pp32-40

2

Speaking with small voices: voice, resistance and difference

Elizabeth Atkinson

Introduction

This chapter explores the significance of voice – and particularly of small voices – in both resisting and recreating social patterns and structures. Sometimes unwittingly, sometimes deliberately, small voices can either seal the boundaries and barriers within a community or open the doors to greater social cohesion and mutual understanding. To illustrate the multi-layered way in which such small voices operate I would like to open this chapter with an edited version of a story by a former student, Allison Hicks, which was written when she was in the final year of an Early Childhood Studies degree programme at the University of Sunderland. Allison wrote this story as part of her assessed work for a module on equality and diversity which required students to put themselves inside the head of an imagined child. Allison's imagined child is David, a 4 year-old British Jew.

Monday

We had PE today and the teacher asked us to get changed. I didn't have any black shoes. Zena wore long trousers and a long top called shalwar-kameez. Zena was last to get changed, the teacher kept telling her to hurry up because we didn't have long, then she said she could get changed in the girls' toilets. James laughed at us and said we couldn't run as fast as he could in his black shoes.

Tuesday

Dad talked about my cousin's Bar Mitzvah tonight, he said it was a coming of age ceremony for boys. Dad says I will have one, but I am four and not a man yet. When I am a man, I am going to marry Zena, she is very pretty. James said she will marry a Paki from her country and he would take his Dad's job. Granddad was talking to Grandma about the Day of Atonement, when Jews don't eat anything. Dad calls it fasting. Granddad says we need to think about things that we have done wrong and try and do better. I wonder if James has a Day of Atonement ...

Thursday

I don't eat ham or pork, well any food that comes from the pig. Dad told me it was because in Israel (where Jews came from) it was hot and pigs carried disease. Granddad eats meat called Kosher. I eat a lot of British things. I am hungry tonight because it was sausage at school today and the dinner lady couldn't say if they were pork free, so was Zena my friend. She is Muslim and doesn't eat pork either. I told the dinner lady I was hungry. She said I should have eaten all my dinner.

Saturday

Today is Saturday, the holy day. James' parents go to work on a Saturday. I know because his Mam works in the paper shop, where Dad gets his newspaper. Mam gave her job up because the manager kept asking her to work on a Saturday. Now I can't get shoes like James' because his Mam works and my Mam stays at home. James says his Dad said we won't spend our money and he called me tight, but my shoes aren't tight. They are just brown, not black like his.

David doesn't exist. He is a figment of Allison's imagination. Nevertheless, his experience is real and Allison's skilful weaving together of discourses of marginalisation speaks clearly of the daily injustices and misunderstandings which serve to maintain social barriers from childhood onwards, while at the same time bringing David's small voice to the fore to speak to us between the lines (as it has done with each successive group of students, to whom I have read David's story) for a vision of a more just world.

David's story speaks primarily of racial and cultural marginalisation. The remainder of this chapter will focus on my own area of research and practice: challenging institutional heteronormativity and homophobia in primary schools. This is a context in which every small step is potentially a giant leap and where those taking the steps may not know whether the giant leap will lead to a better place for them and their pupils or to public criticism and outrage coupled with moral panic. The voices in this research are almost by default speaking the unspeakable and speaking it in a context which, however gently and quietly they do it, potentially makes their voices sound like trumpet calls.

The primary school as a heteronormative pedagogic space

The act of voicing resistance, however quietly, disrupts what Fairclough (1988) calls normalising discourses: the ways of thinking, doing and being that have become so ingrained in our way of life that we think of them as simply common sense. As common sense they seem to become incontrovertibly right. In the field of sexualities equality research, common sense is represented by heterosexuality and its powerful corollary, heteronormativity: viewing the world from a heterosexual perspective. As an unmarked category heterosexuality is invisible in its own environment and the idea that anyone should be thought to be promoting it through heterosexist practices is easily dismissed as laughable. How could and why would anyone want to *promote* heterosexuality? It just *is* ...

Emma Renold describes the primary classroom as a 'heteronormative pedagogic space' (2005, pp153-4) and provides a rich ethnography of the discourses through which compulsory heterosexism and (hetero) gender are played out. Both Renold (*ibid*) and Epstein *et al* (2003) identify schools as sites for the performance and perpetuation of the heteronormative. Our own research has also shown how, through inaction as much as through action, heteronormativity permeates all aspects of primary school life, whether it is recognised or not (Atkinson and DePalma, 2006; DePalma and Atkinson, 2006a, b). In our interviews with primary teachers several of our heterosexual respondents emphasised that they don't teach heterosexuality or flaunt their own sexual identity in school while commenting, sometimes within the same statement, that their pupils knew, of course, that they were married or that they had children[1]. There was not a hint of irony in these statements: they simply did not connect the fact that their heterosexuality was public knowledge with the concept of heteronormativity.

The research I will draw on here, which has been conducted in collaboration with Renée DePalma, has developed over three phases, the third of which is only in its third month at the time of writing. Initially we gathered views from students and academic staff in one university through an online discussion forum on whether issues of sexual orientation should be addressed in the context of schooling[2]. We then interviewed 50 primary teachers and 12 trainee primary teachers in North East England, South West England and London about whether they addressed, or would address, lesbian, gay, bisexual and transgender equality in their own schools and classrooms and if not, what would stop them[3]. In the current phase, *No Outsiders: Researching approaches to sexualities equality in primary schools*, we are working with a team of fifteen teacher-researchers in schools and local authorities in three regions of the country and with nine university researchers based at three institutions[4]. Each teacher-researcher is developing their own strategies to address lesbian, gay, bisexual and transgender equality and to challenge institutional heteronormativity in their own school, with the support of a regional research assistant. Each project will be different, arising as it does from the teacher-researchers' own contexts, needs and interests. Overall the project gives voice in an unprecedented way to a much-needed resistance to heteronormativity in the primary school experience of pupils, parents and teachers.

Voicing difference to make a difference: shouting out quietly against normalising discourses

One effect of voicing resistance is that it shifts the emphasis from the reactive to the proactive: while we found that all the teachers we interviewed in the second phase of our research emphasised the significance of addressing sexualities equality in the classroom and placed it on a par with other aspects of equality and diversity, only two made a point of addressing these issues proactively. This echoes the experience of Kevin Colleary (1999) who found that most teachers in his study, while agreeing in principle with addressing sexualities equality, tended to wait for opportunities (which might never come) to address it rather than creating opportunities themselves.

These two teachers' simple and courageous approaches to addressing sexualities equality effectively illustrate the power of small voices. Their strategies are described in the following extracts from our interview transcripts.

Michael[5], a gay year four (age 8-9) class teacher, describes how he challenges homophobia with his class (E and R are the interviewers, M is Michael):

    E   So do you talk about it in school?

    M   Yeah, all the time but not my own, I mean I haven't told the kids but I
        mean, I had a gay brother, half-brother, and he was killed in 1998,

someone set his house on fire. So when there's homophobia in school I'll talk about that and say 'My brother was killed because someone had your attitude, you know.' So I am always talking about it, I always bring it up in school and I always say, 'We don't tolerate homophobia, not in this school.' ... On my second year teaching practice ... a girl Linda in my class [said], 'Mr. Smith, Tanya called me a lesbian,' and so I said to her, 'Linda, Tanya's actually used the word incorrectly. There's nothing wrong with being a lesbian, and so she's used it wrong.' And the teacher came up to me after the lesson and said, 'You can't say that ... People round here don't like it.' I said, 'Round where, exactly?' And she said, 'Well, you can't do that, that's promoting homosexuality.' I said, 'That's not promoting homosexuality. It's promoting tolerance.'

Although Michael chooses to challenge homophobia proactively by drawing attention to the death of his gay brother, he chooses not to tell his pupils that he too is gay. When asked why he doesn't do so, his very hesitant answer contrasts starkly with his fluent accounts of discussions about other gay people:

E   So what is it that stops you from saying, 'And I'm gay'?

M   Ah. I don't know what it is. I mean I, yeah, it's a relevant issue in schools but my sexuality, I mean, I don't have time to think about it in my day-to-day so I do sometimes think, well, you know, yeah, I'm mean, I'm not sure why, I mean, I'm not really I mean, yeah, I've been single for, I'm dead from the waist down at the moment (laughter), so, you know, I suppose...

The implied suggestion that Michael's sexuality is irrelevant because he does not currently have a partner throws an interesting light on the way in which sexual orientation for non-heterosexuals tends to be conflated with sexual activity and thus gains what Patai describes as *surplus visibility* (1992) which is a concept explored elsewhere in relation to this research (DePalma and Atkinson, 2006a) and later in this chapter. While Michael is prepared to joke about common perceptions of gay sexual activity (see below), his awareness of these perceptions perhaps serves both to prevent him from revealing his own sexual orientation to his pupils and to eliminate himself, at least while he is unpartnered, from the category 'gay'. This is a move which is hard to imagine in a heterosexual context. At the same time he is aware that potentially he has an important role in broadening his pupils' understanding of gay identity:

M   I mean, I'm hoping that each small step would bring us forward. Because the thing is it's all the rumours, isn't it? About gay people, you know, they're predatory and they have sex all the time. Don't they, gay people, they do nothing else, they just have sex all the time (laughter).

R   They don't have time for jobs, actually.

M   With people who don't want to have sex with them. And so if they learnt that you know the gay person is also a teacher and he's got friends and he does *pol* and he's got this interest and he likes reading and da da da da. Then the sex part of it becomes a much smaller percentage.

In spite of his hesitation about revealing his own gay identity, Michael provided the most forthright approach to gay equality in the interviews, demonstrating how a small voice holding an apparently simple conversation can break through barriers which other teachers in our research saw as unmovable. His account of the strategy he uses is reproduced here as a dialogue between himself and his pupils. His first move is to write 'Gay people' on the board:

> Come on, tell us what gay people do.
> And it's (pupils): Kissing.
> Alright, so I'll write 'Loving each other'
> And it's (pupils): Having sex.
> OK, loving each other.
> (Pupils): Holding hands.
> OK, loving each other.

Michael continued to explain his strategy, re-enacting the dialogue between himself and his pupils and pretending to write their responses on the board:

M   And it's all the sex. And I'll say come on, gay people, do they eat? And they'll go (makes face). So OK, gay people eat. So if they eat, they'll need to get food. Do they go shopping? OK (gestures writing on the board) so they go shopping. OK, do gay people, if they go shopping, it means they'll need money. So do gay people have jobs? OK (gestures writing). Gay people have jobs. And we end up having all this stuff about what gay people do, and I cross out the word gay, and I say, 'People do all these things.'

The second example of a proactive approach to sexualities equality comes from Brenda, a lesbian primary head, talking about the approach one of her class teachers takes in sex education lessons with year six pupils (age 10 to 11). B is the head and R and E are the interviewers.

B   Rather than say, say stuff, straight to the kids, they have this question time. And invariably the questions in there will have references to gay and sometimes lesbian and it's always things like, 'What do gay, what do gay people do?' And things like that. And the teacher who works with that, he's really good. He tells it like it is.

E   So he answers the question?

B   Yeah. Yeah.

R   Hmmm, that's rather unusual, too.

E   (laughs) Yes. Are there any questions that he wouldn't answer, is there a kind of a policy on where the boundaries [unclear]?

B   Anything that might suggest S and M or abuse or a sort of non-loving non-caring approach to relationships.

E   So simply saying what it is that men do together or what women do, might do, women might do together, would not in any way be beyond that boundary, there would be answers ...?

B   No, no, no. [This teacher] would, he would be pretty clear with the kids.

R   In a sense, drawing those boundaries in that way I think is sending a really important message.

E   Yes.

R   You know, because you're saying 'we're not, we will not refuse to talk about this, but we will refuse to talk about this,' whereas a lot of times I think gay and lesbian relationships are on the other side of that line [that is, something we refuse to talk about].

This teacher was clearly willing to raise a small voice in acknowledgement of both the existence and the legitimacy of gay sex, in stark contrast to the silence on this issue reported in other interviews where several respondents said that if this question was raised, pupils were told that this was something they should ask their parents about. We were interested to find that this teacher did not talk about lesbian sex in his sex education lessons and that this was a silence that was echoed at first in my own reluctance, as a lesbian researcher, to ask about it:

E   And [does this teacher talk] about lesbian sex?

B   No, definitely not. No.

E   Because I watched myself not even asking that question.

B   Yeah, yeah.

E   Is it because lesbians don't do it? (laughter)

B   Yeah, that's right.

E   And I noticed the invisibility I bought into it in that. Very interesting, speaking as a lesbian researcher I don't know why I don't include myself here (laughing).

Thus while this teacher speaks the unspeakable in relation to gay male sex, layers of silence are wound around the discussion of lesbian sex, rendering the invisible even more so and perhaps sustaining the perception that lesbian sex only has a recognised existence as an activity performed for the heterosexual male gaze.

Storying the small voices: heteronormativity and rhizoanalysis

One of the dangers of speaking out is that of essentialism: speaking the unspeakable may lead us to minimise the complexities in order to be heard. However this is not an inevitable outcome: queer theory and feminist poststructuralism offer us ways of representing ourselves which simultaneously present a recognisable (or what Judith Butler (1993) would describe as intelligible) identity and demonstrate the multiple facets of our selves. This theoretical perspective, exemplified in the work of Bronwen Davies (2003), Glenda MacNaughton (2005), Emma Renold (2005) and others, demonstrates an openness towards the fluidity and instability of gendered and sexualised identities, as well as the complexity of the 'boundary work' (Thorne, 1993) which children and adults undertake in order to negotiate and renegotiate the terrain of sex-gender-sexuality. Such fluidity is reflected in the approaches we are taking within the *No Outsiders* research team to challenging heteronormativity and with it what Renold describes as hetero-gender. In this sense the work of the teacher-researchers is not so much about including the excluded, which may do nothing to shift the centre, as about opening up the boundaries of the 'normal' so that a wider variety and a greater flexibility of subject positions is made available to children, teachers, parents and the wider community.

MacNaughton (2005) draws on the work of Deleuze and Guattari (1987) to explore and apply the concept of *rhizoanalysis* to her field of research: this analysis is based on the lateral, unpredictable logic of the rhizome rather than the predictable, linear logic of the tree with its roots and branches. She states:

> [Thus] rhizoanalysis explains things in terms of a dynamic, ever-changing 'becoming', rather than a fixed and finished 'being'; and a particular rhizo-analysis – e.g. of gender – is never fixed and final, but is always becoming. One meaning expands into another, some meanings become outdated and new meanings shoot forth. (2005, p121)

Such a concept offers particularly rich rewards for the use of small voices to challenge institutional heteronormativity: the effect of each new step reaches out, perhaps imperceptibly, in directions which cannot be anticipated and with results which cannot be known. There are no fixed objectives here, no determinable outcomes to be ticked off: there will be as many approaches as there are researchers – indeed there will probably be more as each teacher-researcher might try out several strategies within their own practice setting. But with these small voices come new meanings and connotations, new connections to new possibilities, opened up through what Judith Butler (1997) calls a politics of *performative resignification.*

One of the richest sources of *performative resignification,* as well as, ironically, of fixing meanings and ideologies, is the multi-layered children's book: meanings can be re-worked and re-shaped through both words and pictures, not only by authorial intent but also by the multiple readings children and adults bring to them. This has been richly explored through the growing body of critical exploration of children's literature (see, for example, Watson and Styles, 1996; Paul, 1998; Chapleau, 2004). With this wealth of interpretive possibilities in mind we have provided a collection of some 25 picture books featuring lesbian and gay identities to each of the teacher-researchers in the No Outsiders project. Rhizomatic logic is at work in these texts as well as a healthy dose of irony, forming a powerful resistance to the operation of heteronormativity. Johnny Valentine's *One Dad, Two Dads, Brown Dad, Blue Dads* (1994/2004) treats the plethora of pseudo-scientific explanations for homosexuality with the lightest of touches, through neatly side-stepping the fact that one of the children in the story has two gay dads and displacing the second child's consternation onto the fact that they are both blue. A fascinating parallel to this was offered by one of our teacher-researchers who recounted a conversation between two young children in his school along the following lines:

> Boy: My dad's in prison.
>
> Girl: I've got two dads but they're not in prison.
>
> Boy: You mean you've got two dads, and *neither* of them is in prison??

Valentine's *One Dad, Two Dads* (pp17-20) allows us to laugh at ourselves and our society for offering ridiculous explanations for things we don't understand:

> 'What I'd like to know now.'
> I went on to say,
> 'is, just how did your dads
> end up looking this way?

Did they go through the wash
With a ballpoint pen?
Or were they both blue
Since the young age of ten?

Did they drink too much
Blueberry juice as young boys?
Or as kids, did they play
With too many blue toys?'

The subtleties and the explicit foregrounding of gay identity offered by these books are not always welcomed. One of our *No Outsiders* teacher-researchers recounted the reactions of her colleagues when she opened the pack of project picture books in her school staffroom. Her account is summarised below in the field notes taken at a regional teacher-re-searchers' meeting:

> A [the teacher-researcher] had unpacked the project books for classroom use in front of other members of staff, many of whom had laughed, pointed out gay stereotypes (big moustaches!) and talked about the way in which they didn't feel that they could use these books in their classroom. Responses included, 'You're joking, not with the children I've got,' 'Oh my god, no, I can't show my children this,' and 'I wouldn't want my child to read this book'. While *Priscilla and the Pink Planet* was thought to be 'OK,' *Daddy's Roommate* was laughed at because of the 'gay moustache' and one teacher said of *The Princesses Have a Ball* (which does not depict gay or lesbian characters): 'No way would I use this with my children.'

Yet these books offer an avenue for exploring gay relationships in the safest of safe spaces: stories about families. In the true story of two male penguins in Central Park Zoo who bring up a chick (Justin Richardson and Peter Parnell's *And Tango Makes Three* 2005, p9) 'Mr Gramzay noticed the two penguins and thought to himself, 'They must be in love.' And in *Daddy's Roommate* (Wilhoite, 1991, pp26-27), Daddy's relationship with Frank is explained in the simplest of terms: 'Being gay is just one more kind of love. And love is the best kind of happiness.' It goes without saying that the depiction of a heterosexual couple, whether human or penguin, would attract no attention at all, being the stuff of which many storybooks are made; but these books show how to speak the unspeakable through story.

Addressing lesbian, gay, bisexual and transgender equality in primary schools: speaking the words and finding the sky doesn't fall in

I have referred elsewhere to the forced silence around non-heterosexual identities in school contexts (Atkinson, 2002) and the 'normalisation of nothingness' (Atkinson, 2004) which pervades educational cultures, particularly in relation to sexualities and sexual identity. From the first phase of our current research we have explored the layers of silence around sexuality and sexual orientation in wider public discourses about education, and the effect of the mistaken assumption that children are asexual beings on shutting down potentially useful discourses in school contexts (DePalma and Atkinson, 2006b). We have also pointed out (2006a) that 'simple visibility' is an impossibility in research and practice related to sexual orientation and sexualities equality. As soon as this particular difference is voiced it gains what Patai (1992) calls surplus visibility when the effect of words and actions, which in other contexts would seem unremarkable, is magnified beyond any possibility of being considered normal. While the simple breaking of the silence or 'permission to talk about it' (DePalma and Atkinson, 2006a) became a pervasive theme in both our earlier and current research with primary teachers, the irony facing these teacher-researchers is that having gained the permission the danger of surplus visibility is ever present. Simply being able to speak the unspeakable *without* attracting surplus visibility has become a project goal in itself.

This is what is already becoming possible in the relatively safe context of the project. In one project school a deputy head, instead of reprimanding a boy outright for calling another boy gay, turned the perpetrator's taunt upside down by asking 'Was that meant as an insult or a compliment?' The same approach was taken by a head in our preparatory research who, on being told bitterly by a child's father that other children were calling him (the father) gay, asked why this was a problem. The child who had called another child gay answered 'An insult, of course' but perhaps he went away with an alternative perception of 'gay' in his mind. In the school where staff reacted with horror to the project book collection one of the teacher-researcher's colleagues came to her saying she would be proud of her, as she had said to a child who called another child gay that she would talk to him/her about what 'gay' meant. This suggests a welcome opening up of possibilities and closing down of taboos: an imagining of the previously unimaginable.

In the context of this project it will become imaginable for a Reception teacher to walk into her/his class of 4 to 5 year-olds and read Michael

Willhoite's *Daddy's Roommate* or Lesléa Newman's *Heather Has Two Mommies* without it being an issue for public debate and concern. It will become imaginable for a teacher of 10 to 11year-olds to share James Howe's *Totally Joe* with their class as a means of exploring individuality, identity and difference. They might take the following exchange between Joe and his friend Skeezie (Howe, pp11-12) as a starting point for a discussion of the rules of being a 'guy-guy':

Skeezie: Stop crossing your legs at the knee.

Me: What does that have to do with being a guy-guy?

Skeezie: It has to do with guys do not cross their legs at the knee. Your aunt Priscilla crosses her legs at the knee.

Me: I don't have an aunt Priscilla. Although I wish I did. I *love* the name.

Skeezie: *You're* an aunt Priscilla, okay? Now, listen up and do what I'm tellin' ya. If you gotta cross your legs, you keep one leg at a right angle to the floor and put your other ankle on the knee of that leg. Like this.

Me: Oh my god, you look just like that gangster in that movie. You know, the one with Al Pacino and all the blood? We saw it at Bobby's that time.

Skeezie: Do it, lame brain.

Me: Ow. It hurts.

Skeezie: Stop waving your hands around.

Me: I'm not waving –

Skeezie: Yes, you are. Guys don't wave their hands around. They keep their hands quiet.

Me: Well, *that's* boring.

Skeezie: What are you doing?

Me: What?

Skeezie: Your hands. You're folding them in your lap.

Me: I'm keeping them quiet.

Skeezie: Your aunt Priscilla sits with her hands folded in her lap.

Me: Not with her legs crossed like this, she doesn't. Where are you going?

Skeezie: I give up. Just be who you are, okay?

Me: But you haven't taught me how to talk sports yet. So, what do you think about those Yankees? Huh, Skeezie? Ho 'bout them Yankies?

Voicing difference – or voicing commonality?

Perhaps one of the greatest ironies of this whole enterprise of voicing difference, whatever the context, is that in the end it is as much about voicing *commonality* as about voicing difference. It is the fact that speaking the unspeakable leads to nods of recognition, that shouting quietly to make a difference sets up ripples of common identity, that is significant. In the same way in which the post-structuralist exploration of multiple identities demonstrates not the fragmentation of the human race but its shared multiplicities, so the act of daring to speak opens the door to an acknowledgement of what the speaker and the listeners have in common. This is the way in which a society which really celebrates diversity might be generated: not through a spurious tolerance of the differences which simply reinforce the norm but through a recognition of what we have in common.

The alternative to voicing resistance is silence. And silence in the field of sexualities equality and its related themes is a dangerous weapon. As King and Scheider put it (1999, p131):

> When we refuse to talk about it, the value of sexual talk of all kinds increases on the black market of linguistic transactions. Ultimately, we are responsible as teachers for what we choose not to teach children.

And as I have pointed out elsewhere (Atkinson 2002, p128):

> The manifestations of [these] dominant heterosexual discourses (including discourses of silence) are multiple and powerful. They are a cause for concern, not because heterosexuality is somehow undesirable, but because heteronormativity so easily masks the possibility of anything else.

Add to this the fact that lessons of intolerance and misunderstanding will find their way into the gaps we leave and we have a clear mandate, whatever the risks, perhaps even whatever the consequences for ourselves, for choosing to speak with small voices.

Acknowledgements

Although Renée DePalma's voice is not directly present in this chapter her insights and interpretations have had a significant effect on my perceptions of our research. And although the voices of the remaining seven members of the universities-based research team and the fifteen teacher-researchers around the country are not literally present here, their echoes are to be heard throughout its pages. I am deeply indebted to all the participants in this research for the illumination they have brought to this thorny area of inquiry. Finally, my grateful thanks to Allison Hicks for allowing me to reproduce *David's Story* as part of this chapter.

Notes

1 As one of the editors has pointed out, plenty of gay people are married and/or have children; but this was not mentioned by any of our heterosexual respondents.

2 This project was supported by a grant from the Nuffield Foundation, Project Code SGS/00853/G, with additional funding from the University of Sunderland School of Education and Lifelong Learning.

3 This project was supported by a Research Development Fellowship, awarded by the University of Sunderland and funded by the Higher Education Funding Council for England (HEFCE).

4 *No Outsiders: Researching approaches to sexualities equality in primary schools*, is funded by the Economic and Social Research council (ESRC) Ref. RES-062-23-0095, and runs from September 2006 to December 2008. The university-based research team comprises Elizabeth Atkinson, Renée DePalma and Elizabeth Brace (University of Sunderland); Judy Hemingway, Deborah Youdell and Michael Reiss (Institute of Education, University of London) and Alexandra Allan, Nick Givens and David Nixon (University of Exeter). For purposes of confidentiality, the teacher-researchers are remaining anonymous at the time of writing. For more information about the project, go to www.nooutsiders.sunderland.ac.uk.

5 Names of the research participants and of the people they mention have been replaced by pseudonyms.

6 A circus skill involving twirling weighted (sometimes flaming) ropes or chains about the head and body.

References

Atkinson, E (2002) Education for diversity in a multisexual society: negotiating the contradictions of contemporary discourse. *Sex Education* 2, 119-132

Atkinson, E (2004) Sexualities and resistance: queer(y)ing identity and discourse in education in J Satterthwaite and E Atkinson (eds) (2004) *Educational Counter-Cultures: confrontations, images, vision.* Stoke-on-Trent: Trentham, pp55-67

Atkinson, E and DePalma, R (2006) Imagining the homonormative: the place of subversive research in education for social justice. Paper presented at the fifth *Discourse Power Resistance* conference. Manchester Metropolitan University 20-22 April

Butler, J (1993) *Bodies That Matter: On the Discursive Limits of 'Sex'.* London: Routledge

Butler, J (1997) *Excitable Speech: a politics of the performative.* London: Routledge

Chapleau, S (ed) (2004) *New Voices in Children's Literature Criticism.* Lichfield: Pied Piper

Colleary, K P (1999) How teachers understand gay and lesbian content in the elementary social studies curriculum in W J Letts and J T Sears (eds) *Queering Elementary Education: advancing the dialogue about sexualities and schooling.* Lanham, MA: Rowman and Littlefield, pp151-164

Davies, B (2003) *Shards of Glass: Children Reading and Writing Beyond Gendered Identities.* New Jersey: Hampton Press

Deleuze, G and Guattari, F (1987) *A thousand plateaus: capitalism and schizophrenia.* London: The Athlone Press

DePalma, R and Atkinson, E (2006a) 'Permission to talk about it:' LGB and straight teachers' narratives of sexual equality. Paper presented at the annual meeting of the British Educational Research Association, University of Warwick, 6-8 September

DePalma, R and Atkinson, E (2006b) The sound of silence: talking about sexual orientation and schooling. *Sex Education* 6, 333-349

Epstein, D, O'Flynn, S and Telford, D (2003) *Silenced Sexualities in Schools and Universities.* Stoke-on-Trent: Trentham Books

Fairclough, N (1988) *Language and power.* London: Longman

Howe, J (2005). *Totally Joe.* New York: Simon and Shuster

King, J R and Schneider, J J (1999) Locating a place for gay and lesbian themes in elementary reading, writing and talking. In W Letts and J T Sears (eds) *Queering elementary education: advancing the dialogue about sexualities and schooling.* Lanham, MA: Rowman and Littlefield, pp125-136

Mac Naughton, G (2005) *Doing Foucault in early childhood studies: applying poststructural ideas.* London: Routledge

Parnell, P, and Richardson, J (2005) *And Tango Makes Three.* New York: Simon and Schuster

Patai, D (1992) Minority status and the stigma of 'surplus visibility'. *Education Digest* 57(5), 35-37

Paul, L (1998) *Reading Otherways.* Stroud: Thimble Press

Renold, E (2005) *Girls, boys and junior sexualities: exploring children's gender and sexual relations in the primary school.* London: RoutledgeFalmer

Thorne, B (1993) *Gender Play: girls and boys in school.* New Brunswick, NJ: Rutgers University Press

Valentine, J (2004) *One Dad, Two Dads, Brown Dad, Blue Dads.* Los Angeles: Alyson Books

Watson, V and Styles, M (eds) (1996) *Talking Pictures: pictorial texts and young readers.* London: Hodder and Stoughton

Willhoite, M (1991) *Daddy's Roommate.* Los Angeles: Alyson Books

3

Giving voice: evidence-informed policy and practice as a democratising process

David Gough

Introduction

An important role of universities is to develop new ways of understanding our physical and social worlds. This may include challenging accepted views and shining light on established orders and powers. Many of the chapters in this volume provide examples of such research which explores social differences and social interests hidden by dominant discourses and revealed by academic inquiry and analysis.

One approach to developing new research perspectives on the world is to involve a greater number of voices in the interpretation, use and conduct of research. Research helps us to understand the world and if this research is only led and understood by certain sections of society its approach and findings are likely to be limited by the ideological and conceptual assumptions and priorities of those groups.

The importance of the different perspectives on knowledge creation and use can be seen in widespread debates about such contested issues as the nature of mental illness or whether doctors or service users should determine the nature of maternity services. In the area of education you would expect policy makers, practitioners, parents and school students to have different perspectives and different research questions about the nature of educational services. Each of these groups would find it easier to engage in debates about research evidence if they were determining the questions driving the evidence being created.

This chapter has similar interests in developing and challenging ways of understanding the world. Its focus is on secondary research, on how we go about finding out what we know already from existing research evidence and how this can be a powerful driver for determining future research agendas. Clarifying what we know is traditionally the role of experts or of literature reviews but these may not be explicit about their assumptions or methods of review. It is therefore important to have formal explicit methods of review just as formal explicit methods are required to ensure that the findings of primary research are accountable. This is not an argument for one method of review but for multiple explicit accountable methods for specifying what we know from research evidence and how we know it. This includes being clear about the questions being asked, by who, and for what purpose.

Systematic research synthesis is an umbrella term for a number of formal explicit methods for reviewing research literature. Such systematic methods have many advantages over traditional informal methods of review and many implications for the creation and use of knowledge, including giving voice to different groups and individual members of society.

Systematic reviews often have a number of common stages that can but not always include:

- Specification of question and the conceptual framework and method of review (though this may not be pre-specified in iterative reviews with emergent methods)

- Definitions of studies to be considered (inclusion criteria)

- A strategy for identifying such studies (search strategy and screening)

- Describing the research field (systematic mapping)

- Quality and relevance appraisal

- Analysis and synthesis

- Communication of review findings

- Interpretation of findings for different needs

- Implementation of interpreted findings for different needs

There are many myths about systematic review one of which being that they are limited to statistical meta analysis of results from quantitative experimental studies. This can lead to the fear that systematic reviews will be used to control the research agenda of what is studied and how. The logic of the need for transparent methods of reviewing what we know and how we know it applies to all research questions and thus all research methods and types of data (Gough and Elbourne, 2002; Gough, 2004). This chapter argues that systematic reviews can be a powerful means to enable access to all potential users of research to research knowledge and more importantly to drive research agendas. Such potential users and beneficiaries of research include researchers, policy makers and practitioners but also include members of the public and all minority groups.

The chapter considers three inter-related issues in relation to systematic research synthesis as a means of giving voice to all research users. First, the role of systematic research synthesis in democratising access to knowledge and in clarifying the values driving research questions, methods and findings. Second, the breadth of questions and evidence that can be considered. Reviews can be concerned with all types of research knowledge, not only those coming from a particular conceptual or methodological standpoint. Third, the potential of systematic research synthesis to allow a greater range of voices to drive research agendas, thus democratising knowledge creation.

If different groups within society had the resources and power to commission systematic research reviews, there would be a range of different perspectives of what we want to know, what we already know already and how we know it, and what more do we want to know and how could we know it? In this way the different groups would drive the research agenda and be active players in knowledge creation and its use. This does not mean that everyone has to be a researcher. It means that different groups need to have the power to contribute as active players and managers and controllers of the research process undertaken by others.

Access to and appraisal of research knowledge
Access
In the past the inability to read or understand specific languages was a barrier to most people accessing knowledge that was written and accumulated by the learned and elite in society. Everyone in a society is a potential beneficiary and thus user of research knowledge so that knowledge should not be held by a few privileged members and groups in society. The problem is not access alone but in making sense of the extraordinary quantity of research that is published each year in a vast

array of different forms (Hillage *et al*, 1998). Research synthesis that brings together all that is known within clear parameters and uses explicit methods of review can enable such research knowledge to be open to all. It enables those making decisions and those affected by decisions to have easier access to research evidence that may be relevant to the arguments made in support of or against any such decision (Smith, 1996).

Trustworthiness and accountability

A basic premise of research is that it has some form of methodology that is made explicit so that the results of the research are accountable in terms of:

- the underlying theoretical and value assumptions of the research

- the methods of the research

- the manner in which these methods have been executed

Explicit reporting enables people to know whether they agree with the theories and other assumptions underlying the research, the methods used, the manner in which these were implemented in practice, the analysis of results and the conclusions drawn: all of this may include ethical objections to aspects of the research. Such explicitness of theory and method has long been a requirement in primary research. But transparency of theory and methods has not traditionally been the expectation from reviews of evidence from these primary studies. Until recently reviews have been relatively silent on their method and dependent on trusting the expertise of the reviewer.

However, there is empirical evidence that the method of review affects the results of the review (Oliver, 1999) which is hardly surprising when considering all the stages and processes of a review that require theoretical or value judgement and decisions. The consequence is that a traditional review may give non-researchers access to research findings but not in an accountable trustworthy or interpretable way. Similar concerns can be made about expert opinion, which may be based on high levels of skill and experience but is difficult to evaluate without an understanding of the basis on which it is made.

In contrast to traditional informal methods of reviewing and also to expert opinion on what is known from the research literature, systematic research synthesis uses explicit and transparent methods to determine what is known from the research literature. Such systematic reviews are pieces of research, which follow standard sets of stages and so are accountable, updateable and in some cases replicable. Systematic research synthesis enables us to be clear about what we know and how we know it within different ideological and theoretical positions.

Conceptual and value positions

The way we understand the world is dependent upon the implicit and explicit theories and assumptions by which we perceive and analyse information so there are many potential understandings or discourses and many types of knowledge.

Being clear about the methods by which knowledge has been identified and synthesised enables the ideological and theoretical assumptions on which the research knowledge is based to be more transparent. The aim is to make these inevitable biases explicit rather than being hidden within the discourse of the account of knowledge. Research and evidence cannot be value-free, but it can be an overt epistemic form of knowledge creation. What systematic reviews aim to eliminate is hidden bias that may mislead the user of the research review.

Research evidence is only one factor influencing policy, practice and individual decisions. Other factors such as ideology, political judgment, experience and resources may be equally if not more important. Being more explicit about what is known about research and the premises on which it is based allows us to be more explicit about the other factors influencing decisions. In this way, non-research factors influence both the creation of research knowledge and its use in decision making (Table 1). Thus, systematic research synthesis highlights rather than hides judgements, values and worldviews so that they can be overtly discussed and debated. It can also reveal where research is being used selectively to support decisions made for other reasons (Weiss, 1979).

Table 1: Factors effecting the research process and interpretation and use of research knowledge it creates

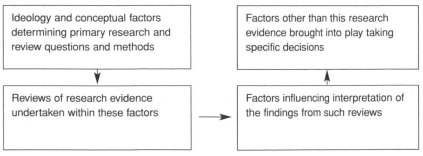

RESEARCH	DECISION MAKING
Ideology and conceptual factors determining primary research and review questions and methods	Factors other than this research evidence brought into play taking specific decisions
Reviews of research evidence undertaken within these factors	Factors influencing interpretation of the findings from such reviews

All types of research knowledge

There are an infinite number of research questions that could be posed by different users of research based on different conceptual and value positions. These different questions need different research methods to answer them: this is reflected by the richness in variation of primary research methods, from ethnography to randomised controlled experiments, and of primary research data and research findings. This richness in methods, data and evidence is mirrored in research reviews so that systematic reviews may be as varied as primary research and require judgment and decision at every stage of the review.

Reviews are undertaken in order to answer questions. The nature of the review question is likely, as in primary research, to influence the method of review and the evidence considered competent to answer the review question. Often the conceptual and value positions in a research question are not fully explicit. But to undertake a systematic review, the question to be answered and its assumptions need to be made clear in order to define what studies to include and how they should be considered by the review.

Different types of question are not only more likely to be related to specific research methodologies but also to particular paradigms of research. Studies asking questions of process or conceptual understanding may be more likely to use descriptive analytic techniques and to create new theories about the world. The question about how mixed ability teaching affects different individuals and in what ways can be explored through small sample qualitative designs. On the other hand, studies asking questions about the efficacy of interventions or of measuring the extent of some phenomena are attempting to ascertain some empirical facts (within the parameters of the conceptual assumptions of the study) and so may use large scale empirical designs. For example, the question about whether mixed ability teaching leads to improved or worse outcomes for certain groups of individuals can be tested with experimental or large group naturalistic research. In this way the variation found in primary research studies is also likely to be reflected in secondary research including systematic reviews. Some of the most important differences between reviews are described in the next section (Gough, 2007).

Type of review question

The range of questions considered by systematic reviews is to date relatively limited, many reviews being concerned with the efficacy of interventions, though an increasing number ask questions of prevalence, need, process and of conceptual understanding and explanation (Dixon-Woods *et al*, 2006; Greenhalgh *et al*, 2005; Pawson, 2006). All questions asked of primary research can be asked of reviews. There is no full account of all these potential questions, so work is underway to examine the range of questions found in journals across the social science disciplines (at the Methods for Research Synthesis Node of the ESRC National Centre for Research Methods, see www.ncrm.ac. uk). This means that reviews can be charted against possible questions and that the actual and potential range of review methods used to address these questions can be explored.

A priori or iterative methodology

For some primary research it is considered important for the research method to be specified well in advance of the research, whilst for other primary research it is important that the method, and to some extent the research question, is flexible and develops iteratively as the research progresses. Research reviews mirror this distinction. For example, reviews on the efficacy of educational interventions by the Campbell Collaboration (www.campbell.org) are more likely to use *a priori* methods using meta analysis of experimental studies to ask questions of empirical efficacy. In contrast, reviews concerned with examining theory are more likely to use iterative approaches (Dixon-Woods *et al*, 2006; Greenhalgh *et al*, 2005; Pawson, 2006).

Research designs, numerical or narrative data, empirical or conceptual data, and relatively homogeneous or heterogeneous data

Primary research varies in the research design and specific methods used to answer different questions and the type of data produced by such methods. Reviews can also vary in their design and method and in the types and range of primary research considered. Even within one type of research design data can vary on dimensions such as topic, concepts and approach, sample, context and measures. If several types of research design are considered there can be considerable heterogeneity in the studies included in a review.

Numerical or narrative analysis of data in synthesis and integrative (meta empirical) or interpretative (meta conceptual) synthesis of data

When a primary study or review includes only numerical data it is possible that the data analysis will be also be numerical but this may not always be the case as when the full data are not available or are too heterogeneous for meaningful numerical analysis. In all cases where numerical analysis is not possible the material for analysis will be words and so will be narrative. This narrative analysis may aim to make empirical statements about the world within a particular conceptual framework thus integrating empirical evidence from individual studies to make an overall meta empirical statement. Alternatively, the analysis may be integrating theoretical understandings to make a new conceptual understanding or meta conceptual synthesis.

Many more distinctions can be made between different methods of systematic review (Gough, 2007) including the appraisal of the quality and relevance of research contributing to the review findings (Gough in press). The purpose here is only to introduce some of the major distinctions to show that reviews cover the whole spectrum of methods of primary research. Reviews are not confined to a particular approach to research; they do not predefine how research is to be undertaken or require a particular world view. Reviews are not atheoretical processes without judgement. They span both what are often termed qualitative and quantitative research. Systematic research synthesis, like primary research, aims to avoid implicit assumptions and to encourage question-driven, transparent, and methods of research which are fit for purpose.

User-led research agendas

The crucial issue for all research is the question being asked. Different questions have different implicit and explicit assumptions and so lead to different answers. It is therefore important to know who is asking the questions and for what purpose. If the questions are in the control of only some parts of society this can alter the research agenda being undertaken. Some sections of society may be directly affected by decisions informed by research but may have had little say in the research agenda that informed the creation of that research knowledge. This is why there have been attempts to involve different groups of citizens in research agenda setting (Oliver *et al*, 2004). Systematic reviews are a powerful means of achieving this objective because they consider all research within certain specified boundaries. They provide greater leverage in considering what we want to know and how we can know it than involvement in single primary studies. The role of users can vary from being powerful managers of the whole process to providing input for some of the stages of a review such as those listed in Table 1 and discussed below (Gough, 2005).

Table 2: Review stage and potential for indirect and direct user input

Stage of knowledge reviews and production	Indirect user input: via new primary research or reviews of user views	Direct user input: inform versus participate versus control
1. Review question	eg priority setting	eg user managed reviews
2. Process of the review	eg mixed methods reviews including user views	eg advisory committees
3. Communication	eg studies of communication and impact	eg user written summaries
4. Interpretation	eg practice surveys	eg user input about context and practice knowledge
5. Application	eg reviews of implementation research	eg concensus development methods for developing intervention guidelines
6. Driving new primary research	eg priority setting	eg user led research agenda setting

Informing the specific focus of the review question

In determining the questions for research review, users of research are determining what we want to know. Even if there is broad agreement about what needs to be studied, the particular focus may be determined by those with particular perspectives such as academic, policy maker or practitioner perspectives. For example, a review on social issues for children driven by a class of school students in London reflected these students' topic interests (Garcia *et al*, 2006)

A review needs to have a specific question, so not all views can be included, but a process of considering many different views clarifies the focus of the review and whose interests it will serve. There is no problem with a plurality of reviews on a topic area but there is a problem if reviews only represent certain sectional interests particularly if this is not explicit. There needs to be open debate about the democracy of review question decision making.

There are several ways in which different perspectives can input into a review. One way is to study the range of views about an issue through new primary research or through systematic reviews of studies of the range of different perspectives about the issue. For example, a systematic map of the effects of travel on children undertook a telephone survey and a focus group with children to identify the range of travel experiences and outcomes that the systematic map should cover (Gough *et al*, 2001). Another way is to represent views on an advisory group to the review with varying degrees of specification of roles, responsibilities and decision making powers including formal consensus formation processes (Oliver *et al*, 2004). The role of users of the review can vary between being consulted and advising on the review to directing the decisions being taken.

Informing the process of undertaking the review

In addition to determining the initial review question there is also much opportunity to impact upon its process. This is particularly so in iterative reviews where the method is being developed during the process of the review but also true of reviews which are predominantly *a priori* with some iterative components. Reviews can have a mapping stage where a broad range of literature is systematically identified and described and then decisions are made as to the most useful and coherent way to undertake a synthesis of the evidence on all or part of this research. If only part of the research map is considered in the synthesis this is a narrowing of the research question. Even when there is little iteration the review question, its conceptual framework and the protocol for review require many decisions to arrive at *a priori* decisions on inclusion criteria, the search strategy, screening of studies, quality appraisal and synthesis.

Communication, interpretation and application of the findings of the review

In order to fulfil the requirements of being explicit and transparent about the methods of the review a full technical explanation of methods is required but shorter summary versions for different audiences can assist communication. These formats may include some aspect of interpretation which provides another potential input for user voice. The interpretation may be undertaken by the authors of the review by guessing different user needs; it may be produced by user groups themselves or there may be an explicit formal deliberative process for considering particular views and other types of knowledge to move from review findings to interpretation for different users and contexts (Gough, 2005). Similar processes may or may not occur in moving from interpretation to action through implementation of review findings in influencing decisions. One example is the use of further research such as implementation surveys to examine the contexts and uses to which the new research evidence might be put (CHSRF, 2006).

Informing new evidence production and synthesis

A systematic review aims to answer a research question but the research evidence may not be adequate for this or the findings and interpretation of the review may lead to new questions. In this way those determining the review question and the process of the review are also able to help determine the new primary research agenda. The different beneficiaries and users of research and research of reviews are thus able to have much greater influence on the nature of research and research findings than they would by being involved in one specific piece of community-based research. They also have a good oversight of the process of research and so develop a capacity to understand the nature and purpose of research.

Conclusions

Systematic reviews are considered by some to be a mechanical and potentially dangerous technique for controlling research agendas. This chapter has shown that their potential is the opposite. They are concerned with all types of research and can vary in terms of question and method as much as in primary research. They can provide access to research findings for all and so allow more democratic involvement in societal debates where research evidence has a role. They can enable the open use of research evidence in debate with all the other factors that are used to make decisions. They can reveal where research evidence is being used opportunistically to support decisions already made for other reasons.

Furthermore, systematic reviews enable different users of research, including members of the public, to be involved in setting the questions asked by reviews and the further primary research that such reviews may lead to. This provides users of research with much greater leverage than could be achieved by involvement with single pieces of research. It also provides those using and influencing research reviews with a good understanding of the purpose and methods of research and the skills to commission and manage it. Not everyone needs the specialist skills of academic researchers: drivers of research agendas just need skills in the management oversight of research done in their name with public resources.

Academic researchers are specialists with much knowledge and skill. They are a major group of users of research and have key roles in developing research agendas as well as having the technical skills to undertake the research. However they should not be the only arbiters of what research is undertaken. We should celebrate and use the dimensions of difference in perspective. We should engage in the debates of the dimensions of difference of knowledge that will be created. Systematic reviews provide a means for this to be achieved that has more leverage and power than debates which are undertaken at the level of individual studies of primary research.

The argument is that systematic reviews can bring about a change in access and power. The trouble is that resources are needed to make this a reality. Some users of research such as funders of research, academics in universities and commercial companies are more likely to have the resources to be able to determine the focus of review questions. We need to share resources more broadly within society to achieve greater plurality in the production and use of research knowledge. Research and research evidence is a democratic issue.

References

CHSRF (Canadian Health Services Research Foundation) (2006) Weighing up the Evidence. Making evidence-informed guidance accurate, achievable, and acceptable *A summary of the workshop held on September 29 2005* (Available at: http://www.chsrf.ca/other_documents/evidence_e.php)

Dixon-Woods, M, Cavers, D, Agarwal, S, Annandale, E, Arthur, A, Harvey, J, Hsu, R, Katbamna, S, Olsen, R, Smith, LK, Riley, R, and Sutton, AJ (2006) Conducting a critical interpretive review of the literature on access to healthcare by vulnerable groups. *BMC Medical Research Methodology* 6, p35

Garcia, J, Sinclair, J, Dickson, K, Thomas, J, Brunton, J, Tidd, M and the PSHE Review Group (2006) *Conflict Resolution, Peer Mediation and Young People's Relationships.* London : EPPI-Centre

Gough, DA (2004) Systematic research synthesis. In Thomas G, Pring R (eds), *Evidence-based Practice in Education.* Buckingham: Open University Press, pp44-62

Gough, D (2005) User led research synthesis: a participative approach to driving research agendas. Presented at the Knowledge Mobilisation for the Human Sciences Symposium, Banff Centre, September/October 2005 (Available at: http://eppi.ioe.ac.uk/)

Gough, D (2007) A typology for systematic reviews. Poster presented at NCRM Conference Manchester January 2007 (Available at: http://eppi.ioe.ac.uk/)

Gough, DA (In press) Weight of evidence: a framework for the appraisal of the quality and relevance of evidence. In J. Furlong, and A. Oancea (eds) Applied and Practice-based Research Special Edition of *Research Papers in Education,* Summer 2007

Gough, D, Elbourne, D (2002) Systematic research synthesis to inform policy, practice and democratic debate. *Social Policy and Society* 1, 1-12

Gough, DA, Oliver, S, Brunton, G, Selai, C, and Schaumberg, H (2001) *The effect of travel modes on children's mental health, cognitive and social development; a systematic review.* Report for DETR EPPI Centre, Social Science Research Unit

Greenhalgh, T, Robert, G, Macfarlane, F, Bate, S P, Kyriakidou, O, and Peacock, R (2005) Storylines of research in diffusion of innovation:a meta-narrative approach to systematic review. *Social Science and Medicine* 61(2), 417-430

Hillage, J, Pearson, R, Anderson, A, and Tamkin P (1998) *Excellence in Research in Schools.* London: Department for Education and Employment/Institute of Employment Studies

Oliver, S (1999) Users of health services: following their agenda. In: Hood, S, Mayall, B, Oliver, S (eds) *Critical Issues in Social Research: Power and Prejudice.* Buckingham: Open University Press

Oliver, S, Clarke Jones, L, Rees, R, Milne, R, Buchanan, P, Gabbay, J, Gyte, G, Oakley, A, and Stein K (2004) Involving consumers in research and development agenda setting for the NHS: developing an evidence-based approach. *Health Technology Assessment Monographs* 8(15), 1-148

Pawson, R (2006) *Evidence-Based Policy: A Realist Perspective.* London: Sage

Smith, AFM (1996) Mad cows and ecstasy: chance and choice in an evidence-based society. *Journal of the Royal Statistical Society* 159, 367-383

Weiss, CH (1979) The many meanings of research utilisation, *Public Administration Review* 39, 426-431

4

Terminal terminology:
the language of assessment

Maddalena Taras

Introduction

Current educational discourse supports learners: learner and learning-centred educational ideals, self-assessment, assessment for learning. Language and assessment seem heavily weighted in favour of learners. However, this chapter argues, that beneath a superficial veneer of supporting learners, discourse, assessment practices and terminology conspire to disadvantage them despite the good intentions and liberalism which inspire arguments based on sound educational principles.

Educational discourse is not static and often fluctuates according to the socio-political agenda: being aware of this discourse allows us to monitor this agenda. The discourse of two aspects of assessment, self-assessment and assessment for learning, are examined to attempt to throw light on the implications for learners and tutors. These paradigms which purport to support learning and empower learners are perpetrating and perpetuating the very problems which they are working so hard to resolve.

In this chapter three aspects of assessment will be examined: first discourse, in particular metaphor, along with the implications for educational contexts, second how language can be used in a dichotomous way and create restrictions of choice, and third self-assessment and assessment for learning imagery. This process will help to show how discourse, power issues and grading within assessment all contribute to the marginalisation and disempowerment of learners.

Metaphor

As a working definition of metaphor, Low's is the clearest and most direct. He affirms that it is a reclassification which involves 'Treating X as if it were, in some ways, Y' (Low, 1988, p126). Metaphor takes the attributes of one term and transfers salient features to another.

The discussion of metaphor has always required a radical choice: either language is a rule-governed mechanism in which metaphor constitutes a malfunction (as Aristotle proposes) or that language is by nature and originally metaphorical. Within the latter belief considering metaphor to be an intrinsic part of language is the strong form; there is a weaker form of this belief which, while acknowledging the importance of metaphor, attributes only an influence as opposed to a determining force. This chapter supports the strong form. Many academics believe in the strong version of the role of metaphor (Fairclough, 1994; Petrie and Oshlag, 2002; Harrison, 2004). Even those who favour the weak form acknowledge the importance of metaphor in discourse.

Four dimensions of metaphor are particularly pertinent to this chapter. Taking a social discourse and cognitive theories paradigm, metaphor has an all-encompassing hold on our thought processes and concepts (Fairclough, 1994; Petrie and Oshlag, 2002; Lakoff and Johnson, 2002). Metaphors have a critical influence in determining our reality (Lakoff and Johnson, 1980, p146) and they are central in helping us to understand and interiorise new concepts and knowledge by linking old and new ideas (Reddy, 1979; Lakoff and Johnson, 2002; Ortony, 1979, 2002): 'Metaphors structure the way we think and the way we act, and our systems of knowledge and belief, in a pervasive and fundamental way' (Fairclough, 1994, p194). On the negative side, metaphors can be so forceful that 'they are taken as literal truth (Petrie and Oshlag, 2002, p581) thus impeding future developments and options, and producing a cognitive straightjacket (Taras, 2007). In addition to imprisoning us within our opinions and realities (Reddy, 1979; Lakoff and Johnson, 1980), networks of metaphors also exclude or preclude new ideas or paradigms thus 'silencing' the lone voice offering new stories (Harrison, 2004).

Linked to this is the fourth dimension of excluding and including: 'what is not acknowledged is the power of metaphor in allowing the emergence of some accounts whilst silencing others' (Harrison, 2004, p175).

46

The partial aspect of metaphorical structuring of concepts necessarily means that some aspects are highlighted by the metaphor and some masked (Low, 1988, p126).

Metaphors of communication

Two metaphoric networks in the English language the conduit metaphor (Reddy, 1979) and the 'argument as war' metaphor (Lakoff and Johnson, 1980) together compound the impact of making disagreement into an aggressive act. Since argument is so central to creating new discourse in the academic context, this has serious implications.

Reddy provides an extensive analysis of the conduit metaphor and finds that it both blames the speaker/writer for communication problems as the one with the more difficult task of packaging meanings/feelings and belittles the work of the listener/hearer who only has to open the package. Psychologically this is negative for both parties who are attempting to communicate: 'communication is considered a 'success without effort' system' when it is an 'energy must be expended' system (Reddy, 1979, p308). Admitting a lack of understanding signals ignorance or lack of intelligence in the listener and speakers feel their efforts have been wasted.

A metaphor within the conduit network is the 'ideas are in the library': 'We have the greatest, most sophisticated system for mass communication of any society that we know about, yet somehow mass communication becomes more and more synonymous with less communication' (*ibid,* 310). This is because the learning or extraction of this information is trivialised in the conduit metaphor.

Like Reddy, Lakoff and Johnson discover an extensive metaphoric network of argument as war. Fairclough notes:

> Some arguments are so profoundly naturalized within a particular culture that people are not only quite unaware of these most of the time, but find it extremely difficult, **even when their attention is drawn to them**, to escape from them in their course, thinking, or action ... Thus the militarization of discourse is also a militarization of thought and social practice ... just as the marketisation of discourse in education referred to above is also a marketisation of thought and practice (Fairclough, 1994, p195)

Therefore, as for Reddy's network, the argument as war metaphor has far-reaching and profound implications, particularly for the academic community. As Harrison notes:

Evidence for metaphor in shaping and structuring how we think and act is provided by the difficulty of imagining a world in which argument is viewed differently, for example as a dance in which the main objective is to achieve an elegant and balanced performance. (Harrison, 2004, p172)

Arguments would hold few threats if we were merely dancing our way through academic papers.

Implications for education

In the academic context, where ideas and arguments are at the heart of academic life, disagreement can be interpreted as a lack of solidarity and support for colleagues: negotiation of meaning in arguments and theories becomes difficult when disagreement is seen as an attack or defence against an attack (Taras, 2007).

Discourse between academics and between tutors and learners is fraught with danger: the two communication metaphors combine to deadly effect. In the conduit and ideas in the library metaphors, learning is trivialised and discourse between academics becomes difficult as the listener/reader will be reluctant to request clarification for fear of being seen as intellectually inferior. In face to face discussions it may be easier to negotiate meaning, accept another viewpoint and agree to differ. Differences of opinion may have greater repercussions when a paper is sent to review for a journal: reviewers may be less favourably disposed to work which challenges their own paradigms. More difficulty in diffusing and rationalising differences is even more likely with published written work because of the difficulty of negotiating meaning. This may lead academics to accept rather than challenge published work, particularly since publishing represents endorsement by the wider community. Reviewing peer work for journals also becomes a possible attack or act of aggression when new paradigms or ideas are offered. Schools of thought and ideologies may form cliques which are difficult to enter or to break up.

For learners of all levels and ages trivialising learning means that lack of conceptual understanding may label the learner as intellectually slow or lazy and evoke little sympathy or support. It also places them in a position of vulnerability which they themselves aggravate because learners are also subject to the metaphoric influence and may blame themselves for not understanding. If assessments require learners to argue a position with which tutors disagree, this may be perceived as negative by tutors and be to the learners' detriment. Although the current business metaphor in higher education (HE) is generally seen as negative to all concerned because learning becomes a commercial enterprise as opposed to a basic tenet of an enlightened society (Fairclough, 1994, p195), it could have the unexpected benefit of providing learners with the right to question since the customer is always right.

From the tutors' perspectives they are the ones who have prepared the ideas and the 'package' and if learning does not take place they are doubly insulted: they have done the work for the learners and the learners have failed to put in the required effort or time or both. These perceptions will influence the relationship between learners and tutors. In class, learners who question opinions and ask questions may not be appreciated.

Dichotomy of language

Language can create dichotomies which tend to exclude other options or viewpoints (Stronach, 1996, p6, 9). This means that instead of discourse which permits a number of options a binary solution is established. In the assessment context, summative and formative assessment as originally presented by Scriven (1967) did not do this but developments in the assessment for learning paradigm present them as alternatives so that even the possibility of them working together is seen as very difficult and problematic (Black and Wiliam, 1998a). Stronach (following Derrida) calls this 'violent hierarchy of the text's opposition' (Stronach, 1996, p6) which sets lines and boundaries in discourse. Academic research communities work within very different sociopolitical contexts which influences practice. However, the internationalisation of research journals and papers means that increasingly common discourse parameters are being set: dichotomies, instead of opening up discourse so that we all benefit from different experience, risk driving the academic community into narrow parameters.

Discourse of difference for assessment

In order to understand how language and perceptions fix and influence our beliefs about assessment, this chapter returns to the primary terminology which governs our basic concepts and assumptions. Presumptions and assumptions which need to be explicit in order to understand their power and to attempt to change and open the discourse are inherent in these terms. The arguments in favour of student self-assessment echo those supporting the use of assessment for learning: both terms contain the word assessment and involve learners. Both are seen as formative procedures although Taras (2005) notes that according to Scriven (1967) and Sadler (1989) self-assessment is the equivalent to summative and not formative assessment. This would make them essentially different exercises although perceptions place them as analogous. Self-assessment is one of four formative assessment interventions in the assessment for learning paradigm. Hierarchically, this would place self-assessment subservient to formative assessment, whereas Taras' classification would reverse the order and require self-assessment to be an essential step prior to formative assessment. Procedures and processes of assessment have been the focus of few discussions: many different perceptions and understandings of the terminology exist (Brookhart, 2004).

Dichotomy between summative and formative assessment across sectors

Self-assessment, generally developed in the HE and professional development context, was intended to wean students from being reliant on the tutor and thus to develop students' autonomy and independence in learning (Boud, 1995). This was the assessment by students of their own work in order to understand assessment protocols, develop their expertise and build-up confidence in their own judgements. It was developed essentially as a formative exercise which excluded students from summative, graded assessment (Boud, 1991; Boud, 1995). As a consequence students have been excluded from the centre and seat of power and self-assessment risks being more of a confessional of weakness than a negotiation of assessment issues (Reynolds and Trehan, 2000).

Assessment for learning was developed in the compulsory sector and was initially a means of extricating teachers and learners from pressures of national and externally accredited assessments and exams. Teachers and learners were increasingly facing a narrowing of the curriculum in order to focus on these final assessments (Black and Wiliam, 1998a; Black et al, 2003). Assessment for learning was a means of returning learning to the classroom, learning which was supported by assessment and not stultified or restricted by it. This was developed as a series of formative exercises by opening the Black Box (Black and Wiliam, 1998b) of the classroom, making learning procedures explicit and providing good feedback. Assessment for learning was put into direct opposition to summative assessment which encompassed external and national exams.

Within the compulsory sector and in HE, although independently of each other, the dichotomy between summative and formative assessment has been progressively reinforced. This is dangerous because this common dichotomy which has different origins and meanings is perceived as representing similar structures and processes. In both the compulsory sector and in HE, the danger is that tutor and learner assessments become mutually exclusive and excluding. We need metaphors, images and processes which are inclusive of options and do not create dichotomies: a discourse of difference which opens up choices.

Self-assessment: words and meaning

Student self-assessment is acknowledged as pivotal in allowing students to develop as independent and autonomous learners (Cowan, 2006; Nicol and Macfarlane-Dick, 2005). The term self-assessment is however misleading and linguistically ambiguous: is it assessment *of* the self, *by* the self or *for* the self or possibly all three? A literal reading could suggest introspection of the human self. In education self-assessment implies student involvement with assessment and innovative practice from the tutor. This burden of innovation could be frightening for tutors and be a contributing factor in limiting its use.

Furthermore, hidden in the word self-assessment is the fact, as will become evident, that it rarely involves learners in summative assessment, i.e. grading. It is often used as a learning instrument and hardly impinges on, questions or shares the tutor's processes or power as an assessor, although this sharing of tutor power is often a primary association with the term. It helps learners understand assessment protocols by involving them in criteria and how their work addresses these but it rarely includes learners in assessments which count for accreditation.

Although self-assessment is used as a learning tool, expectations engendered by the term are misleading: both tutors and learners are lulled into believing that learners are involved in assessment. Because of these connotations tutors are often reluctant to use student self-assessment because they associate it with loss of power: both tutors and students collude to maintain the *status quo* of mutual dependency (Black and Wiliam, 1998a, p20). Unless tutors include learners in grading, it can be disempowering (Reynolds and Trehan, 2000).

Self-assessment and power

Assessment is at the centre of political and power issues: Broadfoot argues that the emphasis in public debate on the 'scientific' nature of assessment has consistently disguised the values and power relations, the interpretative and the idiosyncratic in assessment practices (Broadfoot, 2000).

Heron presents the power issue more strongly: 'The unilateral model of control and assessment in education is a form of political exploitation, of oppression by professionalism' (Heron, 1988, p81). Talbot extends the web of influence of power by using Foucault's metaphor: 'Power is deployed by those who are in a position to define and categorise, to include and exclude' (Talbot *et al*, 2003, p2). The seat of power has resided with the tutor even in contexts where external validation of exams takes place, as in the compulsory sector because tutors maintain power through classroom assessment (Boud, 1995; Brookhart, 2004).

Common sense indicates that assessment is the responsibility of the tutor. In traditional assessment contexts tutors make most of the decisions: curriculum, content, what to assess, how to assess. The assessment itself is decided and rarely contested, particularly by students themselves even at university level (Taras, 2001, 2002). Innovative assessments purport to follow the principles of learner and learning-centredness including learners in assessment with ensuing access to power. This is a common argument in support of self-assessment (Somervell, 1993; Boud, 1995; Cowan, 2006).

The most compelling pedagogic argument for self-assessment with the ensuing greater equality of power between students and staff is that empirical evidence has shown beyond doubt that learning is enhanced by it (Broadfoot and Black, 2004; Nicol and Macfarlane-Dick, 2005; Black and Wiliam, 1998a). For HE Dearing (1997) states the need for learner and learning-centred institutions which produce independent and autonomous students, claims which are made in many university mission statements. This would make student self-assessment become mandatory (Taras, 2002; Nicol and Macfarlane-Dick, 2005).

It is the pedagogic argument which has led to the use of self-assessment in the school sector within the assessment for learning paradigm: Black *et al* (2003) use self-assessment as one of four key procedures of formative assessment to help student learning. It is also a key feature helping to promote deep learning (Cowan, 2006). Closely linked to this is the argument promoting lifelong learning, the necessary skills for professional practice (Taras, 2001; Boud, 1995) and for integrating learners into a democratic and inclusive society.

Self-assessment: power and grading

The current predominant self-assessment discourse in HE in Britain and Australia, which has been promoted and essentially developed by Boud and taken as the flagship of innovation, claims to be a means for students to access the power structures of assessment (Boud, 1995; Somervell, 1993). Two models predominate, neither of which allows student assessments to contribute to the final student mark and are essentially formative exercises: students enumerate strengths and weaknesses against agreed criteria and may provide an expected grade with their work. Alternately students receive a model answer with criteria and a mark sheet as a time-saver device for tutors (Boud, 1985, 1989). The latter is perhaps one of the expectations of tutors who are newcomers to self-assessment, an expectation which is rarely realised and which often results in tutors turning their backs on self-assessment.

However there is one important problem. Boud himself notes: 'Self-assessment contributes to changing power relationships, but only if it is used with a shift of control as, for example, can come about when it is used as part of assessment which counts for formal grading purposes' (Boud, 1995, p44).

Many examples of learner ownership in assessment relegate students to their own assessment process which does not impinge on the summative assessment framework of the tutor and quality processes (Boud, 1991; Boud 1995): Cowan (2006) and Taras (2002, 2003) offer notable exceptions. In one study in 1985, Cowan offers a Learning Contract Design model, where 25 per cent of learning and assessment is in the hands of the learner and contributes to the final mark. Each assessment involves summarising the standards and criteria, describing their performance in comparable terms and reporting the process of judgement by comparing the work with standards and criteria to justify the mark. 'My role in assessment was simply to confirm that the conditions had been met' (Cowan, 2006, p115).

Taras (2001, 2002, 2003) provides the only model which requires learners' involvement in grading. There are four original and distinctive features in this model: using summative assessment tasks, integrated tutor feedback but with no initial mark or grade, peer discussion and feedback to clarify criteria/standards feedback, and the comparison and discussion of the students' and tutor marks. Some benefits are summarised as follows:

> The results showed that while both conditions benefited learning, self-assessment with integrated tutor feedback helped students identify and correct more errors (those that they or peers had not been aware of) than self-assessment prior to peer or tutor feedback. Interestingly, this study not only shows the benefits of integrating external and internal feedback but it also shows ways of helping students internalise and use tutor feedback. (Nicol and Macfarlane-Dick, 2005 p9)

In assessment in HE it is surprising how little contestation there has been of the tutor's power: even when students are included in assessment the role of the tutor as final arbiter of assessment is often unchallenged. This is true of most forms of both self and peer assessment: some include student grades but they are rarely significant enough to challenge tutors' decisions (Boud, 1995). Self-assessment is also rare because formal assessment is seen as the only power tutors still wield: student involvement may be seen as a challenge to this power.

Student self-assessment as it is widely understood and used (Boud, 1995), could be seen as a confessional:

> If self-awareness, consciousness-raising or reflexivity are introduced into the assessment process without power, authority and judgement-making being examined or changed, students have even less control than in more traditional methods. (Reynolds and Trehan, 2000, p271)

Reynolds and Trehan further highlight the dangers of self-assessment as a learning instrument:

> At best, participative methods empower students by constituting them as active learners, responsible for their own learning. Superficial application in the interests of 'student involvement', within an unaltered disciplinary regime of the academic institution, engenders surveillance through self-regulation, especially if students are required to reveal or confess themselves. (Reynolds and Trehan, 2000, p275)

This would seem to confirm that including students in assessment would require them to have access to graded work and to grading, otherwise we risk making them the victims of more injustice and less empowerment.

The assessment for learning imagery

The phrase *assessment for learning* creates powerful imagery for educationalists because it seems to assuage all our fears relating to assessment: like metaphor it transfers attributes of learning which are all positive because they deliver the aims of education. Its other positive aspect is that *for* looks to the future, whereas *of* looks to the past: *for* has an additional favourable connotation (ie not against).

The word assessment has negative and even sinister connotations. Fear of assessment is linked to the term itself; it is often called evaluation to make it sound more benign (Taras, 2005). Other subjects like languages, maths and sciences use testing, which sounds less threatening. It is possible that the term assessment itself was adopted to replace the less impartial examinations, a term with clinical connotations.

Assessment is a judgement; these terms denote something serious, heavyweight and often negative (Scriven, 1967) despite representing a common and universal process (Rowntree, 1987). The contemporary view is that it is politically incorrect to pass any judgement, however important or necessary; it is generally taken to be a condemnation. In education, assessment evokes the finality of exams and accreditation, and the fear of failure. In HE assessment has fallen behind learning and teaching (Nicol and Macfarlane-Dick, 2005) and become the area in which staff are least knowledgeable or expert. The term assessment is not neutral nor does it evoke positive reactions. Assessment for learning seems to have overturned many negative connotations relating to assessment except that all the benign aspects of learning are overshadowed by the negative connotations relating to assessment.

Positive contributions of assessment for learning

Assessment for learning, which has received major funding support in England and through the government's Primary and Secondary National Strategies, provided a key element of the national assessment framework in Wales and has been an important export to the US. It has had important positive effects because it is based on sound educational ideals and principles: the nugget of assessment is feedback, which has been described as the life-blood of learning (Rowntree, 1987). As with assessment, we are bad at producing it and ensuring that it has been understood and used for learning (Broadfoot and Black, 2004; Nicol and Macfarlane-Dick, 2005; Black and Wiliam, 1998a).

Assessment for learning has helped open the Black Box (Black and Wiliam, 1998b) of the classroom and educationally and politically it has re-profiled learning and classroom assessment which is a big achievement. It has fired the imagination of educationalists by using interventions which have been shown through extensive empirical research to be statistically significant in improving learner test scores and it has been developed by a group of respected academics. It acts as an antidote to the conduit metaphor which denigrates and trivialises learning by focusing on empirically tested positive support for learners.

Negative contributions of assessment for learning

However assessment for learning does not deliver on the promise of neutralising the frightening aspects of assessment because it ignores them and focuses on formative rather than on summative assessment. Taras (2007) argues that its positive aspects have led to the whole paradigm being accepted as a panacea by the academic community without scrutiny of process or theory in order to ensure continued improvement.

Biggs' (1998) main criticism of Black and Wiliam's (1998a) world-renowned review, which also applies to Black *et al*, 2003, the bible of assessment for learning is that they have excluded summative assessment from the discussion. Brookhart (2004) shows that good students think of assessment in both summative and formative terms, as does Biggs' work in Hong Kong (1998). By excluding summative assessment from the discourse, Black and Wiliam are trying to render it invisible in the classroom. The dichotomy between summative and formative assessment has created a further divide. Both impede the possibility of a discourse of difference.

The work of Black and Wiliam vilifies and blackens summative assessment as the source of evil because tutors and learners focus on it to the detriment of formative assessment. This distorts the essential neutrality of the assessment process, particularly of summative assessment (Taras, 2005; Rowntree, 1987; Scriven, 1967). It also distorts the essential links between summative and formative assessment which results in duplication of assessment processes in the classroom to the detriment of all (Taras, 2005, 2007). Black *et al* (2003) were forced to integrate summative and formative assessment in classroom practice because teachers refused to separate the two as logistically impractical and impracticable.

The assessment for learning paradigm has become the dominant discourse of assessment despite the theoretical inconsistencies (Taras, 2005, 2007): more seriously, these theoretical inconsistencies are being rationalised and confirmed. It is time to appraise and examine the consequences of the paradigm, particularly as the discourse is being transferred to HE.

Summary and conclusion

This chapter has examined aspects of discourse which dominate our thinking and perceptions. Metaphors create our realities: metaphoric images, particularly metaphoric networks such as 'argument as war' and the conduit metaphor, tend to present disagreement as an attack on the author/speaker and the respondents as lacking in intelligence: this aspect challenges the very heart of academic life which is based on discussion and being aware of the problem is not necessarily a safeguard against its power. Metaphors also silence discourse and dichotomies separate and divide. This would reverse the proverb making it 'speak before you are spoken to' if you wish to have the upper hand.

Assessment discourse has shown how the dichotomy between summative and formative assessment has different origins within sectors and preclude the healthy middle ground where learners and tutors meet. In HE self-assessment is in opposition to tutor assessment. In the compulsory sector assessment for learning separates classroom assessment and learning from external exams. Both have evolved separately and differently across sectors but use common terminology which provides the illusion of parallel and complementary assessment processes.

Other illusions are provided by other assessment terminology, notably 'self-assessment' and 'assessment for learning'. These have meanings which are counter-intuitive: the first, far from making students an integral part of assessment, tend to marginalise their own assessment activity by excluding this from graded work. Self-assessment has the added danger of drawing learners into a confessional form which would further penalise them. Taras is a notable exception requiring student involvement in grading. Assessment for learning has fired the imagination of teachers and academics. Recent work by Taras (2005, 2007) shows that there are dual and disparate definitions of formative assessment in this paradigm, exacerbating the problems created by the summative/formative assessment dichotomy.

Discourse of difference breaks down hierarchies of normative, dominant discourse and offers choices for a forum of open discussion where dialogue develops theories and practices for a more inclusive and democratic society.

This chapter has examined educational assessment and shows how language, particularly metaphor and dichotomy, can dominate and highjack new thoughts and concepts, creating a dominant discourse which it is difficult to challenge: standing on the shoulders of giants (Scriven, 1967) becomes a very dangerous activity.

The pervasive networks of discourse metaphors have a detrimental influence on academic processes both for academics and learners and therefore on the relationship between learners and tutors. A discourse of difference is required to free assessment for learning and self-assessment paradigms from the current impasse created by the summative and formative assessment divide, the erroneous perceptions of the processes which govern them and the misleading expectations created by the terminology. There will be few learner and learning-centred educational realities if assessment, particularly summative assessment, is misunderstood, controlled by tutors and vilified because assessment manipulates and controls learning.

References

Biggs, J (1998) Assessment and Classroom Learning; a role for summative assessment? *Assessment in Education* 5(1), 103-110

Black, P and Wiliam, D (1998a) Assessment and Classroom Learning. *Assessment in Education: Principles, Policy and Practice* 5(1), 7-74

Black, P and Wiliam, D (1998b) Inside the Black Box: Raising Standards Through Classroom Assessment. *Phi Delta Kappan* 80(2), 139-144

Black, P, Harrison, C, Lee, C, Marshall, B and Wiliam, D (2003) *Assessment for learning. Putting it into practice.* Maidenhead: Open University Press

Boud, D J (1985) *Studies in Self-Assessment.* Tertiary Education Research Centre, The University of New South Wales

Boud, D J (1989) The Role of Self-Assessment in Student Grading. *Assessment and Evaluation in Higher Education* 14(1)

Boud, D J (1991) *Implementing Student Self-Assessment* 2nd edition. Sydney: Higher Educational Research and Development Society of Australia

Boud, D J (1995) *Enhancing learning through self assessment.* London: Kogan Page

Broadfoot, P M Preface in Filer, A (ed) (2000) *Assessment: Social Practice and Social Product.* London New York: RoutledgeFalmer

Broadfoot, P and Black, P (2004) Redefining assessment? The first ten years of *Assessment in Education, Assessment in Education*, 11(1), 7-27

Brookhart, S M (2004) Classroom Assessment: Tensions and Intersections in Theory and Practice. *Teachers College Record* 106(3), 429-458

Cowan, J (2006) *On Becoming an Innovative University Teacher Reflection in Action* (Second Edition). Oxford: Oxford University Press

Fairclough, N (1994) *Discourse and Social Change.* Cambridge: Polity Press/Blackwell

Harrison, R (2004) Telling Stories about learners and learning. In Satterthwaite, J, Atkinson, E and Martin, W (eds) *The Disciplining of Education: New Languages of Power and Resistance.* Stoke on Trent UK and Sterling, USA: Trentham Books

Heron, J (1988) Assessment Revisited in Boud, D J (ed) *Developing Student Autonomy in Learning.* London: Kogan Page, Second Edition pp77-90

Lakoff, G and Johnson, M (1980) *Metaphors we live by.* Chicago: University of Chicago Press

Lakoff, G and Johnson, M (2002) The contemporary theory of metaphor in Ortony, A (ed) *Metaphor and Thought.* Cambridge University Press

Low, G D (1988) On Teaching Metaphor. *Applied Linguistics* 9(2)

Nicol, D J and Macfarlane-Dick, D (2005) Formative assessment and self-regulated learning: A model and seven principles of good feedback practice. *Studies in Higher Education* 31(2), 199-218

Ortony, A (1979) (ed) *Metaphor and Thought.* Cambridge: Cambridge University Press

Ortony, A (2002) (ed) *Metaphor and Thought.* Cambridge: Cambridge University Press

Petrie, H G and Oshlag, R S (2002) Metaphor and Learning. In Ortony, A (ed) *Metaphor and Thought.* Cambridge: Cambridge University Press

Reddy, M J (1979) The Conduit Metaphor – A case of frame conflict in our language about language. In Ortony, A (ed) *Metaphor and Thought.* Cambridge: Cambridge University Press

Reynolds, M and Trehan, K (2000) Assessment: a critical perspective. *Studies in Higher Education* volume 25(3), 267-278

Rowntree, D (1987). *Assessing Students: How Shall We Know Them?* London: Harper and Row

Sadler, D R (1989) Formative assessment and the design of instructional systems. *Instructional Science* 18, 145-165

Scriven, M (1967) The methodology of evaluation. In Tyler, R, Gagne, R and Scriven, M. *Perspectives on Curriculum Evaluation* AERA Monograph Series – Curriculum Evaluation. Chicago: Rand McNally and Co

SomervelL, H (1993) Issues in assessment, enterprise and higher education: the case for self, peer and collaborative assessment. *Assessment and Evaluation in Higher Education* 18(3), 221-233

Stronach, I (1996) Fashioning post-modernism, finishing modernism: Tales from the fitting room British Educational Research Journal 22(3), 359-373

Talbot, M, Atkinson, K and Atkinson, D (2003) *Language and Power in the Modern World.* Edinburgh University Press Edinburgh

Taras, M (2001) The use of tutor feedback and student self-assessment in summative assessment tasks: towards transparency for students and for tutors. *Assessment and Evaluation in Higher Education* 26(6), 606-614

Taras, M (2002) Using assessment for learning and learning from assessment. *Assessment and Evaluation in Higher Education* 27(6), 501-510

Taras, M (2003) To feedback or not to feedback in student self-assessment. Assessment and Evaluation in Higher Education, 28(5), 549-565

Taras, M (2005) Assessment: summative and formative, some theoretical reflections. *British Journal of Educational Studies* 53(3), 466-478

Taras, M. (2007) Machinations of assessment: metaphors, myths and realities. *Pedagogy, Culture and Society* 15(1)

Wiliam, D and Black, P (1996) Meanings and consequences: a basis for distinguishing formative and summative functions of assessment? *British Educational Research Journal* 22(5), 537-48

Acknowledgements

I would like to thank Catherine Angela Jones for her support and feedback.

5

Representing the world: difference and science education

Michael J. Reiss

The power of science

I t is difficult to characterise cultures, particularly the culture one in-
habits but in many countries contemporary (natural) science, for all
that it is often critiqued in the media, has a powerful influence on
how people see themselves and understand the world. It is therefore
important for anyone interested in education to consider what science
is and how it is presented as a discipline in schools and elsewhere. One
of the triumphs of science is how many people have taken on board its
big ideas, its metanarratives. For example, most people in Europe
accept that we live in a universe that is billions of years old, that the laws
of nature are the same everywhere and at all times, that all matter is
composed of only a hundred or so elements and that humans have the
other animals as their evolutionary relatives. Such knowledge, most of
it unimaginable only a few centuries ago, is of huge cultural importance.

Despite the importance of science in our lives and in how we understand the world in the UK most university students of science are taught
little explicitly about the nature of science, though school science now
increasingly considers this issue. It is difficult to come up with a definitive answer to the question 'What do scientists study?' (Reiss, 2005a).
Certain things clearly fall into the domain of science: the nature of elec-
tricity, the arrangement of atoms into molecules and human physiology, for example. However, what about such issues as the origin of the

universe, the behaviour of people in society, decisions about whether to build nuclear power plants or go for wind power, the appreciation of music and the nature of love? Do these fall under the domain of science? Some people would argue 'yes', holding the view that science can provide answers for everything.

However most people think that science is but one form of knowledge and that other forms of knowledge complement scientific knowledge. This way of thinking means that the origin of the universe is also a philosophical or religious question or simply unknowable; the behaviour of people in society requires knowledge of the social sciences rather than only of the natural sciences; whether we should go for nuclear or wind power is partly a scientific issue but also requires an understanding of economics, risk and politics; the appreciation of music and the nature of love, while clearly having something to do with our perceptual apparatus and our evolutionary history, cannot be reduced to science.

While historians tell us that what scientists study changes over time, there are certain consistencies. First, science is concerned with the natural world and with certain elements of the manufactured world so that the laws of gravity apply as much to artificial satellites as they do to planets and stars, the laws of chemical bonding as much to nylon tights as to silk stockings. Second, science is concerned with how things are rather than with how they should be. So there is a science of gunpowder and *in vitro* fertilisation without science telling us whether warfare and test tube births are good or bad.

How is science undertaken?

It is difficult too to come up with a clear-cut answer to the question 'How is science undertaken?'. There is, and has been for many decades, active debate about this matter among academic historians, philosophers and sociologists of science.

Robert Merton characterised science as open-minded, universalist, disinterested and communal (Merton, 1973). He saw science as a group activity: even though some scientists work on their own, all scientists contribute to a single body of knowledge accepted by the community of scientists. There are parallels with art, literature and music. After all Cézanne, Gauguin and van Gogh all contributed to post-impressionism. But while it makes no sense to try to combine their paintings, science is largely about combining the contributions of many different scientists to produce an overall coherent model of one aspect of reality.

In this sense science is disinterested and impersonal. The worth of a piece of scientific work can be abstracted from its originator so that scientists should take no notice of individual circumstances in evaluating the validity of a scientist's work.

Individual scientists are passionate about their work and often slow to accept that their cherished ideas are wrong. But science itself is not persuaded by such partiality. While there may be controversy about whether the works of Bach or Mozart are the greater (and the question is pretty meaningless anyway), time shows which of two alternative scientific theories is nearer the truth. While scientists need to retain open mindedness, always being prepared to change their views in the light of new evidence or better explanatory theories, science itself advances over time. This means that, while some scientific knowledge ('frontier science') is contentious, much scientific knowledge can confidently be relied on: it is relatively certain.

Karl Popper emphasised the falsifiability of scientific theories (Popper, 1934/1972). Unless you can imagine collecting data that would refute a theory the theory isn't scientific. The same applies to scientific hypotheses. So, classically, the hypothesis 'All swans are white' is scientific because we can imagine finding a bird that is manifestly a swan in terms of its appearance and behaviour but is not white. This is precisely what happened when early white explorers returned from Australia with tales of black swans.

Popper's ideas easily give rise to a view of science in which scientific knowledge steadily accumulates over time as new theories are proposed and new data collected to discriminate between conflicting theories. Much school experimentation in science is Popperian in essence: we see a rainbow and hypothesise that white light is split up into light of different colours as it is refracted through a transparent medium (water droplets). We test this by attempting to refract white light through a glass prism, we find the same colours of the rainbow are produced and our hypothesis is confirmed. Until some new evidence causes it to be falsified, we accept it.

There is much of value in the work of Thomas Merton and Karl Popper but most academics in the field would argue that there is more to the nature of science. Thomas Kuhn made a number of seminal contributions but is most remembered nowadays for his argument that while the Popperian account of science holds well during periods of *normal science* when a single paradigm holds sway, such as the Ptolemaic model of the structure of the solar system or the Newtonian understanding of motion and gravity, it breaks down when a scientific crisis occurs. At the time of such a crisis, a scientific revolution happens during which a new paradigm, such as the Copernican model of the structure of the solar system or Einstein's theory of relativity, begins to replace the previously accepted paradigm. The central point is that the change of allegiance from scientists believing in one paradigm to their believing in another cannot be fully explained by the Popperian account of falsifiability (Kuhn, 1970).

Kuhn likens the switch from one paradigm to another to a *gestalt* switch when we suddenly see something in a new way or even a religious conversion. As Alan Chalmers puts it:

> There will be no purely logical argument that demonstrates the superiority of one paradigm over another and that thereby compels a rational scientist to make the change. One reason why no such demonstration is possible is the fact that a variety of factors are involved in a scientist's judgment of the merits of a scientific theory. An individual scientist's decision will depend on the priority he or she gives to the various factors. The factors will include such things as simplicity, the connection with some pressing social need, the ability to solve some specified kind of problem, and so on. Thus one scientist might be attracted to the Copernican theory because of the simplicity of certain mathematical features of it. Another might be attracted to it because in it there is the possibility of calendar reform. A third might have been deterred from adopting the Copernican theory because of an involvement with terrestrial mechanics and an awareness of the problems that the Copernican theory posed for it. (Chalmers, 1999, pp115-16)

Kuhn also argued that scientific knowledge is validated by its acceptance in a community of scientists. Often scientists change their views as new evidence persuades them that a previously held theory is wrong. But sometimes they cling obstinately to cherished theories. If these scientists are powerful and can control which papers are published in the most prestigious journals, scientific progress may be impeded until the scientists in question retire or die.

The portrayal of sex and reproduction in school and college textbooks

A good example of the way in which attempts by science to represent reality can distort reality, with consequences that ignore difference and severely disadvantage minority groups, is provided by the way in which human gender, sex and reproduction is represented in school and college textbooks (Reiss, 2005b). School and college biology typically examine issues of human sexuality and femaleness and maleness through the lens of human reproduction. Heterosexuality is assumed. Biology is all too often presumed to be a largely neutral subject which does not assign values so that many biology teachers and lecturers in schools and colleges continue to teach biology as unquestioned fact. Differences between females and males are often presented as clear cut, so that individuals who do not fall neatly into either category are ignored, while the study of school biology textbooks shows that they are often sexist and ignore lesbian and gay issues (Reiss, 1998). For example, GCSE biology textbooks in England often omit all mention of the clitoris or talk of it in a belittling way as the female equivalent of a penis. Males are rendered visible, females less so and the female exists by comparison with the male. When homosexuality is addressed it is as a second best option which the reader may grow out of. However, closer examination of sex in human biology provides plenty of space for critical reflection and allows for a richer understanding of what it is to be a sexual person.

Emily Martin has shown that while menstruation is viewed in scientific textbooks as a failure to get pregnant, sperm maturation is viewed as a wonderful achievement in which countless millions of sperm are manufactured each day (Martin, 1991). Furthermore, sperm are viewed as active and streamlined whereas the egg is large and passive and just drifts along or sits there waiting. It was back in 1948 that Ruth Herschberger argued that the female reproductive organs are viewed as being less autonomous than those of the male. (It is difficult in the scientific discourse around sex to avoid referring to reproduction unless you use the term 'urino-genital organs'.) The way the egg is portrayed in science textbooks has been likened to the fairy tale *Sleeping Beauty*, in which a dormant, virginal bride awaits a male's magic kiss. However, for well over a decade biologists have seen both egg and sperm as active partners. Just as sperm seek out the egg so the vagina discriminates between sperm and the egg seeks out sperm to catch. Nevertheless, as Martin points out, even when acknowledged, such biological equality is still generally described in a language that gives precedence to the sperm. When the egg is presented in an active role, the image is one of a dangerous aggressor 'rather like a spider laying in wait in her web' (Martin, 1991, p498).

Social historical research on sex hormones has also shown how the way that such hormones are presented in textbooks and scientific papers gives messages that go well beyond what the data indicate. Despite the fact that it has been known since the 1920s that each sex contains the other's hormone – ie males contain oestrogen and females testosterone

– school textbooks typically ignore both this fact and the close chemical similarity between oestrogen and testosterone (Roberts, 2002). A different reading of the data from what is usually presented in school textbooks which is more in line with the scientific evidence about the working of sex hormones is that femaleness and maleness lie on a continuum. This model of the consequences of the actions of the sex hormones became common among academic endocrinologists (who study hormones) from the 1940s. While this model can lead to an essentialist understanding of sexuality and sexual orientation it can also be seen as allowing a far more fluid understanding of sexuality which includes some forms of intersexuality. It also correlated with a rise in the number of studies of the presumed femininity of gay men (Oudshoorn, 1994).

The principle of intersexuality dates largely from Magnus Hirschfeld's pioneering work on sexual difference in the first three decades of the twentieth century. By rejecting the discrete categories of male and female and arguing instead that each of us uniquely sits on a continuum, Hirschfeld did not so much give rise to the notion of the third sex as radically deconstruct the sexual binary (Bauer, 2003).

Biological indicators of sexual orientation have long been sought and continue to fascinate commentators while worrying many in the gay and lesbian community. Hardly a month goes by without a report of some such biological indicator. Precisely which indicator is flavour of the month (a hormone, a gene, parental upbringing, relative finger length, etc.) may tell us more about research fashions than anything else. Around the middle of the twentieth century hormones were widely thought to be all powerful and responsible for our sexuality. Hormones are chemicals made in glands; they then circulate in the body and reach target organs where they have their effects. Towards the end of the twentieth century the focus shifted to genes, the building blocks of our chromosomes. Genes are responsible for the chemicals, including hormones, made in the body and a reductionist perspective sees them as determining not just sex and sexuality but almost all of what it is to be ourselves.

Much of the literature about the 'causes' of sexuality concentrates on gayness, though Lynda Birke, a biologist as well as a feminist and a lesbian, provides a valuable review about lesbianism and over the years has 'spent much time and energy refuting the allegations that any social categories (of gender, race or sexuality) are fixed by biology' (Birke, 1997, p58). However, as Birke points out, there are a number of reasons for not entirely rejecting biological notions of sexual orientation. For one thing, some have used the biological argument politically to argue for gay rights though this approach has been hotly contested (Schüklenk and Brookey, 1998). More prosaically, it may well be that there are biological bases to at least some people's sexuality.

All of which leads one to ask how biology can be taught better in schools and colleges. Much biology teaching is focused around the use of textbooks which are consumed uncritically by teachers and students alike. Yet:

> Teachers can read subtextually and resistantly and can help their students to do likewise. Too rarely are students encouraged to critique their science textbooks; too often are textbooks used as if they contained only unquestionable truths. (Reiss, 1998, p148)

This is a simple message but one that provides a teacher and her/his students with a powerful tool because it avoids buying into the general assumption of the teacher as the expert repository of facts and allows for more emancipatory understandings of education. This is more satisfying for teacher and students alike and fits well with an information society which provides students with opportunities to obtain many of the facts they need to know at their own pace.

For anyone, including teachers, to change their practice is rarely straightforward. The literature on continuing professional development and teacher change shows that a whole range of factors are needed otherwise their best intentions are unlikely to be embedded in subsequent practice (Joyce and Showers, 1995; Bianchini *et al*, 2002; Loucks-Horsley *et al*, 2003).

An account of what biology teachers can do is provided by Anne-Marie Scholer in her published description of her teaching programme for a two semester intermediate level college course in anatomy and physiology, required for first-year students in nursing, athletic training and physical therapy majors (Scholer, 2002). Scholer begins with the idea that male/female is not a dichotomy. She draws on the various causes of indeterminate gender in humans, the sex hormone theory outlined above, the existence of breast cancer in men, and the occurrence of transgender. As she says:

> While the foregoing material is undoubtedly familiar to individuals in the fields of sexuality education, it is quite new to most of my students and peers. I have found such examples to work well in class, creating vocal displays of cognitive dissonance. (Scholer, 2002, p78)

Every teacher knows that cognitive dissonance if well handled can be a powerful incentive to learning. Handled badly it can reinforce prejudice or be rejected as confusing. Scholer goes on to challenge the prevailing stereotype of eggs as passive objects, to discuss how sex is not just anatomy and hormones, to avoid heteronormativity and generally to 'create an inclusive environment in my classroom' (p82).

There may be some who think that school and college biology is not an important battle ground, and that to fight discrimination and injustice on this front risks that the predominant discourse will be determined by conservatives. However, as Marianne Whatley points out in a chapter in Debbie Epstein's and James Sears' *A Dangerous Knowing*, 'Using science to attack comprehensive sexuality education and to support abstinence-only education is one strategy being used currently' (Whatley, 1999, p238). Similarly, Will Letts (2001) explores how school science structures and is structured by norms of heterosexual masculinity.

Letts' work is particularly valuable as he focuses on classroom examples of primary school science which might be assumed to be fairly neutral. He argues that science, including school science, functions as a grand narrative that seduces students and teachers and concludes:

> As a plan of action, I advocate that school science becomes an active and generative site for critical science literacy. The words 'science literacy' in this phrase are intended quite differently than popular utterances of them have come to mean. 'Science literacy' does not simply mean an intake and consumption of science texts and 'facts', either purposefully or through acts of seduction. I am using critical science literacy to denote something akin to critical media literacy. (Letts, 2001, p270)

The ideal teaching space for critical science literacy would be one where the traditional virtues of science, its open mindedness and refusal to accept tradition on trust, were more widely (reflexively) applied. It would allow students to think about themselves and their sexuality more meaningfully. It would help those who are uncomfortable with traditional descriptions of masculinity and femininity to realise that they are not alone in their rejection of such simple dichotomies. All this can be achieved without harming those students who are comfortable with conventional descriptions. Indeed, it might be good for these students to explore alternatives even if they reject them. At least they would know that they have made a decision rather than presume that there was none to be made. Sadly such innovative classrooms and labs are still rare although this kind of teaching would make the world a better place both overall and for the many individuals who otherwise find they don't fit in.

Representations of reality

In the nineteenth century William Whewell, who coined the word 'scientist', believed so strongly in the provisional nature of scientific truth that he argued that until a century had passed we could not be sure that scientific theories were true (Annan, 1999/2000). Scientific truth, although it may be reliable for most purposes, is by its very nature provisional. Newtonian thinking may have ruled for three hundred years but it eventually bowed to Einstein's views. What is less often appreciated is the way in which physics, chemistry and biology represent reality by means of conceptual models. In one of Lewis Carroll's *Alice* books one of the characters talks about what would happen if a map was produced to the same scale and in as much detail as the ground. Would it still be a map? The same point holds about scientific models. They are abstractions of reality, they represent reality in the way that a delegation represents those who send it: the relationship is one of a correspondence, not of identity.

Just as we don't all write the same sort of poetry, even if we are writing in the same language, on the same subject and in the same form, so not all scientists generate the same representations. This is not to imply that all representations are equally valid (your haiku may be better than mine) but it does mean – and this is an important point for education – that a better science is likely to result from having a diversity of people with a diversity of viewpoints, just as you can't have a very good rugby team if everyone is the same height and weight. This is not the only argument for encouraging diversity within science any more than the business argument for equal opportunities is the only argument for equal opportunities but it is not an argument appreciated by many young people or by many of their science teachers. Immigration over the last hundred years has probably been what has kept the USA at the top of the scientific league table. It will be interesting to see, post 9/11, whether this continues. Early indications are that the USA may be losing its scientific leadership for this very reason (cf. King, 2004).

The language of science

It is rarely appreciated that the choice of the language in which scientific concepts are expressed is significant. What is widely recognised is that scientific language is generally impenetrable unless you have spent a long time learning how to read it: this is as true of the visual representations of science (graphs and diagrams) and its use of mathematics as it is of scientific prose. As Halliday and Martin put it 'The language of science, though forward looking in its origins, has become increasingly anti-democratic: its arcane grammatical metaphor sets apart those who understand it and shields them from those who do not' (Halliday and Martin, 1993, p21).

Clive Sutton (1992) points out that the motto of the Royal Society, *Nullius in verba,* can be read as 'Take nobody's word for it' which is almost certainly how it was intended but also as 'Put not your trust in words'. He continues:

> To readers unlearned in Latin the motto suggests strongly a distrust of words ... In contradiction of any such idea, my own preferred message for learners would be 'Out of words, may things have come' or even, more strongly:
>
> > *Out of words, many **things** have been brought into being.* (Sutton, 1992, p31)

In case these points about language and science may seem to have little relevance to the everyday teaching of science in schools, here is a passage about the teaching of energy at KS3 (ie to 11 to 14 year-olds in England and Wales) written by someone working for a mainstream science education charity:

> Many school textbooks introduce energy by starting that it is difficult to state exactly what it is. This is a very reasonable place to start, since there is no easy answer to the question 'What is energy?'. There are formal definitions, but these don't really help pupils to understand what it is. It may be better to think of understanding energy as coming to know the character in a drama or a novel – getting to know the concept bit by bit as more of the story about its characteristics unfolds. However, there are at least three broad ways to think about the nature of energy.
>
> *Energy as a value*
> One way of thinking about energy is simply as a *value* that can be calculated. Many different kinds of change take place – a candle burning, a ball rolling downhill, an electric kettle boiling some water – but for each of these you can calculate the total energy before and find that it is the same as the total energy after. We could think of this as a 'book-keeping' approach.
>
> It is interesting to note that many chemists in the 19th century viewed the concept of an atom simply as a 'book-keeping' device to make calculations on reacting quantities. It was only in the 20th century that atoms came to be seen as entities with some kind of independent existence rather than as a convenient fiction.

Energy in many guises

Another approach sees energy not as an abstract value, but as more 'entity-like'. However, it manifests itself in many ways – hot things are seen as having 'heat energy', moving things as having 'kinetic energy', and so on. Though these manifestations appear to be very different, energy can change itself from one 'guise' to another – for example, when a fuel burns, 'chemical energy' is changed into 'heat energy'.

Energy is energy

A third approach is to think of energy as 'fluid-like' – and the same kind of things whether it is in a hot object or a moving one. It doesn't change its *nature* – energy is energy is energy – but *where it is* does change. So, we can talk of energy as being in a certain region, moving from one place to another, having a lot of it or a little of it, making it concentrated in one region or letting it spread out. For example, temperature can be seen as being a measure of the 'concentration of energy', and energy is what flows from hot or cold as temperature differences disappear. (Boohan, 2002, p4)

Unfortunately this rich discussion about what energy really is is unlikely ever to take place in a school science classroom. The source from which the quote is taken is a booklet for teachers not pupils. School science continues to present an unproblematic account of science. It is little wonder that most young people conclude it is not for them. This is a great shame for young people, for science and for all of us. Attempts to impose a single scientific language need to be rejected in schools and elsewhere. A richer vision is provided by listening to the complexity and difference in the world and by recognising the role of scientists in knowledge production. Scientific models of the world tell us about those who produce them as well as about the world they model more explicitly. Realising this has a number of benefits. It increases the chance that science education can engage a broader range of students, and it helps us realise the extent to which scientific accounts of reality have their own power as they project themselves back onto reality. The result is that subsequent viewers see the models along with the realities, the representations along with the presentations.

References

Annan, N (1999/2000) *The Dons: Mentors, Eccentrics and Geniuses.* London: HarperCollins

Bauer, J E (2003) Magnus Hirschfeld's doctrine of sexual intermediaries and the transgender politics of identity. Paper given at the Conference: Past and Present of Radical Sexual Politics Amsterdam 3-4 October, 2003 Available at www.iisg.nl/~womhist/hirschfeld. doc. (Last accessed 22 October 2006)

Bianchini, J A, Hilton-Brown, B A and Breton, T D (2002) Professional development for university scientists around issues of equity and diversity: investigating dissent within community. *Journal of Research in Science Teaching* 39, 738-771

Birke, L (1997) Born queer? Lesbians interrogate biology. In Griffin, G and Andermahr, S (eds) *Straight Studies Modified: Lesbian Interventions in the Academy.* London: Cassell, pp57-70

Boohan, R (2002) *Energy Transfer Kit.* London: Science Enhancement Programme

Chalmers, A F (1999) *What is this Thing called Science?* 3rd edn. Buckingham: Open University Press

Halliday, M A K and Martin, J R (1993) *Writing Science: Literacy and Discursive Power.* London: Falmer Press

Joyce, B and Showers, B (1995) *Student Achievement through Staff Development.* White Plains New York: Longman

King, D (2004) The scientific impact of nations: what different countries get for their research spending. *Nature* 430, 311-316

Kuhn, T S (1970) *The Structure of Scientific Revolutions* 2nd edn. Chicago: University of Chicago Press

Letts, W (2001) When science is strangely alluring: interrogating the masculinist and heter-normative nature of primary school science. *Gender and Education* 13, 261-274

Loucks-Horsley, S, Love, N, Stiles, K E, Mundry, S and Hewson, P W (2003) *Designing Professional Development for Teachers of Science and Mathematics* 2nd edn. Thousand Oaks CA: Corwin Press

Martin, E (1991) The egg and the sperm: how science has constructed a romance based on stereotypical male-female roles. *Signs: Journal of Women in Culture and Society* 16, 485-501

Merton, R K (1973) *The Sociology of Science: Theoretical and Empirical Investigations.* Chicago: University of Chicago Press

Oudshoorn, N (1994) *Beyond the Natural Body: An Archeology of Sex Hormones.* London: Routledge

Popper, K R (1934/1972) *The Logic of Scientific Discovery.* London: Hutchinson

Reiss, M J (1998) The representation of human sexuality in some science textbooks for 14-16 year-olds. *Research in Science and Technological Education* 16, 137-149

Reiss, M (2005a) The nature of science. In Frost, J and Turner, T (eds) *Learning to Teach Science in the Secondary School: A Companion to School Experience* 2nd edn. London: RoutledgeFalmer, pp44-53

Reiss, M J (2005b) Biology, teaching of. In Sears, J T (ed) *Youth, Education, and Sexualities: An International Encyclopedia,* Volume One, A-J. Westport: Greenwood, pp81-84

Roberts, C (2002) 'A matter of embodied fact': sex hormones and the history of bodies. *Feminist Theory* 3, 7-26

Scholer, A-M (2002) Sexuality in the science classroom: one teacher's methods in a college biology course *Sex Education* 2, 75-86

Schüklenk, U and Brookey, R A (1998) Biomedical research on sexual orientation: researchers taking our chances in homophobic societies. *Journal of the Gay and Lesbian Medical Association* 2(2), 79-84

Science Enhancement Programme (2002) *Energy Transfer Kit.* London: Science Enhancement Programme

Sutton, C (1992) *Words, Science and Learning.* Buckingham: Open University Press

Whatley, M H (1999) The 'homosexual agenda' goes to school. In Epstein, D and Sears, J T (eds). *A Dangerous Knowing: Sexuality, Pedagogy and Popular Culture.* London: Cassell, pp229-241

6

Discourses of masculinity and femininity: implications for equality and difference

Carrie Paechter

Introduction: the nature of discourses

Whereof one cannot speak, thereof one must be silent.
(Wittgenstein, 1922, p189)

Discourses of masculinity and femininity are fundamental to social life. They structure how we think about ourselves and each other, how we expect people to react and how we understand who we are. This chapter looks in detail at how some specific discourses operate and at the implications for equality and difference. First, however, it is important to consider the nature of discourses in general: what discourses do and why it is important to examine them.

A discourse is essentially a structuring device for thought. It governs what is thinkable. This is the case at a deep level. A discourse is not just the box that we are encouraged to think outside; it is another box beyond that, so that to step beyond the discourse is to move into a space of unthinkability. Stepping outside a particular discourse is to try to speak of that 'whereof one cannot' (Wittgenstein, 1922), refusing silence. This is clearly difficult and dangerous; discourses bring with them a form of ethical authority. Foucault notes that:

It is not enough to say that science is a set of procedures by which propositions may be falsified, errors demonstrated, myths demystified, etc. Science also exercises power: it is, literally, a power that forces you to say

73

certain things, if you are not to be disqualified not only as being wrong, but, more seriously than that, as being a charlatan. (Foucault, 1988, pp106-7)

Here the discourses of science are so powerful that thinking outside them is a moral transgression; one is in some way cheating one's readers or hearers. To make good a claim to be a scientist, by operating within the scientific discourse, one has to 'say certain things' and only these things: what cannot be said is at least as important as what can.

As always, while discourses exert coercive force they also act in positive ways (Foucault, 1978). We do need to know what counts as science and what does not if we are to be able to rely on it for decision making. Adopting particular discourses can also have positive effects in terms of power/knowledge relations. For example, Gordon *et al* (2005) note that in Nordic countries discourses around equality mean that women with children are more likely to participate in the paid workforce than their counterparts in the UK. The discourses considered in this chapter are similarly positioned. While they all have problematic coercive force, this is only because they were originally of enormous importance in prising apart previous discourse structures and acted as a positive force in power/knowledge relations. They are now in some ways acting restrictively and need to be questioned.

The chapter focuses on three central discourses about masculinity and femininity. The first, the sex/gender distinction discourse, is now so well established that it has permeated everyday speech and writing; it is no longer in any way a specialist discourse. The problems with this distinction have been apparent for some time and there have been attempts to address them through an alternative, second, discourse of masculinity and femininity, which has developed into a related discourse of masculinities and femininities. While this remains useful and is certainly an improvement on the sex/gender discourse, it brings with it another set of problems, which will also be explored. The third discourse is that of hegemonic masculinity (Connell, 1987, 1995) and its near-counterpart, emphasised femininity, both of which are useful in many ways, particularly in the 'pure' form in which they were developed by Connell. However, as they become part of broader, less precise discourses, they are beginning to restrict theorising in this area.

These discourses are all valuable, and continue to act as important tools in the dismantling of power/knowledge systems. However, this also makes them problematic. The most useful discourses are also potentially the most restrictive because of their ability to capture us, to take us into themselves so that we can no longer see beyond them. Some discourses, including discussed in this chapter, are exciting and empowering as well as restrictive. They make certain kinds of thought so much easier that we do not notice that they outlaw others. By examining their workings we can resist this process, while continuing to use them when they still have explanatory or emancipatory force.

The sex/gender distinction

It is not entirely clear when the distinction between sex and gender first emerged in western literature. It is highly language-specific, being taken very seriously by English speakers but less important to other language communities (Moi, 1999; Rhedding-Jones, 2003). It was only in the second half of the twentieth century that it really took hold, initially in psychological work on people with intersex conditions and on transsexuals. Stoller (1968: viiii-ix) delineates the distinction thus:

> The word *sexual* will have connotations of anatomy and physiology. This ob viously leaves tremendous areas of behavior, feelings, thoughts, and fantasies that are related to the sexes and yet do not have primarily biological connotations. It is for some of these psychological phenomena that the term *gender* will be used.

He also relates gender, which he states is independent of biological sex, specifically to masculinity and femininity and to ideas about what these might be, that anticipate some of the problems arising from this discourse:

> Gender is the amount of masculinity or femininity found in a person, and, obviously, while there are mixtures of both in many humans, the normal male has a preponderance of masculinity and the normal female a preponderance of femininity. (Stoller, 1968, pp9-10)

This distinction between sex as pertaining to the body and gender as pertaining to the mind was taken up by two major groups: feminists and transsexuals. For both it served essential purposes in the battles being fought at the time. For feminists it was an important part of the argument that biology was not destiny, that women's lives did not have to follow their biological functions as childbearers. For transsexuals it allowed the possibility of their existence by reinforcing the idea that a fundamental aspect of identity could be separated from the physical appearance and functioning of the body. It made transsexualism a coherent possibility.

Both groups constructed the sex/gender distinction as a dualism, as did many psychologists of gender. In a formal dualism one term is not simply set up against another. Instead one side of the dualistic relation is understood as the negation of the other in equal balance, so that not only is there a hierarchy between the two terms but a negation of the second term (Gatens, 1991). In a formal dualism, therefore:

> categories are not only constituted hierarchically (for example in gender categories the masculine/male is given superiority), but one of the categories is *constituted within binary logic as nothing.* (McFarlane, 1998, p206, emphasis in original)

The relation between sex and gender is an unusual dualism because either half can be the main term, depending on one's theoretical position. When the distinction was first posited, sex was the negated term following the Cartesian dominance of mind over body (Paechter, 2006). Gender was seen as all-important although this has been challenged more recently by the rise of sociobiology. When this distinction first became widely used gender was seen as malleable, because it was all-important for identity and as learned, as culturally determined (Stoller, 1968). This left bodily form as something that was more or less arbitrary in the development of gender identity. Such an approach resulted in attempts to manipulate the gender identities of intersex babies by assigning them to the most convenient gender from the point of view of surgery. Despite the supposed independence of sex and gender there is a constant urge to make outward bodily form conform to assigned gender and to and construct bodies that (in theory at least) match the assignment (Money and Ehrhardt, 1972). In most cases this was successful with the children indeed growing up secure in their assigned sex despite their mutilated bodies (Kessler, 1998; Preves, 2003).

There are a number of advantages to the separation of sex and gender although the dualistic nature of this split is more problematic. We still encounter the suggestion that women would be happier if their lives, or even their educational opportunities, were restricted on the grounds of their biology (Tooley, 2002). Similarly, the continued dominance of gender over sex in public understandings of identity is what has allowed the gradual increase in equal rights for transsexuals in many western countries, including, in some cases, the right to make changes to birth certificates. Sex/gender could therefore be argued to be one of the few benign dualisms, one that has allowed considerable moves towards greater equality for a number of oppressed groups.

However, all is not as simple or as fine as it seems, as is often the case with such dualistic and pervasive discourses. First, the dualism allows a split of the mind from the body that is not grounded in reality. There is now a lot of evidence that bodily functions and mental states are closely intertwined (Damasio, 1994) and that mental states are experienced in the body and vice versa. Furthermore, gender itself is related to our bodies. Most people grow up with a gender identity that conforms to their initial gender assignment, which in almost all cases is made on the basis of outward bodily form. We do not decide which gender a new baby will be independently of what it looks like; we have a quick look at its genitals and make an assignment accordingly. Throughout life gender is much more a matter of embodied self than something that is entirely in the mind: while having a particular female body form is not fundamental to my identity as a woman, the particular form that my body actually has is fundamental to my sense of self, including myself as a woman.

Even for transsexuals their sense of gender is not really experienced as independent of the body but is closely bound up with it. Prosser (1998) argues that the image of a transsexual as being in the wrong body is not just a discursive construction: 'being trapped in the wrong body is just what transsexuality feels like' (p69). This suggests that having the wrong body is actually fundamental to many transsexuals' experience of self. If it were not, there would be no reason for people to undergo expensive, difficult and painful operations in an attempt to make the body correspond to an individual's idea of it. Prosser argues that the desire of the transsexual is not for a new body, but for a body that is already in existence psychically:

> What makes the transsexual able and willing to submit to the knife – the splitting, cutting, removal, and reshaping of organs, tissues, and skin that another might conceive as mutilation – is the drive to get the body back to what it should have been. What makes possible the psychic translation of the surgical incursions into the body into a poetics of healing is a kind of transsexual somatic memory. Surgery is made sense of as a literal and figural remembering, a restorative drive that is indeed common to accounts of reconstructive surgeries among nontranssexual subjects and perhaps inherent in the very notion of *reconstructive* surgery. (Prosser, 1998, p83, emphasis in original)

Second, the dualistic nature of the sex/gender split has led us to ignore the subordinate term, sex, in our overwhelming focus on gender. This has had a number of effects. While gender has always been conceptualised as a continuum between masculinity and femininity, sex continues to be treated as dichotomous, so that one is either, and exclusively, male or female, despite our increasing understanding of a variety of forms of intersexuality. Sex has also been constructed simultaneously as to do with what the body looks like that can be altered at will to conform to the gender as individually experienced or medically assigned, and as an internal characteristic that is given, unchanging and rooted in the facts of biology. Thus the predominant negation of sex as a term within sex/gender dualism has led to considerable confusion about its meaning. This is further complicated by the ways in which dichotomous sexes are themselves in a dualistic relation, with femaleness being treated as the negation or absence of maleness (Kessler and McKenna, 1978), even in descriptions of foetal development (Fausto-Sterling, 2000):

> Usually, the development of specific tissue types is understood to involve the activation of specific genes or gene sequences. Yet, the generally accepted theory of sex determination claims that female differentiation is determined by the absence of something, that a female develops when something is lacking. I suggest that the pervasiveness of our cultural construction of female as absence, seen in everything from Freudian theory to the non-equivalence of male and female words in our language (the opposite of male is not female, but non-male) has also insinuated itself into biological theories about male and female development. (Fausto-Sterling, 1989, pp328-329)

Third, the discourse of the sex/gender distinction has had a tendency to separate the body from even its own performances. While it seems reasonable to argue (Butler, 1990; 1993) that gender is performative, that it is in many ways a constantly reiterated public and private construction of particular ways of acting and being, such performances are performances of and by a body, and what that body is like remains important. The power of the sex/gender distinction, combined with the idea of gender as performance, leads to the unfortunate impression that anyone can perform any identity they like. This is patently not the case. Part of the performative nature of gender is that it is a reciprocal act (Paechter, 2003, 2007) in which there is a recognition of the performance as of maleness or femaleness (or drag, or deliberate androgyny), which reflects an unseen inner state and, in most cases, bodily configuration. It should allow us to ascribe 'cultural genitals' (Kessler and McKenna, 1978, p153), those which we assume are present, to the body in question. The performance has to be understood as an authentic performance of that gender, or as transparently inauthentic, as in drag. Otherwise, it is a failed performance: the point of the performative nature of gender is that it is not acknowledged as such but treated as if it were a natural expression of an inner state. What this means is that what can be performed is both restricted and enabled by bodily form: with suitable dress, walk, hairstyle and breast-binding, I might be able to make a reasonable job of performing male, at least until I spoke. I would not, in my late forties, be able to present myself convincingly as a *young* male. I am betrayed by the lines on my face and the sag of my jaw.

In recent years a further problem has arisen from the ways in which the discourse of the sex/gender distinction has developed and been taken into public consciousness. In particular, gender seems to be increasingly used as a sort of politically correct term for sex, so that we now find uses of gender that do not in any sense refer to anything socially constructed. There is an example of this in the following news item from the BBC website:

> The entire male fish population of some European rivers show feminising effects from so-called 'gender-bending' chemicals, according to new research.

> Freshwater fish in five out of seven northern European countries surveyed so far showed some signs of exposure to the chemicals, which mimic female hormones and are present in sewage effluents. (Briggs, 2000)

If this really is a comprehensible use of gender-bending, then gender has broadened its meaning considerably in the past few years. If it is all right to use gender-bending to mean that certain chemical pollutants in rivers can cause fish to change sex (Birke, 2000), then it is unclear whether and where the line between sex and gender can be drawn: it is presumably not being argued that the chemicals lead fish to change the way they construct their identities. It may be that we are coming to a point at which even the sex/gender distinction itself, even leaving aside its dualism, has outlived its usefulness.

The discourse of the sex/gender distinction is thus both powerfully emancipating and seriously limiting. It has captured us so thoroughly that it is hard to think beyond it, while at the same time it has become increasingly obvious that we have to. In response to this, several authors (Buchbinder, 1994; Mac an Ghaill, 1994; Connell, 1995; Bourdieu, 2001; Skelton, 2001; Martino and Pallotta-Chiarolli, 2003; Paechter, 2006, 2007) have started to work with the ideas of masculinity and femininity, which were already encompassed by the term gender but are seen as less all-embracing and so less powerful – but also less dangerous. It is to the discourses that we have built up around them that I now turn.

Masculinity/femininity, masculinities/femininities

The move from discourses of sex/gender to those of masculinity/femininity and masculinities/femininities seems at first sight to be liberating. This is because these terms deal more directly with a person's sense of self and who they are, and with their behaviours, not with some undefined, if socially constructed, essence. Furthermore, they have the potential to include the body, as it is certainly possible to speak of embodied masculinities and femininities (Connell, 1987). The move to a multiplicity of masculinities and femininities is also useful in many ways: it allows us to move away from monolithic and normalising ideas about what it is to be male or female and to re-think masculinity and femininity not as externally-defined qualities that one might have more or less of (Stoller, 1968), but as collectively constructed ways of 'doing' male and female (West and Zimmerman, 1987).

The shift from masculinity and femininity to masculinities and femininities needs to be treated with care. I have argued (Paechter, 2006, 2007) that we need to see masculinity and femininity as co-constructed ideal types specific to local communities while treating masculinities and femininities as the related identities that individuals construct and inhabit within these communities. The local nature of this conception is important: without it we fall once more into a discourse of masculinity and femininity as universals of which we can have different amounts in our psychological makeup. This restricts the ways in which we can construct both them and ourselves. This emphasis on local constructions requires those of us who work in the field to consider specifically what constitutes the ideal type(s) of masculinity in the particular site(s) under consideration; we can no longer fall back on a universal shorthand idea of what constitutes masculinity or femininity. At the same time we cannot treat these as masculinities or femininities; there has to be a distinction between what pertains to the group and what to the individual.

This approach has some advantages. It allows for the possibility of masculine femininities and feminine masculinities or, masculine ways of 'doing' girl or woman and feminine ways of 'doing' boy or man (Skelton and Francis, 2003; Paechter, 2006), in which ideal typical performances of one gender are incorporated into the identity of an individual who sees her or himself as 'doing' the other. This allows for greater fluidity not only of performance and identity but of theoretical and practical understanding of what is going on. In my own research, 10 and 11 year old girls were clear that they constructed themselves as 'a bit tomboy', which included significant aspects of local forms of masculinity in their individual femininities (Paechter and Clark, forthcoming).

80

At the same time, and while this formulation is useful, there are already some concerns about where this approach might lead. In particular, there is a need to explore further what we really mean by phrases such as 'masculine femininities'. There is still a need to decide what constitutes 'masculine' in this context. While we continue to emphasise local constructions of masculinity, we may be at the same time repeatedly falling back on univeralised concepts, which take us right back to sex/gender or, at best, masculinity/femininity. This needs to be addressed before this discourse becomes monolithic.

An example of how this might work, that seems to me to be even more problematic can be seen with Halberstam's concept of 'female masculinity' (Halberstam, 1998). It is important to understand that the attractiveness of this concept lies in its embeddedness in discourses by which we are already ensnared, while at the same time appearing to challenge them. First, it rests on an assumption that we already know what masculinity is, to an extent that what is in question is not masculinity, but what it means for it to be manifested by females. Second, while Halberstam makes the important point that we need to uncouple masculinity from maleness so that it is not simply 'what men do', she relies on an implicit definition of it which seems to be just that. Saying what masculinity is, if it is not treated as a local phenomenon, and therefore as different in different contexts, seems to be highly problematic. Halberstam herself gives some examples, but these seem to be more closely related to an idealised and imagined middle-class male childhood, treated as both real and universal, than to anything else:

> If masculinity were a kind of default category for children, surely we would have more girls running around and playing sports and experimenting with chemistry sets and building things and fixing things and learning about finances and so on. (p269)

The problem with 'female masculinity' is twofold. First, it goes along with the wider discourses of masculinity and femininity in fooling us that we think that we know what masculinity is, as a general and universal term, when we do not. Second, in Halberstam's formulation at least, it is posited it as a positive term that dualistically negates the feminine for both males and females. It returns us to a masculine/feminine dualism that, while uncoupled from maleness/femaleness, continues to deny the importance and power of the feminine. This example makes clear that discourses of masculinity/femininity, masculinities/femininities, while not yet as monolithic and problematic as those of sex/gender, have the potential to be so and we should take care when we use them.

Hegemonic masculinity/emphasised femininity

Hegemonic masculinity, and its dualistic Other, emphasised femininity, are another pair of useful concepts which are in danger of developing into a capturing discourse. This is partly because, as with all conceptually useful ideas, they have a tendency to slide away from their original definitions as they pass into widespread use. Hegemonic masculinity is defined by Connell (1995, p77) as:

> The configuration of gender practice which embodies the currently accepted answer to the problem of the legitimation of patriarchy, which guarantees (or is taken to guarantee) the dominant position of men and the subordination of women.

Hegemonic masculinity in this definition is not a universal: it is specific to a particular time or social configuration. It is also not necessarily a masculinity that is frequently found in practice: Connell argues that 'the number of men rigorously practising the hegemonic pattern in its entirety may be quite small' (79). Nevertheless, it is a form of ideal-typical masculinity which is presented as being at least partially cross-cultural, as is its dualistic Other, emphasised femininity (Connell, 1987), though this has an even fuzzier definition and lacks the role in supporting power structures taken by hegemonic masculinity.

Both hegemonic masculinity and emphasised femininity as terms stand in specific relation to how we understand masculinity and femininity in everyday speech. This raises the problem discussed in the last section: in practice they depend in part for their definitions on what men and women actually do. With emphasised femininity this is quite an oblique relation: ideal-typical emphasised femininity seems to be what we refer to simply as 'femininity' in everyday speech, and therefore far removed from the practices of many 21st century women. Nevertheless, when it is not being equated with forms of femininity that are more akin to drag than to anything performed by the majority of women (Butler, 2004; Paechter, 2006), the discourse of emphasised femininity allows the reification of one specific form of femininity, with an unspoken understanding of what it means to enact it. Suddenly this discourse does not seem to be taking us as far as we might have hoped.

Hegemonic masculinity is a slightly different case, though its reification of particular forms of masculinity is the same. Although Connell sets up the definition partly to make clear that it is a relational term, the precise instantiation of which depends on particular social configurations, its use has become so widespread that it has become a shorthand for a small number of modes of dominant masculinity that deal with male power in its various forms. Thus, while strictly what constitutes hegemonic masculinity should be discussed in terms of its manifestation in a specific, local social group, this is not what tends to happen in practice. The discourse of hegemonic masculinity has become so powerful that what it represents is now treated as universal, as something that we all understand and can recognise, that does not vary across time, place and culture. The discourses around hegemonic masculinity, rather than preserving its relational nature, have given it too much solidity so that it has developed a tendency to attach itself to specific forms of masculinity which are seen as its cross-cultural attributes.

Implications for equality and difference

All three discourses discussed above have been, and remain in many ways, useful tools for deconstructing dominating patterns of gender and power. They allow us to cut through other powerful discourses to construct alternative, counter-discourses with the potential to allow people to live differently, to think and speak outside dominant modes. These counter-discourses were extraordinarily important for emancipatory theory and practice. A successful counter-discourse, however, has the potential to become dominant. This has happened to sex/gender and seems also to be happening to masculinity/femininity and hegemonic masculinity/emphasised femininity.

One reason why these have all become dominant and ensnaring discourses in their own right is that they are all still caught up in the extraordinarily powerful discourse of dualistic thinking. Even as counter-discourses to binary dualisms they operate within that overall framework, constructing their own dualistic power relations and keeping our thinking trapped within it. We need to challenge the dualistic forms of binary thinking, to construct counter-discourses to it which will loosen the hold of these lesser dualisms.

The power of these discourses lies also in their continued usefulness. We need to use our tools according to circumstances. It is still important to use the discourse of sex/gender, emphasising the importance of gender, when dealing with policy issues and questions of equal opportunities. The language of masculinity and femininity, masculinities and femininities allows us to see that ways of being male and female are not universal but need to be addressed in local ways through local actions and forces. The concepts of hegemonic masculinity and emphasised femininity are powerful reminders that these ways of being are also not equal and cannot be treated as such. We should not abandon these discourses but use them with care, with scepticism and with vigilance.

References

Birke, L (2000). Sitting on the fence: biology, feminism and gender-bending environments. *Women's Studies International Forum* 23(5), 587-599

Bourdieu, P (2001) *Masculine Domination.* Cambridge: Polity Press

Briggs, H (2000). 'Gender-bender' fish problem widens. London, British Broadcasting Corporation http://news.bbc.co.uk/1/hi/in_depth/sci_tech/2000/festival_of_science/913273. stm accessed 13/1/2005

Buchbinder, D (1994) *Masculinities and Identities.* Melbourne: Melbourne University Press

Butler, J (1990) *Gender Trouble: feminism and the subversion of identity.* London, Routledge

Butler, J (1993) *Bodies that Matter: on the discursive limits of 'sex'.* London: Routledge

Butler, J (2004) *Undoing Gender.* New York: Routledge

Connell, R W (1987) *Gender and Power.* Cambridge: Polity Press

Connell, R W (1995) *Masculinities.* Cambridge: Polity Press

Damasio, A R (1994) *Descartes' Error: emotion, reason and the human brain.* London: Papermac

Fausto-Sterling, A (1989) Life in the XY corral. *Women's Studies International Forum* 12(3), 319-331

Fausto-Sterling, A (2000) *Sexing the Body: gender politics and the construction of sexuality.* New York: Basic Books

Foucault, M (1978) *The History of Sexuality Volume One.* London: Penguin

Foucault, M (1988) On Power. *Politics, Philosophy, Culture: Interviews and Other Writings 1977-1984.* Kritzman, L. D. (ed). London: Routledge pp96-109

Gatens, M (1991) *Feminism and Philosophy: perspectives on difference and equality.* Cambridge: Polity Press

Gordon, T, J Holland *et al* (2005) Imagining gendered adulthood: anxiety, ambivalence, avoidance and anticipation. *European Journal of Women's Studies* 12(1) 83-103

Halberstam, J (1998) *Female Masculinity.* Durham: Duke University Press

Kessler, S (1998) *Lessons from the Intersexed.* New Brunswick: Rutgers University Press

Kessler, S and W. McKenna (1978) *Gender: an Ethnomethodological Approach.* New York: John Wiley and Sons

Mac an Ghaill, M (1994) *The Making of Men: masculinities, sexualities and schooling.* Buckingham: Open University Press

Martino, W and M Pallotta-Chiarolli (2003) *So What's a Boy? Addressing issues of masculinity and schooling.* Maidenhead: Open University Press

McFarlane, J (1998) Looking through a glass darkly: a reading of Bronwyn Davies' Shards of Glass: children reading and writing beyond gendered identities. *Women's Studies International Forum* 21(2), 199-208

Moi, T (1999) *What is a Woman?* Oxford: Oxford University Press

Money, J and A A Ehrhardt (1972). *Man and Woman Boy and Girl: the differentiation and dimorphism of gender identity from conception to maturity.* Baltimore: Johns Hopkins University Press

Paechter, C (2003) Learning masculinities and femininities: power/knowledge and legitimate peripheral participation. *Women's Studies International Forum* 26(6), 541-552

Paechter, C (2006) Femininities and Schooling. *Handbook of Gender and Education.* Skelton, C, Francis, B and Smulyan, L. London, Sage pp365-377

Paechter, C (2006) Masculine femininities/feminine masculinities: power, identities and gender. *Gender and Education* 18(3), 253-263

Paechter, C (2006) Reconceptualizing the gendered body: learning and constructing masculinities and femininities in school.' *Gender and Education* 18(2), 121-135

Paechter, C (2007) *Being Boys, Being Girls: learning masculinities and femininities.* Buckingham: Open University Press

Paechter, C and S Clark (forthcoming) Who are tomboys, and how do we recognise them? *Women's Studies International Forum*

Preves, S E (2003) *Intersex and Identity.* New Brunswick: Rutgers University Press

Prosser, J (1998) *Second Skins: the body narratives of transsexuality.* New York: Columbia University Press

Rhedding-Jones, J (2003) *Reconceptualizing gender: new theorizations from early childhood education data.* British Educational Research Association Annual Conference, Edinburgh, 10-13 September 2003

Skelton, C (2001) *Schooling the Boys: masculinities and primary education.* Buckingham: Open University Press

Skelton, C and B Francis (2003). Introduction: boys and girls in the primary classroom. *Boys and Girls in the Primary Classroom.* C Skelton and B Francis Maidenhead, Berks: Open University Press

Stoller, R J (1968) *Sex and Gender: on the development of masculinity and femininity.* New York: Science House

Tooley, J (2002) *The Miseducation of Women.* London: Continuum

West, C and D H Zimmerman (1987) Doing Gender. *Gender and Society* 1(2), 125-151

Wittgenstein, L (1922) *Tractatus Logico-Philosophicus.* London: Routledge and Kegan Paul

PART TWO:
Educational imperialism
and its legacy

7

'Ya daddy ain't ya daddy': Socio-cultural norms and sex education: voicing the need for difference in sex education practice in the Caribbean

Ruby Greene

What and how do individuals learn, particularly about the most intimate behaviour in sexual relations? This question, especially as it relates to sex education, underlies this chapter. Informal socio-cultural dynamics provide at least as much influence if not more than formal sex education in this environment. This is reflected in culturally accepted behaviours such as fluid conjugal relationships, multiple concurrent sexual partner relationships and ages mixing, which are traditional norms associated with Caribbean sexuality. They have been such an integral part of the culture that Calypsonians (persons assuming sobriquets, who perform calypsoes) sing about them and Caribbean people dance with gay abandon to the lyrics delivered with tantalising rhythm. This controversial difference in Caribbean sexuality is often discussed in humorous anecdotes among men and women in the region. Religious leaders and members of other cultures tend to associate these cultural practices with immorality and sex educators link them with the rapid and persistent spread of HIV/ AIDS. Despite the existence of this difference in both family structure and socio-sexual practices, except for prohibitive messages, their inclusion in formal targeted Caribbean sex education is not focused upon. Ostensibly this is because of the tensions which exist between acceptance and denial of these phenomena as cultural norms.

Ethnographic research between November 2003 and January 2004 into the socio-cultural factors impacting on sex education in Guyana found that transactional sex , recreational multiple concurrent partner sexual relationships and gender violence are all cultural practices which formal targeted sex education relegates to embarrassed silence.

The main argument of the chapter is that the socio-cultural factors which impact on sexuality, sexual identity, and the sexual behaviours of Caribbean people in general, and African Guyanese as a case study in this instance, are negatively articulated in discourses of formal sex education. These discourses are more typical of northern rather than of Caribbean cultures. Furthermore the different levels of meanings and understanding of Caribbean discourses about sex/sexuality cannot be articulated through the present formats and contents of this northern-styled sex education.

The main focus of this type of sex education is to present sex/sexuality in a censorious way, in order to prevent unplanned and unprotected sexual intercourse and its possible detrimental consequences. This for-mat also serves to allay the anxieties of adults who fear that constructive information surrounding sexual intercourse, sexual feelings, eroticism and positive aspects of sexuality will act as a catalyst for young people to engage in premature sexual activities. Messages targeted towards HIV/AIDS prevention and spread are mainly the ABC messages which advocate abstinence from sexual intercourse, being faithful (sticking to one mutually faithful partner) and using a condom in every act of inter-course. These messages appear to be ineffective if the rapid and persistent spread of HIV/AIDS in the Caribbean region is used as an indicator.

The findings of this research suggest that sex education, including education about culturally acceptable gender roles, gender identities and eroticism is delivered all over the Caribbean on a daily basis. This is done informally and unintentionally through calypsoes, folk songs and culturally acceptable behaviours. Although this education is untargeted in that it is not intended as an education strategy for any particular group, anecdotal evidence suggests that this informal way of learning about sex and sexuality is considerably more effective and enjoyable than contemporary planned forms of targeted sex education which is delivered too little too late. The former contains culturally relevant sex/sexuality discourses. However, this informal social learning also contains erroneous messages that can and should be redressed in similar cultural formats by contemporary targeted sex education .

In order to understand the relevance of effective sex education in the Caribbean in this context, it is first necessary to have an insight into the problem facing African-Caribbean women in relation to HIV/AIDS.

Background to the study: HIV/AIDS and women in the Caribbean

HIV/AIDS is increasingly becoming an illness of women as well as of racial, ethnic, and sexual minorities (Schneider *et al*, 2002, p408). Research reports and the current available literature suggest that HIV/AIDS is affecting Black women disproportionately (Dougan *et al*, 2004; African American Health Articles, 2003; The Balm of Gilead, 2003; Kaiser Daily, 2001). Trends show a dramatic and persistent increase of HIV/AIDS in women and their offspring, with the Caribbean now having one of the highest incidences of female AIDS cases among the sub-regions of the Western Hemisphere (UNAIDS, 2004). In the Caribbean heterosexual contact has been the primary path of HIV transmission aided by cultural norms that tolerate unprotected sex and frequent partner exchange (*ibid*). HIV transmission rates in the Caribbean are the second highest in the world, surpassed only by the rates in sub-Saharan Africa (UNAIDS, 2004). In 1996 in the English-speaking Caribbean, the overall female to male ratio of HIV infection was 2 to 1, doubling from the rates in 1985 (McEvoy, 2000, p3). This trend has continued, especially in adolescents, with the figures for the year 2000 revealing that 7 per cent of pregnant women in rural Guyana tested positive for HIV. The incidence of the disease is five times higher in girls than in boys aged 15-19 in Trinidad and Tobago and in Jamaica girls in their teens had almost twice the prevalence rates of older women (UNAIDS, 2000)[1]. Among young people in this region, 2.9 per cent of women and 1.9% of men were living with HIV/AIDS by the end of 2003 (UNAIDS, 2004, p37).

The extent of Women's vulnerability to HIV/AIDS in the Caribbean is notable given that most of the major HIV/AIDS prevention strategies are linked to sex education which has been in place in the region for more than two decades. These women have high literacy rates, outnumbering their male counterparts at all levels of educational and professional attainment (Danns *et al*, 1997; World Bank Group, 2000). It would therefore be logical to assume that given such high levels of education and the increased thrust in HIV/AIDS education, African-Caribbean women would be less vulnerable to the disease. The fact that this is not the case is cause for concern and merits further investigation.

Rationale for the study

The theoretical base for research about this phenomenon was that the African-Caribbean family is generally viewed as being matrifocal (Gonzalez, 1960; Greenfield, 1973; Smith, 1973; Barrow, 1996). The negative impact of a potentially fatal disease on these women would therefore extend primarily to their offspring and ultimately to the development of countries in the region. It seemed that African-Caribbean women were powerless to negotiate safer sex practices because of cultural norms and societal expectations. Among these is the stigmatisation of childless women, the disregard for educational and professional achievements of a woman if 'she does not have a man' and the theory that those independent Black women who chose singledom are 'penis-hating lesbians' or, are in some way dysfunctional.

In investigating sex education in the Caribbean, it became evident that there is a blurring of boundaries between sex education and HIV/AIDS education. Sex education, is categorised as education related to gender roles, gender identity and the erotic (Calderone, 1989, p131). Among other things, it should inform and educate about the body including how to understand and appreciate it, about sexual feelings and about love and other relationships. However, this is not permissible even in the era of HIV/AIDS. The only widely approved education related to sex and sexuality, especially for young people, is focused on prevention and halting the spread of the disease. This is referred to as HIV/AIDS education which was one focal point of the study. A brief overview of the methodology used in the research is presented below.

Methodology

Because this research was ethnographic, it was organised through a large organisation in Guyana, which is responsible for the major thrust of sex education. After an official introduction to possible network organisations and formal and informal referrals, recruitment of participants for the research assumed a snowballing effect. Twelve snapshot interviews were conducted in order to test the research environment. There was daily interaction with these people who included school children, gardeners, domestic helps, visitors and staff at an Internet café and businessmen. Other methods used in this research were nineteen focus group discussions with a variety of groups including adolescents, religious and gendered groups. There were three group discussions with professionals in the field and nineteen key informant interviews with people positioned to give reliable information on the topic by virtue of their professional or strategic position in the field of sex/HIV/AIDS education. There were also six opportunistic unstructured interviews with people who had heard about the research and wanted to speak about issues which they thought were relevant to the research. One of these was a woman who needed some information about an embarrassing reproductive health issue and this interaction culminated in an extensive unstructured interview. An integral part of this ethnographic research was being involved in ongoing observation of behaviours, practices and the context in which research interaction occurred. Existing research reports and newspaper and journal articles were also reviewed.

Analysis of the data involved thematic aggregation. Implicit and explicit recurrent themes were identified. Using coding frames, I then chose the most regular themes on which to focus. The relevant themes were not only decided on by the regularity of recurrence in the data sets, but also with the help of research notes which determined the context in which they occurred. Following Mason (1997, p149) the concept of triangulation through use of multiple methods helped to approach research questions from different angles and to explore their intellectual puzzles in a rounded and multi-faceted way.

Utilising calypso

In this paper, calypso is used, both to illustrate the normality of the practices highlighted in the findings and to demonstrate their role in forming cultural scripts which relate to the understanding and acceptability of gender roles, identity and behaviours.

Calypso is a powerful medium of social learning because it facilitates freedom of expression through verbalisation and body language to produce effective social commentary or just to reflect the taboo issues which are unspoken. Originally history and literature have been transmitted from one generation to another, since African slavery as part of the oral tradition. This has always been a way of cascading values and norms inter-generationally. Calypso owes much of its renown to the music that accompanies it (Warner, 1999, p33) and consists of a rhythmic pulsating beat that makes the repetitious lyrics an unconscious internalisation of socio-cultural norms and practices.

Its relevance to this discourse is the cultural universality of this medium of social learning. Calypso is a universal form of entertainment and a reflection of the cultural norms in the Caribbean. It is also a form of social learning in the region. The fact that socio-sexual practices are reflected in calypso indicates that they are a part of accepted cultural norms. The messages and values verbalised in calypsoes are inter-nalised by both females and males as a part of the cultural scripts that comprise Caribbean socio-sexual norms.

While calypso reflects social commentary related to all spheres of Caribbean life, the focus of this chapter is only on calypsoes that might be directly and indirectly related to sex education.

The title of this chapter is taken from a calypso, *Ya daddy ain't ya daddy*, which was popular in many Caribbean territories. The practices it des-cribes have always been and are still a fundamental part of Caribbean socio-sexual culture:

> The calypso tells the story of a young man who fell in love with a certain young lady whom he decided to marry. On telling his father the happy news the father advised him that this was not possible because 'the girl is your sister but mammy don't know'.

> The young man had no other option but to obey his father and re-start his quest for love. This situation recurred twice. The young man became so des-pondent that his mother, noticing her son's unhappiness enquired what the problem was. The young man reluctantly told the mother but begged her not to tell his father as his father had told him that she did not know about it. The mother's response to her son was that he had no problem as 'ya daddy ain't ya daddy but ya daddy don't know!!'

> From: *Shame and Scandal in the family – Sir Lancelot 1943 – Remade by Lord Melody 1960s*

This calypso-based anecdote reflects the normality of multiple con-current sexual partner relationships for both men and women.

Multiple concurrent sexual partner relationships
Multiple concurrent sexual partners and fluid conjugal relationships are immortalised in many calypsoes. Below is an excerpt from one calypso with origins in Barbados, and popularised some time ago:

> Well I like to have me fun
> Take a little bit and then I run
> Nimble nimble nimble nimble like kimble
> *The Fugitive by Calypsonians: The Merry Men CD 1992*

The research findings did not suggest that behaviour had changed significantly, as illustrated in the next quote from an unstructured inter-view:

> There was this ting, which was so well packaged that any self-respecting man would want to taste. This friend, 'being a real man', used to have a little

ting outside every now and then. However he never meddled with anything that would break up his marriage or cause complications. This ting that I am telling you about was like a vintage dish and was accustomed to being approached by hungry men. She took pleasure in saying no. Just so men could beg. *Kareem 52 year-old Guyanese businessman*

While the above indicates the penchant by both men and women for engaging in multiple concurrent sexual partner relationships, the main reason Kareem related this anecdote was to justify his assertion that the message given by HIV/AIDS educators about sticking to one faithful partner is unrealistic. Against this, he explained to me that 'a man has got to know when and how to tief a ting.' He pointed out that his friend always ensured that he avoided complications in these matters. Kareem summed up the incident by pointing out that his friend was wise enough to spot this as a potentially detrimental situation to his marriage and avoided it. He concluded:

There are too many other willing tings that understand a man's situation and are willing to facilitate.

This commentary embodies many issues including men's perception of women and the way gender roles and culturally acceptable behaviours are perceived. The difficulty in sticking to one partner in the face of existing socio-cultural norms as articulated by Kareem was repeatedly expressed by men. Another example of men's attitude to such relationships is reflected in the following commentary from one opportunistic snapshot interview

Joe:
I never give my present partner blow (cheated on) yet. 4 years. It is morally incorrect.

Interviewer:
How do you feel about that?

Joe (euphorically):
I feel great. That is the greatest thing I have ever done. That is a major achievement on my part. I must be the only man in this country who has ever done this. I must be 1 in 100 men. There are very few men in this country who are capable of doing that.
Joe: 46 year-old gardener

While in many cultures a four year period of monogamy may not be a significant achievement on the part of a man, it was a triumph in self-discipline for this man in this socio-cultural environment.

During the focus group discussion participants voiced the fact that monogamy was good, although many of them commented after the session that this message 'was unrealistic'. They explained that this was not a practical thing, 'not in this society' and that everyone knew who was having sexual relationships with whom as 'this is a small village.' The men also said that even if they were willing to have only one partner the women in the village 'rushed them.' as they 'always needed something'. These responses reflect of the superficial acceptance of HIV/AIDS messages that do not translate into corresponding behaviour change as is illustrated by the example below.

> Interviewer:
> Do you think that men should have more than one sexual partner?
>
> Tom:
> Yes, because the women in Guyana always want whatever they see some-one else with and they cannot afford to buy it, and they always want you to give them money for it. They are never satisfied. So what are you getting for it?
> *Tom: 54 year-old professional man*

This seems to suggest that men saw women's financial and material dependency on them as a form of currency to be exchanged for sex. In these cases there is a blurring of boundaries between sex which fulfils perceptions of masculinity, and transactional sex which will be discussed next.

Transactional sex

The excerpt below from a calypso illustrates that sexuality related messages are a part of Caribbean culture and that they help to constitute the scripts that Caribbean people write for themselves to understand and construct their sexuality including their gender roles and identity:

> A deputy essential
> To make your living vital
> If boredom is a threat
> Don't stay home and regret
> A deputy is what you must get
> No sweat
> *Calypso by The Mighty Penguin (1982)*

The subtle use of the double entendres in this calypso obscures the message that 'a deputy' can also be a sexual partner. This calypso explains that this type of relationship although necessary must not interfere with an existing long-term relationship or marriage. Applying this discourse to the phenomenon of transactional sex 'a deputy' is an additional partner. Many Guyanese women see the necessity of having an additional man in order to fulfill their financial and other obligations related to heading households. Initially this seemed like another form of commercial sex work, which is reinforced by quotes similar to the one below:

> At least we are honest, we say who and what we are and we go out there and face the music. We make do with whatever little money we earn. We are not like those teachers and civil servants who are drawing a big government salary, pretending to be so respectable and then going in the night jostling us for our clients.
> *Cassie: female community social worker*

transactional sex exists in Guyana, as it has always existed at some level throughout the Caribbean. The excerpt below from the Royal Commission in 1945 suggests that the form of non-commercial prostitution described here would in different circumstances have been categorised as transactional sex. The report reflects a lack of cultural understanding surrounding socio-sexual norms:

> Commercial prostitution is not common as a profession in the West Indies. The high percentage of promiscuity in the colonies puts prostitution into the category of a luxury profession. When this profession is followed, it is usually for economic reasons and because the wages earned by the woman in her other occupation are often too low to obtain the necessities of life for her. She is therefore to be found by night at the docks when ships put in, while carrying out her own work as well in the daytime.
> *(Great Britain 1945 cited in Rohlehr, 1988 p239)*

In all cases, cited reasons for transactional sex are directly and indirectly associated with poverty and the need to use sex as a bartering agent, as demonstrated by the following quotations from research (Greene, 2006 p216):

> Because of the economic situation in the country today women have to depend on three/four men. One to pay her light bill, one to pay her telephone bill, one to pay her rent. One to provide food ... for God's sake what about cooking? What if she has children? Women are working for $25,000 per month (approximately £70) ... and their rent is $35,000. So that is what is making them not have the power to bargain with their partners for safe sex.
> *Female member of the National AIDS committee*

Another related view was that:

> We have males coming over from Suriname, having a good time and then returning to their homeland. Whatsoever they bring they leave in the form of

diseases, because they come here without their wives and then they go back over. We can also see the great influence of Brazilians coming into the country and dwelling in Georgetown. And to have sex in our country, you do not need to speak the language. The green US dollars will do it. They come and they have a good time with our Guyanese women and then they go back and they leave what they bring in most cases.
Male community worker

The above findings illustrated one major disadvantage of women engaging in transactional sex. Another is their vulnerability to gender violence. Detailed below are some research findings associated with this phenomenon.

Gender violence

Gender violence here refers to physical violence by men against women. In many cases this violence is closely linked to women's powerlessness although this may not be always obvious. In some instances women thought that violence was justified. A number of key personnel, including programme planners, policy makers and officials of Non-governmental Organisations reported that not only is violence against women by men prevalent, in many cases it is accepted by women and seen by some men as an attribute of their masculinity. At the time of the research, there were daily radio programmes about gender violence from the feminist organisation, Red Thread. These programmes were meant to empower women to deal with this problem and the issue was portrayed in a culturally explicit way, using local dialect behaviours and with appropriate amounts of local humour. However, newspaper reports of men maiming and killing women were common (Kaiteur News, 2003; Stabroek News, 2003). Red Thread conducted research among 237 respondents in Guyana. Of the 65 per cent currently involved in a relationship, 28 per cent had experienced physical abuse, 26 per cent had experienced verbal abuse and 13 per cent had suffered sexual violence (Red Thread, 2000).

On one occasion a group of men at a market, who were discussing one such incident, were asked about their opinions of a particularly gruesome murder of an unfaithful wife and the attempted suicide of the aggrieved husband. One man responded:

Lady, you do not know the whole story. That woman looked for that. She was bad. We know her. You don't.

On another occasion a 21-year-old man, who was discussing another man chopping his wife to death said that the man was justified in his action. His rationale for this was that 'the woman gave him blow with the neighbour who lived opposite and that was really too much'. When asked why the man could not have just left the woman, he was appalled and retorted 'because he is a man'.

This understanding of the construction of masculinity is not new. The twin phenomena of multiple concurrent sexual partner relationships and gender violence have long been a part of Caribbean cultural norms as seen in the excerpt of this calypso, written a few decades ago and recently re-released.

> We like it
> It's West Indian pleasure
> We like it
> Let's get together
> To see man-beating woman, is not uncommon
> And woman horning husband to mind she sweet man
> *Lord Nelson 1983 from CD-The Best of Nelson (2001)*

Cultural justification of gender violence

The need for a man to keep face and assert his masculinity under the circumstances verbalised above is closely associated with men's physical violence against women. When a group of men in a focus group discussion were asked whether a man was justified in beating a woman, they all asserted he was not. Further probing brought the following responses:

> Only if you come home and the house is dirty, your food is not ready and she is looking at the Young and Restless (a popular soap opera)
> *Jack (26 years old)*

> Well if she is giving you blow, you got to put a hand on she. You got to show she who is man.
> *Sean (32 years old)*

Some women thought gendered violence was justified.

> Some men spoil women and they get out of hand. In such cases they (the men) need to give them a good beating to remind them of their place.
> *Janice (48 years old)*

In relating her experience with gender violence one woman explained that she was having an affair with a man because he used to 'help her financially'. She said that one morning her husband was sitting at the table smoking and asked her:

> I heard you are screwing Tom. Is it true?

She said she became angry because she thought he was being pre-sumptuous as he knew that he was not giving her enough money to maintain the standard of living he was presently enjoying. So she asked him:

> How do you think you can afford to eat the type of food you are demanding? Do you think that the little money you give me could mind the children and buy that type of food?

He became enraged at this and got up, hitting her furiously and burning her with his cigarette butt. She did not say anything as she thought she deserved it. She said she was lucky he did not kill her.

The fact that women involved see these actions as justifiable has impli-cations for the understanding of sexual moralities. While men gain social status for having multiple concurrent sexual relationships and many are open about it, women are socially castigated and conduct these relationships in a clandestine manner. Can sex education related to gender roles and identities address this?

The pertinence of these research findings to sex education in the Carib-bean is now discussed.

The research and sex education

Multiple concurrent sexual partner relationships is a well-documented phenomenon of Caribbean socio-sexual relationships (Brown *et al*, 1993; Barrow, 1996, 1998; Chevannes, 2001, 2002; UNAIDS, 2004). How-ever, the phenomenon of transactional sex has been relatively unmen-tioned primarily because it is a clandestine practice. In this instance, it also affects a racial sub-group that is already highly stigmatised.

Superficially, the prevalence of multiple concurrent sexual partner relationships by men would suggests power asymmetry between men and women with men wielding the power. Power in this case is concep-tualised as power to control or to dominate either overtly or covertly. However, the prevalence of transactional sex among women challenges this power. In transactional sex, women utilise their agency to initiate or negotiate arrangements that suit them in terms of money and other material things. But they lack the power to negotiate safe sex with their partners because of their high level of dependency on the material and financial benefits of these relationships. This is consistent with the findings of other researchers (Cote *et al*, 2004; Luke, 2003; Gupta, 2002). The link between transactional sex and gender violence is also sup-ported by research findings.

Societal tolerance of gender violence against women is not peculiar to Guyana nor limited only to incidences of infidelity or transactional sex. A review of fourteen different societies (Cromwell *et al*, 1996, p67) found that physical chastisement of wives was tolerated in all of them and considered necessary in many societies. Another study of male violence in Uganda found that male violence has become socially sanctioned by the community in specific circumstances (Luke, 2003, p75). These examples imply that men in these societies have the power to subjugate women. One theory is that violence and sexuality are closely linked in the social construction of western heterosexualities (Holland *et al*, 1998, p130) and is the case in the Caribbean.

If women cannot protect themselves from a potentially fatal disease what factors render them so powerless? One theory is that the economic and psychological dependency on men is driven by cultural norms, including a lack of appropriate policies to support and protect women n this predominantly patriarchal society.

In the Caribbean there is a high level of HIV/AIDS education but what is really necessary is sex education. This is not being delivered because of factors related to sexual morality, significantly that:

- this type of education is stigmatised and seen as both unnecessary and immoral in many cases

- because of the fear of corrupting young minds, the formal sex education being delivered is 'too little too late'

One solution to this problem might be the recommendation by Gupta (2002, p3) that for sex education to be meaningful to adolescents, it must go beyond public health goals of disease prevention to the promotion of positive and pleasurable sex, which is rooted in values that are fundamental to both AIDS prevention and to health and personal development.

Young people discover the pleasurable side of sexual activity to the detriment of the educator's credibility. Schneider *et al* (2002, pp408-9) posit that a moral panic is accompanying the HIV/AIDS epidemic. Consequently HIV/AIDS education policy attempts to exert social control on female sexuality by the construction of 'good girls' and 'bad girls'. Researchers argue that the fields of medicine and psychology have heavily influenced sex education and sexuality by putting forward essentially deterministic models of social behaviour that are not flexible enough to capture the variation and dynamism of sexuality and social interaction (*ibid*).

Referring to specific cultural contexts, Adams and Pigg (2005, pp1-3) argue against the practice of misinterpreting sexual practices by viewing them through the lens of inappropriate assumptions. They argue that in social analyses of sexuality too often the history of western sexualities takes centre stage against the rhetorically constructed backdrop of other cultures.

Conclusion

This chapter has presented the complex situation of socio-sexual practices, moralities and contradictions in gendered power. In relating this to the HIV/AIDS situation in the Caribbean, it has highlighted the fact that after more than two decades of aggressive sex education, significant sexual behaviour change in the Caribbean remains little more than a theory.

While Caribbean people from childhood to death are singing and dancing to rhythmic sensuous calypsoes, they are also receiving messages which contribute to the writing of culturally defined sexual scripts. These inform the peculiar construction of their sexuality through this specific understanding of their sexual roles, identity, and behaviours. By the time targeted formal sex education begins these sexual scripts are already written and socio-cultural norms are already internalised as an integral part of their sexual behaviours. Formal, targeted sex education ignores the influence of this informal learning.

It is prescribed by northern moralities and dictated by foreign donor funding and it ignores, except in a censorious way, the peculiar construction of Caribbean sexualities. Meanwhile parallel forms of sexual learning which verbalise and support these sexualities are taking place through informal and enjoyable channels such as calypsoes. Supported by cultural customs and practices, they contribute to the construction of cultural sexual scripts which have become intergenerational norms. Combined with economic poverty and women's learnt dependency on men, whether direct or indirect, they speak to behaviours, which can result in potentially life-threatening consequences such as contracting HIV.

There are no easy solutions to these issues. Not all African-Caribbean men and women indulge in transactional sex and multiple concurrent sexual partner relationships. But, although the Caribbean is not a homogenous society, the phenomena described in this chapter are widespread. The need to acknowledge, understand and positively address the peculiar construction of this sexuality is crucial if these negative outcomes are to be dealt with effectively. Denial of their existence, based on fear of stigmatisation, further complicates sex education. The interlocking issues of social and formal learning also need to be examined more closely to maximize the effects of both.

Sexual dominance is not only determined by ability to control through financial wealth and administrative power. Power also controls through sexual behaviours and practices. The public humiliating of women, unintentional though it might be, through the practice of multiple concurrent sexual partners is the exercise of power to control. The inability of a woman to negotiate safe sex, because of limited options in her bartering position due to financial and material need, and the lack of choice in heading households, also highlights power asymmetries which subjugates poor women.

In the Caribbean, the predominantly male decision-making elite also appear to be insensitive to women's needs by failing to formulate and implement policies, which will ensure comprehensive, culturally appropriate sex education.

Recognition of the need for effective culture-specific sex education is necessary from a multi-sectoral administrative perspective. Policies which ensure a robust social support system for women will alleviate the heavy dependency on men for financial and material support. This will ensure that the laws which are designed to protect women can be effective when they can be assured of financial and material provision for themselves and children. Egalitarian policies to ensure equal remuneration for women and men are also necessary in a society where many women are heading households.

The above raises the question:

> Is this situation peculiar to Guyana or the wider Caribbean, or is it a minute representation of a more pervasive phenomenon?

It is clear that much more research needs to be done in order to ascertain accurate positions and interventions for effective culture-specific sex education.

Note

1 This is a fact sheet with no page numbers.

References

Adams, V and Pigg, S (eds) (2005) *Sex in Development: Science, Sexuality and Morality in Global Perspective.* London: Duke University Press

African American Health Articles (2003) *AIDS Grows Up, But Black Community Takes a Hit* Retrieved from http://www.journeytowellness.com/aids3.html on 13/08/03

Barrow, C (ed) (1996) *Family in the Caribbean: Themes and Perspectives.* Kingston: Ian Randle Publishers

Barrow, C (ed) (1998) *Caribbean Portrait.* Kingston: Ian Randle Publishers

Brown, J, Anderson, P. and Chevannes, B (1993) *Report on the Contribution of Caribbean Men to the Family; a Jamaican Pilot Study.* Jamaica: The Caribbean Child Development Centre, School of Continuing Studies University of the West Indies

Calderone, M (1989) Above and beyond politics: the sexual socialization of children. In Vance, C (ed) *Pleasure, and Danger: Exploring Female Sexuality.* London: Pandora Press

Chevannes B (2001) *Learning to be a man: Culture, Socialization, and Gender Identity in Five Caribbean Communities.* Kingston: University of the West Indies Press

Chevannes B (2002) Gender and adult sexuality. In P Mohammed (ed) *Gendered Realities: Essays in Caribbean Feminist Thought.* Mona: University of the West Indies Press

Cote A Sobela, F Dzokoto, A Nzambi, K, Asamoah-Adu, C, Labbe, A, Masse, B, Mensah, J, Frost, E, Pepin, J (2004) Transactional Sex is the driving force in the dynamics of HIV in Accra, Ghana. *AIDS* 18(6), 917-925.

Cromwell, N and Burgess, A (1996) *Understanding Violence Against Women.* Washington D C: National Academy Press

Danns, GK Henry, B and Le Fleur, P (1997). *Tomorrow's Adults: A Situational Analysis of Youth in the Commonwealth Caribbean.* London: Commonwealth Secretariat

Dougan, S Payne, J, Brown, A, Fenton K, Logan B., Evans, B and Gill, O (2004) Black Caribbean Adults with HIV in England, Wales, and Northern Ireland: an emerging epidemic? *Sexually Transmitted Infections* 80, 18-23 Retrieved from http://sti.bmjjournals.com/egi/content/full/80/1/18 on 10/02/04

Gonzalez, N L (1960) Household and Family in the Caribbean. *Social and Economic Studies* 9, 101-106.

Greene, R (2006) Anywhere Sancho Want Me: a feminist ethnographic study of the socio-cultural factors that influence se-education in Guyana. Unpublished EdD Thesis, Keele University

Greenfield, S (1973) Dominance, focality and the characteristics of domestic groups: some reflections on matrifocality in the Caribbean. In Gerber, S N (ed) *The Family in the Caribbean.* Rio Peidras: University of Puerto Rico

Gupta, G R (2002) Cross-Generational and Transactional Sex: A public Health Crisis and a Moral Dilemma. Keynote Address ICRW conference and PSI 10/09/02

Hawkes, G (2004) *Sex and Pleasure in Western Culture.* Cambridge: Polity Press

Holland, J, Ramazanoglu, C, Sharpe, S and Thomson, R (1998) *The Male in The Head: Young People, Heterosexuality, and Power.* London: The Tufnell Press

Kaiser Daily (2001) Secret Bisexuality Among Black Men Contributes to Rising Number of AIDS Cases in Black Women HIV/AIDS Report Retrieved from http://report.kff.org/archive/aids/2001/3/kh010316.1.htm on 13/08/03

Kaiteur News (2003) Husbands kill at least 26 wives this year 21/12/03 p11

Luke, N (2003). Age and economic asymmetries in the sexual relationships of adolescent girls in sub-Saharan Africa. *Studies in Family Planning*, 32(2), 67-86.

Mason, J (1997) *Qualitative Researching*. London: Sage Publications

McEvoy, P (2000) Heightening awareness of HIV/AIDS in the Caribbean Region Bridging the Gap from Denial to Acceptance to Prevention. Speech: Preparing for the Next Millennium. St. Thomas, US Virgin Islands New York: UNAIDS

Red Thread (2000) Women and Sex Work in Guyana (Unpublished report)

Schneider, B, and Jenness, V (2002) Social control, civil liberties and women's sexuality. In Williams, C and Stein, A (eds) *Sexuality and Gender*. Oxford: Blackwell Publishers

Smith, R T (1973) The matrifocal family. In J Goody (ed) *The Character of Kinship*. Cambridge: Cambridge University Press

Stabroek News (2003) Gender violence must be approached as men's issue say Shadick 26/11/03 p3

The Balm in Gilead (2003) *AIDS Facts* Retrieved from http://www.balmingilead.org/aidsfacts/aidsfacts.asp on 13/08/03

UNAIDS (2000) HIV/AIDS-related programmes/activities in the Caribbean: Caribbean meeting on HIV/AIDS Bridgetown: Barbados, 11-12/09/02

UNAIDS (2004) *Report on the Global AIDS Epidemic*: 4th Global Report. Geneva: UNAIDS

Warner, K Q (1999) Kaiso – *The Trinidad Calypso: A Study of Calypso as Oral Literature*. Colorado: Passeggiata Press

World Bank (2000) *HIV/AIDS in the Caribbean: Issues and Options: A Background Report*. New York: World Bank

8

Reflections on doing educational research in a post-colonial setting

Jennifer M. Lavia

Introduction

This chapter is written as a critical, reflexive work that examines the ways in which participation on a doctoral programme in education allowed for a challenge and interrogation of common assumptions about Caribbean identities. In this light, doing research and engaging in the research process constituted acts of agency that confronted traditional research practice. In conceptualising a practice of research in this way this chapter seeks to unpack the complexity involved in the struggles to articulate meaning, re-discover self and negotiate access within the context of a small, post-colonial state.

Specifically, post-colonial and feminist theories are the theoretical threads that allow me to articulate three major considerations. First, issues of positionality are addressed within the context of crafting images of a post-colonial, gendered self. Second, doing research in small states has its own characteristics which will be explored within a discourse of difference. Elaborating the experience of being in the field presents the third set of discussions. The discussion concludes with a return to the issue of positionality, this time with a reflection of the lessons of the field and the emerging and recurring agendas for research in small states and post-colonial settings.

Crafting the post-colonial gendered self

The researcher, as architect of the process and eventually author of the text, brings to the process interpretations of the world that influence the nature of the study, the theoretical and methodological frameworks and the choices made about how to construct the story that is represented by the text. Such interpretations are the manifestations of how history and biography intersect.

According to Griffiths:

> The self I am – the identity I have – is affected by the politics of gender, race, class, sexuality, disability and world justice. In other words, the feelings I have, the reasons I recognise the wants I act upon – they are all deeply political. (Griffiths, 1995, p1)

Like Morwenna Griffiths I have always felt that teaching, my career of choice, was deeply political. My reasoning about this was to do with my understanding of my location within society as a social being and how I chose to articulate values by speaking up against oppression and injustice. This process is never easy and requires the commitment to confront a culture of silence within a specific set of political, cultural, historical and gendered structures.

These structures have been marked by the legacies of colonialism which have perpetuated elitism, acriticality and dependency. Colonialism is not only a form of direct control of external structures and resources, it is also and more importantly a range of complex structures designed to 'generate conceptions of personhood and identity' (London, 2002, p95). This conception of colonialism embraces Freire's (1985, p72), articulation of 'the culture of silence'. Implicit in this 'culture of silence' are issues of dependency and the power relationships between dependent and metropolitan societies in which forms of 'being, thinking and expression' (*ibid*, p73) evolve and are forged.

This study incorporates three basic elements: a sense of history, a challenge to common assumptions about Caribbean civilisation and identities, and a focus on discontinuities in the social practice of teachers that could offer a pedagogy of hope. Hearing the stories of teachers, particularly the elders and unearthing evidence of progressive practice which was largely unrecorded was an absorbing experience. Brief encounters with the limited local literature was enough to ignite a spark that prompted a search for a largely unrecorded range of images of teacher professionalism. These images emerged out of the anti-colonial, nationalist struggle of the 1940s, 50s and 60s in Trinidad and Tobago. Progressive practice came to mean a situation where teachers employed a practice of critical professionalism in which the personal and professional were seamlessly constructed as political.

My own sense of social justice was also shaped by a number of other factors including a process of being socialised into being aware of being black, being Caribbean and being female. There was an intangible way in which the family framework and schooling combined to convey these messages that foresaw and understood the social and structural impediments that created difference, marginalisation and exclusion. Yet there was a sense in which it was important to 'beat them at their own game'. There was fearlessness in that statement of them and about them that resisted victim roles and the feeling of being excluded from any aspect of social and political life.

A second factor that influenced my philosophical reasons for adopting an emancipatory approach to my research was the shared values that emerged from the discussions and academic innovations undertaken by the group of doctoral students who had embarked on this journey together. There were seven of us initially, five women and two men, and we had decided that during the first phase of our course of study we would meet regularly to discuss key topics on how to understand our local and regional conditions in the light of international literature. Arising from those discussions was a commitment that each of our studies would in some way reflect a 'writing back' discourse which assumed 'that the centre does not necessarily have to be located at the imperial centre' (Smith, 1999, p36). The commitment undertaken was to allow our studies to locate the Caribbean context at the centre of our theorising.

In the course of navigating our way through the process of 'writing back' challenges emerged that caused us to rethink our own insularity and in-securities. The diverse nature of the group meant that we had to negotiate and re-negotiate access through issues of gender, race, class, geography and other aspects of ethnicity for which we did not have a language to explain. What sustained the group was the sharing of common values about contributing to the wider social good and of being insider researchers. What also sustained me was being able to confront and come to terms with notions of post-colonialism and feminism and grappling to find a language suitable to articulate these.

Conducting research in small developing states requires a re-inter-pretation of post-colonialism. This re-interpretation can provide the fillip for critically challenging the political and cultural values that in-form social systems within these states. Similarly, I favour a stance which provides for gendered accounts of teacher professionalism in which attention is paid to 'the ideas of subjectivity, personal and political identity, experience and political commitment' (Griffiths, 1998, p62). As a corollary to these discourses, theoretical and methodological spaces were created to historicise educational policy and teacher professionalism within the contexts of contestation, continuity and change (McCulloch, 1994; McCulloch, Helsby and Knight, 2000).

Characterising difference

Doing research in small states brings with it peculiarities and challenges that can be characterised by a discourse of difference. In this case three such characterisations can be made: the experience of research itself, size and role multiplicity, and notions about what constitutes evidence.

Experiencing research

Firstly, what is the historical experience of research in the Caribbean? The rubric that provided the framework for conducting the study began with the traditional guidelines and references that sought to provide various definitions of research and the procedures that would govern original scholarship. It became imperative to challenge the very notion of the word 'research' and to notice what research meant within the context of where the study was to be located.

To a large extent research has been an instrument of colonisation where, as Smith (1999, p1) points out, 'scientific research is implicated in the worst excesses of colonialism and remains a powerful remembered history for many of the world's colonised peoples'. In the Caribbean it is not long ago since our history books described our indigenous peoples as fierce and warlike when they resisted European colonisers and peaceful and friendly where they succumbed to their brutish onslaught. The frequency with which the islands changed hands between occupiers from 1498 onwards caused one of our eminent historians, Eric Williams (1962), to describe the machinations of the colonialists as perceiving the colonies as a workshop and plaything of the colonisers. It is not surprising that small states have been portrayed in international literature as 'constrained, remote and dependent' (Louisy, 1997, p202).

Education has been shaped by interpretations of the metropolis about who should be taught, what they should be taught, by whom they should be taught and where they should be taught. Such questions about educational aims have persisted to the extent that education policy continues to be largely shaped by policy development strategies developed around appeals for external funding for educational development: this practice has not transcended the post-independence and post-republican periods.

The significance of the debate about research is that it provides another interpretation to the way in which 'scientific research' has been used as a tool of marginalisation, image building and suppression.

Size and transitions

Notwithstanding the colonising effects of research on small states, the indigenous researcher has ample opportunity to contribute to re-framing images of their contexts and to reference post-colonial experiences of the small state in the light of current international debates. Attention must be drawn to the ways in which difference is constructed within the social world of small states where intricate webs and networks of relationships exist and close proximity forces us to learn to live with each other.

Bray and Packer (1993) extend this point when they describe societies in small states as being highly personalised and where it is accepted that individuals play a multiplicity of roles which complement each other at times and conflict at others. These multi-layered, complex connections are relevant both to those who allow their stories to emerge and also to the insider researcher. Thus, the process of research is coloured by seamless, sometimes unconscious and simultaneous transitions of roles, expectations and meanings between the field and the researcher. This interaction is amplified by the direct encounter between the researched and the researcher.

Crossley and Holmes (2001), Crossley and Vulliamy (1997) and Louisy (1997, 2004) have identified constraints and opportunities posed by the size of societies in small states. Treating the familiar as strange is essentially problematic and raises issues of anonymity and confidentiality. If a policy has been drafted by an official who works alone it is impossible to preserve her/his anonymity and this could turn out to have dire consequences. Or, as Louisy (1997) suggests, what about states of 'transparency and visibility' that exercise significant influence over any social interaction? The presence of the insider researcher is announced even before her/his arrival upon the scene!

On the other hand, negotiating access by being familiar with the cultural, organisational and political terrain places the insider researcher in an advantageous position. Brock and Parker (1985, p54) suggest that 'such visibility may be associated with notions of relevance and adaptability which are able to inform networks of communication and decision-making'.

What constitutes evidence?

Smith (1999) has suggested that history and writing as processes of research are bound up with a discourse about epistemological imperialism and interpretations of what constitutes evidence. But how does one go about researching education policy which involves decision making and its relation to teachers in Trinidad and Tobago during the period 1956-1966? The decision to proceed was guided by adopting a critical approach to the legacies of colonialism, based on confronting common assumptions and pursuing an interpretation of 'colonial imagination' from the perspective of change, contestation and continuity.

In discussing what constitutes evidence, concerns about whether evidence can be generated must be considered. Here, Liverpool's experience is appropriate for insertion as it expresses the dilemma of the researcher who is working in small states in which colonial ideology among academic gatekeepers still runs rampant. Liverpool relates his story:

> After completing my master's degree ... I went one day to see a leading professor to discuss plans to complete my PhD studies. He informed me that because of the lack of documentation and sources, I ought not to embark on a doctoral dissertation on Carnival, but should opt for the MPhil award instead. His views were in keeping with the strategy of up to the mid-20th century colonial educators and European dominant groups who sought to convince the colonised that knowledge, whether in the sphere of culture, science or technology, could be acquired only through the mediation of the colonial rulers. (Liverpool, 2001, pxi)

Evidently Liverpool was not daunted. But the notion of re-creating methodology raises the question of where to get the data? E H Carr (1961) proceeds from the position of questioning what a historical fact is. He concedes that 'facts are a necessary condition for historical work but not the essential function of the historian' (Carr, 1961, p11). He advises the use of what he calls 'auxiliary sciences' and invites a multi-disciplinary approach to historical research. He selects the primacy of the researcher when he acknowledges that 'the necessity to establish these basic facts rests not on any quality in the facts themselves but on *a priori* decisions of the historian' (Carr, 1961, p11).

In addressing the methodological problem of what constitutes evidence I am reminded of the ways in which my own voice and the voices of a society have been shaped by imperial schooling. The education system in Trinidad has largely been shaped by the British system where academic standards were set by external examinations administered by Oxford and Cambridge. We had to learn world history and world geography in which the world was Britain. There was a time when it would have been inconceivable for Caribbean history to be written by insider accounts from the colonies. Accounts of West Indian History written by white, male, British academics and educators were given priority.

The relationship between western academy and the colony was one in which western academy assumed the role of authority and its task was to bring the colony up to standard. In this sense issues of history and writing can be seen as tools of silencing. The research revealed a dearth of local texts about education and teacher professionalism which raised the following questions: Who are the educational thinkers and writers in the Caribbean? Where are they? How have they contributed to educational thought in and about the Caribbean? These questions hit at the heart of the ways in which competing colonial interests privilege Eurocentric hegemonic ideas which are globalised and recognised as authority.

During the course of conversations with the elders in the study it became evident that their politics of involvement in the anti-colonial and nationalist movement shaped their conceptions of their professional identity. Their representations of how they confronted their own history and engaged in the movement for the development of insider accounts of West Indian history were lucid and constituted evidence. Through dialogue, it was possible to listen to the elders represent their own understanding of how they experienced the world, how they confronted history and how they experienced disappointment and betrayal. It was not a set of stories that were unfamiliar. As a teacher and social activist I was able to empathise with their struggle to be recognised. I used my own biography as well to inform the study. Indeed, I had conceptualised that my research would represent an act of one teacher speaking up and about injustice and reclaiming a position that challenged invisibility and otherness.

In this struggle with meaning, language and other interpretations of the world it became clear that doing research in a small state requires a commitment to research practices that are engaged in:

> creating a new language, rupturing disciplinary boundaries, decentering authority and rewriting the institutional and discursive borderlands in which politics becomes a condition for asserting the relationship between agency, power and struggle. (Giroux and McLaren, 1994, pix)

Experiencing the field

> She remained poised on the interface between familiarity and strangeness. ... The reality of fieldwork and the nature of estrangement is far more complex than many accounts suggests. Straightforward readings ... imply a position of ethnographer-as-stranger, progressing towards a familiarity and eventually enlightenment, while simultaneously achieving a professional and personal distance. (Coffey, 1999, p19)

My sense of strangeness was associated with my understanding of my emotional space as I experienced the field. I was a neophyte who was attempting 'to be permanently accepted or at least tolerated by the group' that I approached (Schultz, 1971, p27). The self-selected group comprised 24 retired teachers and public servants who were in active practice during the period 1956 to 1966. But strangeness did not only apply to that group, it also applied to the engagement in the research process and the rigours of a critical paradigm which challenged the core of my schooling and methods of thinking, both in form and content.

This strangeness also included an awareness of the need at times to maintain epistemological distance from the subject, not to think as usual but to treat the familiar as strange. Coffey (1990, p20) suggests that the researcher 'is able, and encouraged, to adopt the position of ignorant outsider' when strangeness brings about purposeful mortification of self in which she/he 'initially and purposely divests herself/himself of knowledge and personhood in order to achieve eventual understanding' (*ibid*, p20).

Though she argues her case well, Coffey may not have considered specific dilemmas that face researchers in small states where the entire society is 'personalised' and the researcher's family background and social standing have currency. In my case I was seen as a junior member of a family that had invested years of generational experience in education and most of the respondents were the colleagues and contemporaries of my parents and grandparents.

Louisy (1997) reflects on the dilemma of doing research in small states by problematising the case of the insider researcher. She states:

> The dilemma I faced is best expressed in the juxtaposition of the different approaches that the outsider and the indigenous researcher are perceived to bring to ethnographic inquiry. On the one hand, the outsider attempts to make the strange familiar, while, on the other the local researcher is asked to treat the familiar as strange. (Louisy, 1997, p200)

Louisy (1997) highlights the significance of the insider researcher in small states to ethical concerns. She states that she 'accepted that there was not any possibility of all respondents remaining completely anonymous although [she] adhered to the convention of using anonymised references to specific individuals in the report' (*ibid*). In other words, how does the researcher play the dual role of fringe-dweller and insider in the research context in which she was socialised?

My experience of the field, as it relates to the movement from strangeness to familiarity, from ignoramus researcher to enlightened researcher, from experience to understanding, is encapsulated in the following reflection from my journal that I made while in the field:

> It seems to me that the value of the researcher's value system (ethics), immersion or 'fringe-dwelling' is the choice that will determine the level of connectedness between researcher and the subject of the research. The research cannot be divorced from its social context. In a society like ours, I see research so closely linked to the 're-creation' of an identity, of a people – a nation. That the researcher is part of re-building of a subjugated yet resilient people is central to my research act. (Lavia, 2004, p102)

There were times when I felt that I was being entrusted to continue a heritage for the elderly women. They expressed their delight that I was pursuing doctoral studies because they had not been afforded the opportunity so to do. The institutional barriers and lack of opportunity had impeded the progress of some of them who had wanted to pursue higher education, except in one case where the respondent was fortunate to be assisted by the Canadian Missions to pursue undergraduate studies in the 1940s in Canada and England which was a rarity at that time for a woman.

I considered the conversations with the elders to be a celebration of their lives and a means of baton passing from one generation to the next. It was an extremely emotional experience for me listening to their accounts of their efforts to forge a professional identity in the face of colonial attitudes and practice. So many efforts to bring change had been frustrated by being ignored at the hands of political expediency.

Despite this I managed to maintain my distance and remain focused and incisive in my listening and questioning. Smith articulates this point when she says:

> Each individual story is powerful ... The point about the stories is not that they simply tell a story or tell a story simply ... [but that] the story and the story-teller both serve to connect the past with the future, one generation with the other, the land with the people, the people with the story. (Smith, 1999, p145)

The risky business of positionality

Given the characteristics of the societies in small states it is not surprising that explaining oneself and identifying one's positionality is a risky business. The riskiness for the researcher in the context of the Caribbean is about being aware that the interconnectedness of structures within people's lives and aspirations only allows for a small margin of error, knowing that 'if actions go wrong they will have nowhere to hide' (Louisy, 1997, p203). This presents a dilemma for the insider researcher, especially when to critique can be misconstrued as a an act of disrespect and personal affront and critiquing ideas can be mistaken for criticism of practice. The configuration of networks can determine whether you are included or excluded from the mainstream and respected or ridiculed by society.

According to Holmes and Albert (2001):

> In view of the dangers and dilemmas arising from the uncritical international transfer of research findings and methodologies, there is a strong case for strengthening research in St. Lucia. More democratic forms of 'research' are already taking shape within governmental, educational and civil society arenas.

This perspective was adopted earlier by Smith (1999) in her discourse on research and indigenous peoples. She says:

> Coming to know the past has been part of the critical pedagogy of de-colonisation. To hold alternative histories is to hold alternative knowledges. The pedagogical implication of this access to alternative knowledges is that they can form the basis of alternative ways of doing things. (Smith, 1999, p35)

The essence of Smith's thinking closely resembles Eric Williams' claim that education and educational research cannot be divorced from the colonial question and Edward Said's notion that history and the concept of the oriental has largely been shaped through the eyes of the west. In this context the use of qualitative genres enables a dialogic approach aimed at 'developing voice among those who have been silenced historically' (Gitlin and Russell, 1994, p186).

Post-colonial critic Gyatri Spivak raises the problematic issue of voice in the context of the dilemmas faced by post-colonial intellectuals. Spivak recasts the location of the colonised by problematising the conditions of post-coloniality. She raises the question of whether the subaltern can speak (Spivak, 1993). The concept of the subaltern refers to 'a range of different subject positions which are not predefined by dominant political discourses' (Morton, 2003, p45). Spivak seeks to provide a critical vocabulary and methodology to encompass the histories and experiences of disempowered and marginalised individuals and groups and emphasises the political responsibility of the post-colonial intellectual to expose historical and political relationships that shape representation.

The post-colonial intellectual, who is committed to using critical historiography from the perspective of the colonised (the subaltern) and as a form of agency, transgression and re-presentation, has to negotiate states of being that are unsettling and contested. The conditions of post coloniality required me to pay attention to the plurality involved in writing and researching and the subtle forms of dissonance that might emerge. The task of writing is always tension-filled yet it is a critical reflexive space where my Caribbean educational background and my race, class and gender intersect with the expectations of western academy. It is indeed risky business in which the historically oppressive structures being critiqued might subtly be perpetuated through deeply entrenched power relationships, between post-colonial doctoral students and a British university. It is a paradox. Nonetheless, the contested nature of the post-colonial condition provides opportunities for dialogic spaces to be negotiated, mediated and created, which must be seized. The risk involved is in falling prey to dominant structures of knowledge and representation (Morton, 2003). Rather than give up because of this risk, it is important to acknowledge the risk as inevitable if we are to confront and expose ways of experiencing and understanding the dominant structures.

Armstrong (2003, p201), responding to the debate about voice and positionality, argues for 'a critical history' which should be based on considerations of cultural studies through which voice is represented in terms of 'a contested struggle for legitimacy'. According to Armstrong (2003), legitimacy is related to the ways in which meanings and understandings are constructed and expressed and supports Fulcher's statement (1999) that policy is struggle. The challenge for research in small state settings is to be 'concerned with unpacking the social spaces of dissent' in which power is interrogated 'as a meditative relationship between social interests' (Armstrong, 2003, p217). Critical history therefore proceeds on the basis of theorising 'relationships between structure and agency, policy and experience, power and resistance' (*ibid*, p217).

Gitlin and Russell (1994), like Smith (1999) and Armstrong (2003), assert the significance of the dialogical process in the pursuit of alternative methodologies. Gitlin and Russell formulate their contribution in this way:

> The opportunity to speak, to question, and to explore issues is an important part of this process. But the notion of voice can go beyond the opportunity to speak; it can be about protest. Understood in this way, voice becomes politicised; its aim is to question what is taken for granted and to act on what is seen to be unjust in an attempt to shape and aide future educational directions. Injustice or oppression cannot be defined outside of a historical context. (Gitlin and Russell, 1994, p186)

In facilitating a macro-analysis of an education problem (public issues) through the lived experience of colonialism (personal knowledge and practice), I sought to locate my research and my writing as a form of agency which provided a re-presentation (as opposed to a representation) of the conditions of post-coloniality. Recognition of the social construction of identity and research was emphasised.

Conclusion

During my doctoral studies I embarked upon a journey that was life changing. In using such a clichéd remark, I do not mean to romaticise the process or to oversimplify the case. The process held out the possibility of re-examining the post-colonial condition in terms of the ways in which research can be reflected and experienced as agency and provided glimpses of ways in which de-colonising methodologies can be forged. These can and must be articulations of research projects which involve:

- celebrating the elders and recognising survival

- resistance and resilience

- recognising the ways in which each story reflected the experience of change, innovation and development

- connecting with the elders in a respectful manner

- honouring their dignity and facilitating a humanising process

- negotiating a space and seeking their tacit and formal permission to create spaces for their voices.

In this chapter I have elaborated the context within which the study took place and highlighted the fact that conducting research in a small state in a post-colonial setting has unique characteristics which at times conform to the expectations of western academic tradition but most times do not. Critical reflections on theoretical and methodological endeavours draw attention to the interconnection between educational research, history and biography. Indeed, involvement on the doctoral programme opened up spaces where I was able to use dialogue and engagement as a basis for critical conversations that provided 'a model of possibility' (hooks, 1994, p131).

Note

1 This chapter is based on excerpts and adaptations from Lavia (2004).

References

Armstrong, D (2003) Historical voices: philosophical idealism and the methodology of 'voice' in the history of education, *History of Education*, 32(2) 201-217

Bray, M and Packer, S (1993) *Education in Small States: concepts, challenges and strategies*. Oxford: Pergamon Press

Brock, C and Parker, R (1985) School and community in situations of close proximity: the question of small states. In Lillis, K (ed) *School and Community in Less Developed Areas*. London: Croom Helm pp42-56

Carr, E H (1961) *What is History?* London: Penguin Books

Coffey, A (1999) *The Ethnographic Self: Fieldwork and the Representation of Identity*. London: Sage Publications

Crossley, M and Holmes, K (2001) Challenges for educational research: international development, partnerships and capacity building in small states. *Oxford Review of Education* 27(3), 395-409

Crossley, M and Vulliamy, G (eds) (1997) *Qualitative Educational Research in Developing Countries: Current Perspectives*. New York: Garland

Freire, P (1985) *The Politics of Education*. New York: Bergin and Garvey

Fulcher, G (1999) *Disabling Policies? A comparative approach to education policy and disability*. Sheffield: Phillip Armstrong

Giroux, H and McLaren, P (1994) *Between Borders: Pedagogy and the politics of Cultural Studies*. Routledge: New York

Gitlin, A and Russell, R (1994) Alternative methodologies and the research context. In Gitlin, A (ed) *Power and Method: Political Activism and Educational Research*. London: Routledge pp181-202

Griffiths, M (1995) *Feminisms and the Self: The Web of Identity.* London: Routledge

Griffiths, M (1998) *Educational Research for Social Justice: Getting off the Fence.* Buckingham: Open University Press

Holmes, K and Albert, C (2001) *Rethinking Research.* Available online from: http://www.educatin.gov.lc/home/features/rethinking_research.htm Accessed July 2002

hooks, b (1994) *Teaching to Transgress: education as the practice of freedom.* London: Routledge

Lavia, J (2004) Education Policy and Teacher Professionalism in Trinidad and Tobago in a Period of Transition – 1956-1966. Unpublished PhD Thesis University of Sheffield, UK

Liverpool, H (2001) *Rituals of Power and Rebellion: The Carnival Tradition in Trinidad and Tobago 1763-1962.* Chicago: Research Associates School Times Publications/Frontline Distribution International Inc.

London, N. (2002) Curriculum and pedagogy in the development of colonial imagination: a case study. *Pedagogy, Culture and Society* 10(1), 95-121

Louisy, P (2004) Whose context for what quality? Informing education strategies for the Caribbean. *Compare* 34(3), 285-292

Louisy, P (1997) Dilemmas of Insider Research in a Small-Country Setting: Tertiary Education in St. Lucia. In Crossley, M and Vulliamy, M (eds), *Qualitative Educational Research in Developing Countries: Current Perspectives.* New York and London: Garland Publishing pp199-220

McCulloch, G. (1994) *Education Reconstruction: The 1944 Education Act and the Twenty-First Century.* London: The Woburn Press

McCulloch, G, Helsby, G and Knight, P (2000) *The Politics of Professionalism: Teachers and the Curriculum.* London: Continuum

Morton, S (2003) *Gayatri Chakravorty Spivak.* London: Routledge

Schultz, A (1971) The stranger: an essay in social psychology. In Cosin, B *et al* (eds) *School and Society: A Sociological Reader* 2nd edition. London: Routledge and Kegan Paul

Smith, L (1999) *Decolonizing Methodologies: Research and Indigenous Peoples.* London: Zed Books

Spivak, G (1993) Can the subaltern speak? In Williams, P and Chrisman, L (eds) *Colonial Discourse and Post-colonial Theory: A Reader.* New York: Harvester, Wheatsheaf pp66-111

Williams, E (1962) *History of the People of Trinidad and Tobago.* Port of Spain: PNM Publishing Co. Ltd

9

'She went too far': civility, complaint and dialoguing with the Other

Renée DePalma

According to the National Association of State Boards of Education the typical student graduating from a teacher training programme in the US can be characterised as 'white, female, 21 years old, speaks only English, from a small town and wanting to teach in the same' (Latham, 1999, p85). Nevertheless, the National Council for Accreditation of Teacher Education (NCATE)[1] specifically requires that teachers be prepared to teach 'all students ...(which) ... includes students with exceptionalities and of different ethnic, racial, gender, language, religious, socio-economic, and regional/geographic origins' (2002, p10). In 1972 the American Association of Colleges for Teacher Education (AACTE) specifically endorsed multicultural education through both the creation of a Commission on Multicultural Education and an official policy statement specifically recognising not only ethnic, racial, and linguistic diversity but also 'the support of explorations in alternative and emerging lifestyles' (1972, p2).

In an attempt to prepare future teachers to work effectively with children from backgrounds different from their own and in accordance with accreditation agency requirements, teacher preparation programmes in the US often have a explicit multicultural component to their curriculum, sometimes devoting an entire module to multicultural education which is sometimes referred to as diversity[2] education. Yet there are various definitions of multicultural or diversity education and these imply different conceptions of good teaching (Sleeter and Grant, 2003).

The university teacher-training diversity module described in this chapter was designed based on a Multicultural Social Reconstructionism (MCSR) paradigm:

> MCSR education extends the multicultural paradigm in that it attempts to transform traditional relationships of power and domination, attends to the representative voices of historically marginalized groups, and calls for critical dialogue and the counter-hegemonic actions of principles that translate society and its institutions into democratic sites that are truly democratic, just, and humane. (Martin and Van Gunten, 2002, p45)

As the module tutor I found this paradigm of multiculturalism to be most closely aligned with my own philosophy, but the instantiation of MCSR within my specific (higher) educational institution has proved to be problematic. The notion of critical dialogue is crucial for transforming hegemonic power structures, but who is invited to this dialogue? This chapter will describe and analyse the kinds of discourse afforded and constrained among a group of teacher trainees who are predominantly members of privileged majority groups and for whom the social realities being discussed and supposedly transformed have been largely unproblematic.

The module, students and tutor

I am a white heterosexual native English-speaking female born in the US; from my own personal history I have little to share from a minority perspective. Students preparing to be elementary school teachers at the US university where I taught overwhelmingly represented majority groups. This follows the national trend. The notable exception is gender; the great majority of our elementary teacher candidates have been women, again following the national trend. A demographic cross-section of my students during one semester paints a typical picture: of 84 students enrolled in my modules during the Fall semester of 2003, twelve were men. One student self-identified as Filipina (born in the US), another was from India (immigrated at age 2) and another was Mexican American (born in the US). The rest of the students (81) all self-identified as both white and US-born. No student self-identified as gay, lesbian, bisexual or transgendered and no one reported having any kind of disability.

The module was entitled *Cultural Diversity, Schooling, and Teaching* and was structured around the following core questions:

- Why do so many children, especially those from minority and poor families, fail in school? What makes them fail?

■ What constitutes culture? Can one person have culture? What is the relationship between the individual and culture, society and culture?

■ How can we learn about children's backgrounds, interests, and strengths through guidance in the classroom?

■ What are our own philosophies and approaches to teaching and how will these guide our teaching practices?

■ How can we as teachers become agents of positive change?

(excerpted from syllabus, 2004)

The first question reflects clearly the MCSR paradigm's conviction that inequalities must be recognised in terms of patterns of race, ethnicity, gender, sexuality and gender characteristics that are socially constructed as meaningful. Statistics reveal disturbing patterns of school experiences across majority/minority lines. African-American boys are more likely to be diagnosed with behaviour or learning disorders (Jordan, 2005), gay teenagers are more likely to be depressed and commit suicide (Russell, 2005) and Latino pupils are more likely to drop out of school (Fry, 2003). If we fail to consider these patterns as systemic phenomena, we run the risk of applying a deficit approach to minority children. Based on the assumption that children receive fair and equal treatment in schools regardless of their backgrounds, this deficit approach assumes that certain children 'require some form of 'special' instruction since they obviously have not been able to succeed under 'regular' or 'normal' instructional conditions' (Bartolome, 1994, p174).

The following section analyses some of the particularistic discourse produced by teacher trainees to explain the systematic failure of minority pupils in US schools and then illustrates the difficulties encountered by one student who tried to challenge this normative discourse.

Personalising inequality

A discourse of individualism is deeply ingrained in American culture with its tendency to ignore the effects of society and history (Télliz and O'Malley, 1998). This 'dehistorization and fragmentation' (Bell *et al*, 1999, p27) of socially and historically positioned differences is not so easily addressed through dialogue among those whose stories confirm each other's experiences and reinforce this particularistic and ahistorical interpretive framework.

Therefore, while the module's planned curriculum focused on identifying systemic inequalities that affect children's experiences in school, students generally saw discrimination as a personal rather than a systemic phenomenon (Bell *et al*, 1999). They tended to see disadvantage and racism in relation to individuals and as caused by a particular individual who is incompetent and/or uncaring. Instead of recognising and interrogating systemic inequities they tended to view failure and success on a strictly interpersonal level.

For example, students were asked to reflect in their reading response journals on two interview-based portraits of young men who failed in traditional school and later achieved some success in alternative school settings. These portraits can be found in their entirety in Nieto (2000). Ron is African-American and Paul is Latino. In their interviews both men speak of gang membership and prison and they also talk of their past and present schooling experience. In their reading responses students usually sought to find someone to blame for their past problems or to praise for their more recent successes. In either case the critical gaze focuses on an individual, while systemic, structural and historical factors tend to be ignored.

Sometimes students gave credit for Ron's and Paul's recent school success to teachers at the alternative schools, at the same time placing the blame for the men's earlier failure on former bad teachers:

> While there are a lot of caring teachers out there, it is in some cases very true that teachers do not care about the full well-being of their students, they only care about getting them through the year. In Ron's case, and the situations of many other students like Ron, I think it is so important for their educators to show interest in their students. (response journal)[3]

Students also tended to consider the men's parents to be sources of failure or success. For example, one student attributed both men's eventual success to their strong mothers:

> These guys live in a life threatening environment, but because they both have strong helpful mothers and have been lucky to get into progressive schools, there is hope for their success. (response journal)

Another student considered blaming both men's earlier failure on absent fathers:

> A common aspect of the Ron and Paul articles that I just have to mention is the family life. Both Ron and Paul had no strong father figures in their lives, which might have been the reason for the gang. (response journal)

Ron and Paul had similar family situations; they each described a caring and concerned mother and an absent father. The first student chose to focus on praising the 'strong helpful mothers' for their sons' success, while the second chose to emphasise the fathers' responsibility for their sons' failure. The fact that either success or failure can be attributed to the same parental situation exposes a weakness in the individual blame/praise discourse.

Students also tended to attribute responsibility to the individual who, through personal effort and refusing to complain, rises to success:

> Paul is thankful for what he does have, and isn't negative about life even though he is very poor. He feels it is up to him to get a good education and he shouldn't blame it on where he lives. (response journal)

This commitment to the idea that individual hard work and motivation are the key to success is not at all uncommon among trainee teachers (Smith, 1998) and can lead to conceptualising an immorality of difference that conflates good fortune with morality, since less fortunate people are simply those 'who did not know the 'right values' on which to focus' (Cannella, 1998, p99).

Sometimes students reflected on their own relative privilege but without casting it as a systemic phenomenon: they did not reflect explicitly on the systemic distribution of privilege and disadvantage along racial, ethnic, or class lines. For example:

> The Kozol article reminds me of how truly privileged I have been to grow up in a thriving community. (response journal)

Since the student does not speculate anywhere in her reflection on the reasons for her privilege this comment suggests the interpretation of privilege as the result of superior merit or effort by hard-working or especially clever parents and grandparents which has resulted in a thriving community. This deep-seated cultural narrative has been referred to in American contexts as the Horatio Alger myth, referring to the 'rags to riches' stories of a popular nineteenth century novelist whose characters sum up the American dream by turning hard work and ambition into material success (Pitofsky, 1998).

Other students did speculate as to the source of this good fortune, referring to it as a question of good fortune. One student expressed gratitude for her good luck as she compared her own privileged situation with those of Ron and Paul:

> When you compare my school to the schools that either Leon or Paul attended, I was soooo lucky to have gone to O*** High School ... There was

never any concern with gangs in my high school, and my school was not racially segregated. It did not matter what colour you were, everyone was friends with everyone- white, black, Hispanic etc, and I am so grateful for that as well. (response journal)

All these students' comments have been excerpted from responses from the same group of students to the same readings. There were certainly enough different views to begin a discussion. This group of students brought several viewpoints to the discussion table in their initial analysis of racial inequality in the US: individual effort, personal fortune, good (or bad) teachers, presence (or lack) of parental support. What is missing is any mention of the systematic distribution of resources and power along race, class, gender, or racial lines. This could have been applied to these analyses of the school experiences of minority men raised in single-parent households in impoverished urban neighbourhoods.

Breaking the silence: 'Don't get me started on discrimination'

Those of us who interpret teaching and learning in institutional settings as a process of power imposition and negotiation (Giroux, 1981; McLaren, 1989) cannot ignore these processes at the university level. Not only are power dynamics between the instructor and students constructed through institutional policies such as degree requirements and assessment but power dynamics among peers reflect socially-constructed power differentials: 'A classroom contains a culture of power to the extent that social relations in the classroom reproduce social relations in the wider society' (Anderson *et al*, 1998, p276). In a university classroom which is dominated by majority students who interpret privilege as a personal matter unrelated to social factors, an alternative view is risky. This section will examine an incident in which one student's personal experiences moved her to express anger and frustration at what she interpreted as majority (white male) privilege.

Ellen[4], a young woman of Asian parentage who was adopted as an infant by an American couple, told the class that our readings and discussions had inspired her to examine her own complex ethnic identity critically and in ways she had not done before. She had also recently experienced some personal conflicts around gender relations that had given her reason to examine gender issues critically. For Ellen the issues of ethnicity and gender that we discussed in our public classroom space had moved from the realm of the academic to the realm of the personal.

During one class meeting the subtleties of gender discrimination expressed in a network news special broadcast (1994) were discussed. Hidden cameras recorded the unequal treatment received by a man and a woman as they conducted various daily transactions including interviewing for jobs and buying a car. The students engaged in a rather heated discussion focusing on Ellen's claims that society was not only discriminatory towards women but also to ethnic and racial minorities. The counter-argument was spearheaded by Connor, a white male, who insisted that American society was now favouring women and ethnic minorities in a misguided attempt to redress inequities that no longer existed. My perception was that during the class discussion Connor was more upset and aggressive than Ellen, even though she started this argument by expressing her generalised anger at what she perceived as the social injustice revealed by the news programme. I was concerned that he kept interrupting her, which was surprising because he was usually such a respectful participant. After the class discussion students continued their debate on the internet discussion board. Ellen wrote:

> I don't agree with a lot of what Connor says. Hence why he got irritated on what I said. I understand that he thinks it's not a big deal, but have you thought about what he is? He's a white, Caucasian male. DUH he's not going to see a big deal with it. He hasn't experienced discrimination before ever because he doesn't have to worry about it!!! GRRRRR ... Because this society is a white male, society. please ... don't get me started. (Webtalk posting)

Several other students joined in, continuing the analysis of the news program and reflecting on what happened during the class discussion. Two women supported Ellen's argument. The first focused on her class participation and expressed concerns about Conner's anger:

> I totally followed what Ellen was saying and think that she made some very good points however I think it was very rude of Connor to interrupt her and put her down the way he did. I hope next time we have a class discussion maybe we could be a little more respectful towards each other. (Webtalk posting)

The second woman focused on the content of Ellen's argument, supporting her claim that white men, as majority group members, have difficulty in seeing discrimination:

> Gender differences, and more specifically how men and women view different things, will always be heated and offend people in one way or another. I think that Ellen made a good point about this. She used race as an issue and stated that people that aren't discriminated against don't fully understand what others are going through. Given that point, it is harder for guys to understand what a woman sees in situations like that. (Webtalk posting)

Aside from these two comments, there were eight others from women who took a more critical stance toward Ellen's views and her manner of expressing them. A few criticised Ellen for initiating a 'heated discussion' that 'got a little out of hand' and that she 'took it a little too far'. Some argued that the discrimination illustrated in the video was misleading because it was too dated (the broadcast had aired nine years earlier). One woman posted a link to an article entitled *Woman's work? Almost anything.* The article notes that Harvard University for the first time in history had admitted a Freshman class with more woman than men, citing this as evidence that women are achieving 'educational and professional parity with men' (Sahadi, 2004).

Defining discrimination as an individual attack, one woman referred to a scene in the documentary where a car dealer offered the same car to a woman at a higher price than to a man. She pointed out that it was unfair to consider a car dealer taking advantage of a woman to be an instance of discrimination because that was his job:

> A car dealership is not necessarily the best setting to conduct this experiment. It is a car salesman's job to get the most money out of people and it is his job to use a person's weaknesses against them in order to do so (as sad as that sounds, its true!). (Webtalk posting)

This comment shifts the focus from the systematic focus of the broadcast to the individual focus generally advocated by students. The broadcast, as exemplified by the car dealership segment, suggests that discrimination is enacted as everyday actions based on socially-constructed common assumptions such as the assumption that women are less likely to be good at bargaining over car prices than men. The student's comment re-situates discrimination within particular aggressions based on personal beliefs. According to this individualistic philosophy unequal treatment based on gender is not discrimination if it is based on business practices and not personal belief. That business practices can be discriminatory is an impossible conclusion as long as we limit ourselves to the individual as a unit of analysis. This student's use of 'a person's weakness' to refer to her gender highlights that systematic discrimination is at play here: since the woman was personally unknown to the salesman he drew upon a culturally-available social positioning of women as weak, inept and vulnerable car buyers to decide how to treat her. An individualistic discourse automatically exempts this kind of practice since it is, as the expression goes, nothing personal.

Before this class discussion about gender discrimination I had perceived Connor as an easy-going person who was friendly and funny and quite popular. I was surprised by his unaccustomed anger that day and even more surprised to find that he did not interpret his behaviour as angry. Instead, in response to the first woman's criticism that he had 'interrupted' Ellen and put her down,' he posted a message on the class discussion board claiming that he had been strategically trying to lighten the mood:

> well M*** I was actually trying to just lighten the situation a bit since it WAS getting so heated. I apologise if I offended you or anyone else but what she was saying offended me a bit as well. (Webtalk posting)

The impassioned message posted by another white male student really surprised me, given that Bill had never shared any strong feelings or opinions in the class until this point. While Conner had shared in discussions cheerfully and openly throughout the semester, Bill was quiet and rarely participated in oral or web-based discussions. The title of Bill's unexpected message was 'EMPOWER YOURSELF and break the SELF-FULFILLING PROPHESY' (capital letters in original):

> If you think white males don't get discriminated against you are completely wrong. And don't start talking about this 'white male society' and using it as an excuse to emphasise discrimination of other groups of people. Ever hear of the self-fulfilling prophecy?, probably not. I'll explain, it's when everyone believes in something so much that isn't really true, that it actually becomes true. Maybe if minorities, especially women SAW themselves as equals, discrimination would occur less often. But you expressing the idea of a white male society is just showing me that you personally don't feel strong and empowered as a female. You saying that is actually putting women down below men. (Webtalk posting)

Bill's message echoed the belief that an individual is fully responsible for his or her own success, as was expressed in the response journal reflections. Ellen is implicated in actively perpetuating not only her own discrimination but that of all women and minorities since by complaining she contributes to the 'self-fulfilling prophecy' of discrimination. Later in the same long posting he expressed his belief that white males were a minority and were marginalised in this module, praised Connor for speaking out and promised to contribute more to class discussion now that he recognised his responsibility to express the minoritised white male view:

> I generally choose not to talk as much in our class because I know many of my opinions will be put down or criticized because I am a guy, but I realise

now that me not speaking is hypocritical and goes against everything I've said in this posting. So even though there's not much time left this semester, you can plan on hearing a lot more controversial opinions from myself. (Web-talk posting)

Despite his promise and Ellen's and Connor's apparent willingness to spar, this discussion was never revived either in class or on the Webtalk. It simply died away. I wondered how to provide space for the voices of the angry white males and the rather sheepish angry minority woman as well as the rest of the students who seemed uncomfortable about participating in a heated discussion. However, worried that Ellen might develop into something of a pariah, I decided not to broach the issues raised by the angry men unless she did. She didn't. Neither did I.

Toward a pedagogy of incivility

Mayo explains this silencing phenomenon as the discourse of civility (Mayo, 2002). While civility is typically considered to be a positive force (Plank *et al*, 2001), maintaining the fabric of society in the face of the potentially disruptive effects of controversial differences, Mayo acknowledges the potential for civility to become hegemonic practice:

> The discourse of civility asserts that teachers, students, and administrators ought to be kind, respectful, and tolerant of everyone without having to specify to whom they are being kind, respectful, and tolerant. This practice serves to neglect issues that appear to be in and of themselves uncivil or dis-tasteful. If civility requires leaving unspoken things that would disturb placid social interactions, the practice of civility will necessarily leave out those whose presence disrupts the bias that presumes their absence (Mayo, 2002, p174).

Civility in this sense poses a serious threat to classroom dialogue since it assures that certain voices are not invited into the dialogue even when present in the classroom. When minority students voice their resistance to majority assumptions they may end up apologising for bringing into the public sphere issues that are expected to remain unsaid (Sujo de Montes *et al*, 2002). Teachers may feel apologetic for bringing up topics that majority students aggressively refuse to discuss (Smith, 1998). Given the instructor-student power dynamic, teachers may also hesitate to support students like Ellen who voice uncomfortable and unpopular opinions because teacher support can result in further marginalisation of isolated students (Ahlquist, 1991). In this sense, a university module on multiculturalism can have the detrimental effect of further marginalising people who should be empowered.

While I'm not advocating that dialogue be abandoned as a pedagogical practice, the discursive processes which are analysed are meant to provide a note of caution and healthy scepticism toward what Burbules has referred to as the fetishisation of dialogue:

> One could call this 'the hegemony of reasonableness': that precisely because dialogue seems to hold out the hand of inclusiveness and respect for all points of view, it makes those suspicious of its tacit rules of engagement ... its scope of what is and is not up for discussion, appear as if they are at fault for remaining outside the conversation (Burbules, 2000).

Dialogue will not automatically be a democratic, empowering and enriching process. Elsewhere I have made suggestions for fostering dialogue in multicultural teacher training both among students (Hayes, 2004) and with community members (DePalma *et al*, 2006) but in this chapter I deliberately engage my own earlier arguments to emphasise the existence of genuine and persistent challenges and to refute the illusion of easy solutions. This is not to deconstruct the notion of dialogue to the point where we become immobilised by uncertainty and cynicism, but rather to where healthy scepticism and constant negotiation prevent us from becoming too comfortable with ourselves.

This particular case analysis illustrates a more general tension I always felt in pursuing what I hoped would be a dialogic approach to teaching about multiculturalism. Ellen represents an uncomfortable presence in the class. As the present and vocal Other, she speaks the unpleasant (Chávez and O'Donnell, 1998) and invites the kind of dialogue that can be quite uncivil: it mentions things that we are trying to forget. It asks questions that we'd rather not ask (is there something to minority and majority besides numbers?) and it makes us angry and uncomfortable. Eventually Ellen stopped speaking the unpleasant and I colluded in this self-censorship in an attempt to protect her and to protect myself as well. The white men also censored themselves: Connor recast his own angry response as an attempt to lighten the mood and Bill never followed up his promise to continue to speak out for white male teacher trainees. In a collective attempt to avoid the uncomfortable, we all succumbed to the forces of civility and stuck to safer, less unpleasant dialogue. We continued to discuss social issues as described in the class syllabus but without the kind of passionate, personally-invested and therefore riskier exchanges initiated by Ellen.

Wilma Mankiller (Mankiller and Wallis, 1993), first female chief of the Cherokee nation, once said that she was especially proud of her middle name, Pearl, because a pearl is a beautiful and valuable thing that is only made possible by an irritation to the oyster. Mankiller sees discomfort as a powerful and necessary prerequisite for activism and social justice and I see it as a fundamental aspect of liberatory dialogue. The question that I pose, and that I will continue to struggle with as a researcher and instructor, is how to foster a discomfort that leads to dialogue, an incivility that expands the civil, an irritation that ultimately leads to something beautiful?

Notes

1 In the US, teaching certificates are conceded by individual states, which set their own requirements for both coursework and testing. NCATE-approved teacher education programs have reciprocity agreements with various states so that candidates have greater flexibility upon graduation. See http://www.ncate.org/ for more information about the relationship between teacher certification and NCATE requirements.

2 This close association of 'multicultural' and 'diversity' in US terminology is exemplified by the AACTE Commission on Multicultural Education's 'Best Practice Award in Support of Diversity' as found on their website (http://www.aacte.org/programs/multicultural/multi cultural_comm.htm).

3 Students were encouraged not to worry too much about spelling and grammar for their reading reflections and web discussion postings. Therefore, I have made some minor spelling and grammar corrections to make the reading easier.

4 Student names are pseudonyms.

References

Ahlquist, R (1991) Position and imposition: power relations in a multicultural foundations class. *The Journal of Negro Education* 60, 158-169

American Association Of Colleges For Teacher Education (1972) 'No one model American': A statement on multicultural education

Anderson, G L, Bentley, M, Gallegos, B, Herr, K and Saavedra, E (1998) Teaching within/ against the backlash: a group dialogue about power and pedagogy in the 1990s. In Chavez, R C and O´Donnell, J (eds) *Speaking the unpleasant: The politics of (non) engagement in the multicultural education terrain.* Albany NY: State University of New York Press

Bartolome, L I (1994) Beyond the methods fetish: toward a humanizing pedagogy. *Harvard Education Review* 64, 173-194

Bell, S, Morrow, M and Tastsoglou, E (1999) Teaching in environments of resistance. In Mayberry, M and Rose, E C (Eds) *Meeting the challenge: innovative feminist pedagogies in action.* New York Routledge

Burbules, N C (2000) The limits of dialogue as a critical pedagogy. In Trifonas, P P (ed) *Revolutionary pedagogies: cultural politics, instituting education, and the discourse of theory.* New York: Routledge

Cannella, G S (1998) Fosering engagement: barriers in teacher education. In Chavez, R C and O´Donnell, J (eds) *Speaking the unpleasant: The politics of (non) engagement in the multicultural education terrain.* Albany NY: State University of New York Press

Chavez, R C and O'Donnell, J (eds) (1998) *Speaking the unpleasant: the politics of (non)engagement in the multicultural education terrain.* Albany NY: State University of New York Press

DePalma, R, Santos Rego, M and Lorenzo Moledo, M (2006) Not just any direct experience will do: recasting the multicultural teaching practicum as active, collaborative, and trans-formative. *Intercultural Education* 17, 327-339

Fry, R (2003) *Hispanic youth dropping out of US schools: measuring the challenge.* Washington, DC: Pew Hispanic Center

Giroux, H A (1981) *Ideology, culture, and the process of schooling.* Philadelphia Pa: Temple University Press

Hayes, R (2004) *Toward a practice of polyphonic dialogue: avoiding relativism and dog-matism in multicultural teacher education.* American Educational Research Association San Diego USA

Jordan, K (2005) Constructions of difference and Black overrepresentation in Special Education. *Twelfth International Conference on Learning.* Granada, Spain

Latham, A S (1999) The teacher-student mismatch: what the research says about diversity. *Educational Leadership* 56, 84-85

Mankiller, W P and Wallis, M (1993) *Mankiller: a chief and her people.* New York: St. Martin's Press

Martin, R J and Van Gunten, D M (2002) Reflected identities: applying positionality and multicultural social reconstructionism in teacher education. *Journal of Teacher Education* 53, 45-54

Mayo, C (2002) The binds that tie: civility and social difference. *Educational Theory* 52, 169-186

McLaren, P (1989) *Life in schools: introduction to critical pedagogy in the foundations of education.* New York: Longman

National Council For Accreditation Of Teacher Education (2002) Professional Standards for the Accreditation of Schools, Colleges, and Departments of Education University of Virginia

Nieto, S (2000) *Affirming diversity: the sociopolitical context of multicultural education* New York: Longman

Pitofsky, A (1998) Dreiser's 'The Financier' and the Horatio Alger myth. *Twentieth Century Literature* 44, 276-277

Plank, S B, McDill, E L, McPartland, J M and Jordan, W J (2001) Situation and repertoire: civility, incivility, cursing, and politeness in an urban high school. *Teachers College Record* 103, 504-524

Russell, S T (2005) Beyond risk: resilience in the lives of sexual minority youth. *Journal of Gay and Lesbian Issues in Education* 2, 5-18

Sahadi, J (2004) Woman's work? Almost anything. CNN

Sleeter, C E and Grant, C A (2003) *Making choices for multicultural education: five ap-proaches to race, class, and gender.* New York: J Wiley and Sons

Smith, R (1998) Challenging privilege: white male middle class opposition in the multi-cultural education terrain. In Chavez, R C and O'Donnell, J (eds) *Speaking the unpleasant: The politics of (non) engagement in the multicultural education terrain.* Albany NY: State University of New York Press

Sujo De Montes, L E, Oran, S M and Willis, E M (2002) Power, language, and identity: Voices from an online course. *Computers and Composition* 19, 251-271

Télliz, K and O'Malley, S (1998) Exploring the use of history in multicultural/multilingual teacher education. In Chavez, R C and O'Donnell, J (eds) *Speaking the unpleasant: The politics of (non) engagement in the multicultural education terrain.* Albany NY: State Univer-sity of New York Press

The Fairer Sex? (1994) *ABC News.* Prime Time Live ed New York

10

Power on the page: examining embedded power relations in English textbooks for Iranian students

Ahmad Nazari

Introduction

One of the factors affecting the participation of students in class activities and thereby influencing institutional relationships (ie power relations between the students and educators) in the classroom is the use of artefacts such as textbooks (Lave and Wenger, 1991). These relationships are one of the reasons students engage in or withdraw from academic efforts because according to Cummins institutional relationships are 'at the heart of schooling' (2000, p40). Since the textbooks in Iranian high schools are the main artefact used in English as a Foreign Language (EFL) literacy practices in the classroom and since one of my aims is to explore how these artefacts may affect those literacy practices, this chapter attempts to probe the relationships between EFL textbooks and EFL practices in the classroom. As the concept of power also relates to issues of gender and class, my second aim is to unpack gender-constructed roles and social class representations in Iranian high school EFL textbooks (Talbot *et al*, 2003, p4). The result of this analysis suggests that Iranian high school EFL textbooks are ideologically invested, which contributes to the construction of certain identities for students, teachers and textbook writers. It also demonstrates that a particular sexist ideology is inscribed in the passages of the textbooks which are also invested mainly with representations of the middle social class.

To analyse these textbooks, Fairclough's three dimensional model of Critical Discourse Analysis (description, interpretation and explanation, D-I-E) is used because this model enables the analyst to deal with the ideologies invested in texts and the consequent power relations and identity construction (Fairclough, 1995).

Fairclough's D-I-E

Applying Fairclough's three dimensional discourse analysis approach, the analyst first describes the text linguistically. Linguistic description involves depicting the linguistic properties of the text and dealing with the choices that have been made in the presentation of the text. At the interpretation phase, the analyst interprets the relationship between the text and the features of discourse practice such as text production, distribution and consumption. Finally, the analyst explains the relationship between the properties of the text and pedagogical and socio-cultural practices. In this way the critical discourse analyst

> sets out to make visible through analysis, and to criticise connections between properties of texts and social processes and relations (ideologies, power relations) which are generally not obvious to people who produce and interpret those texts. (Fairclough, 1995, p97)

The analyst makes an attempt to 'denaturalise' the ideologies which are 'naturalised' through texts (Fairclough, 1995, p27; Talbot *et al*, 2003, pp5-6). Temple (2005) and Wiltshire (2006), discussing the critical literacy movement in Australia, imply that the critical analyst endeavours to unmask the true purposes of the text within a particular context to raise the awareness of the text users so that they understand the true meaning of the text. The critical discourse analyst seeks to empower text users to emancipate themselves from its effects: she or he 'intervenes in social practice and attempts to reveal connections between language use, power, and ideology' (Cots, 2006, p336).

In the analysis which follows, the properties of Iranian high school EFL textbooks as well as embedded EFL pedagogies and socio-cultural ideologies are investigated in an attempt to explain how these teaching artefacts act as a means of student pedagogisation. Pedagogisation means how students are placed in the pedagogic discourse in terms of the roles and the social relations assigned to them. Ideologisation means how and what meanings, values, ideas and power relations are constituted, frame classroom practices and are transmitted to students (Dendrinos, 1992).

Textbook description

As far as language learning theories incorporated in Iranian high school EFL textbooks are concerned, a browse through the textbooks shows that the theory of habit formation through pattern practice and over-learning embedded in audio-lingual exercises dominates the activities included in the textbook. Most of the exercises involve repetitions, substitutions, transformations, matchings and fill-in-the-blanks. These exercises as activities assigned to the learner are of the closed-ended type: they constrain the learner in his/her learning activities and restrict his/her ability to manoeuvre and enter the process of negotiation and meaning production. Similarly, the overall form and organisation of the books is rigid, fixed and invariable through the lessons (Fairclough, 1995, p185). The different sections of all the lessons follow the same format. All the lessons start with some new vocabulary, then there is a reading text followed by comprehension questions and afterwards there are speaking and writing drills. These drills are followed by dia-logues as language functions, pronunciation practice and vocabulary review. This absence of variability and flexibility is also seen in the type of language used in the content of the sections on language functions, reading texts and exercises. The language functions are presented in the form of dialogues and like the passages of the reading texts and the con-tent of the exercises are in standard formal language. Here is an example from page 43, *Textbook I*:

A: Do you come from a large family?

B: Yes, I do.

A: How many are there in your family?

B: Seven.

A: What does your father do?

B: He's a doctor.

A: What about your mother?

B: She's a teacher

These dialogues are devoid of the natural fluctuations of normal con-versations such as interruptions, hesitations, false starts, fillers, ironies, metaphors and other types of figurative language. They are also out of context because neither the settings nor the communicants are recog-nised through the dialogues. The linguistic description of the form and content of the textbooks indicates that the audio-lingual method with some shades of the communicative approach has been chosen in the process of producing the textbooks. This pedagogical choice is ideo-logical in that it may bring about certain social relations in the EFL classrooms. This point will be discussed further in the section dealing with the explanation phase of Critical Discourse Analysis, which centres on social practices and power relations in the classroom.

Textbook interpretation

The second phase of Critical Discourse Analysis deals with the interpretation of the relationship between the text and the features of discourse practice. The first step towards the interpretation phase is intertextual analysis which means paying attention to the choice of the narratives in the textbook, which will show that certain ideologies are invested in the textbook. The narratives of most of the reading texts in the textbooks are of the 'closed' type in that all the information is present in the narratives and little chance is given for the student readers to make different interpretations (Luke, 1988, p87). The reading text in Lesson Three in *Textbook I* (A Story About Newton) is an example of a closed text where the interpretation is given at the outset of the text: even great and wise men sometimes forget small things. Another example is in the reading passage in Lesson Six in *Textbook I*, The Boy Who Made Steam Work. This is also closed in terms of the number of interpretations the reader can make: that curiosity is the mother of discoveries and inventions and the eyes, ears and minds of discoverers and inventors are more open than those of average people. Likewise, the reading text in Lesson Eight in *Textbook I*, Eat, Clothes, Eat!, is a closed text because the main interpretation which could be made of it is that people should not be judged by their appearance nor humiliated because of their poor clothes.

Thus the informational content of these narratives is inflexible and they do not involve the student reader in the process of text production, negotiation, interpretation and meaning making. These narratives are end products which do not invite the reader to interact. Closed ended activities constrain students' output and linguistic creativity whereas open ended activities inspire students' linguistic creativity and output (Swain and Lapkin, 2001). Even at lower intermediate levels such as high school EFL classes students need to present their viewpoints and participate in and contribute to literacy practices to improve their language ability.

Content analysis of these narratives indicates that a certain social order is fabricated through the choice of contents. The societies presented in the narratives seem invariable and flat in that they are devoid of conflicts, tensions, diversities, different ethnic groups, different social classes and cultural differences. This absence of social diversity creates and naturalises a false social reality in which everything is even, nothing goes wrong and all events result in happy endings. A certain social ideology is incorporated into the narratives of the textbooks. This issue will be illustrated in the section below headed: Textbooks, gender relations and social class.

The choice of narrative may be ideological in terms of privileging certain social relations in EFL classrooms. As Luke (1988) and Dendrinos (1992) point out, closed texts are ideological in what they do not only to the reading activity but to the role of the reader. The task of the critical discourse analyst is to explore and construct the possible ideological effects by 'reconstructing the role of the reader implicitly prescribed by text structure' (Luke, 1988, p39). This will be discussed further in the section focusing on social practices and power relations in EFL classrooms.

At a macro-level of analysis the discourse practices of textbook production, distribution and consumption could be described as follows: the Ministry of Education asks its expert consultants to write the EFL high school textbooks with certain objectives in mind. These are written, reviewed, revised, edited and illustrated by the textbook writers and their associates. The final version is submitted to the Publication Organisation of Iranian School Textbooks, one of the associated organisations of the Ministry of Education which is responsible for the publication and distribution of the school textbooks. The textbooks are printed and published by this organisation and distributed among bookshops or schools nationwide to be sold to students.

This system of producing and distributing textbooks contributes to the centralisation and nationalisation of the school curriculum and causes a kind of hegemony exercised by the Ministry of Education in that alliances are brought about among the schools as far as textbook selection and consumption are concerned. All schools have to select and consume the same textbooks produced and distributed by the Ministry of Education.

This process will now be described at a micro-level of analysis. To explore how the EFL textbooks were used in Iranian high schools, forty EFL classes taught by ten teachers in three high schools over two months were observed. Open-ended observations were carried out on the use of the textbooks and student-teacher relationships. During the observations, notes were taken in shorthand to record verbatim whatever was seen and heard in the classrooms. The class observations demonstrate that the textbooks are used in the classrooms as a major source of instruction rather than a resource. Education and communication are lateralised and the students are passive institutional consumers who take a submissive role and follow the instructions of the tutor, which are mainly derived from the content of the textbooks. Since instructional artefacts can provide access to activities and opportunities for participation, the pedagogical ideologies invested in the EFL textbooks have created hegemonic relations in the Iranian educational institutes in that the students find little space to take part in the ongoing practices (Lave and Wenger, 1991). Consequently, the link between EFL textbook consumption and hegemonic relations is examined in the following section, centring on the explanation of social relations and institutional practices.

Textbook explanation

The theory of audio-lingualism with some aspects of the communicative approach is dominant in the textbooks so that the activities assigned to the student are the closed-ended sort typical of the audio-lingual method such as repetitions, substitutions, transformations, fill-in-the-blanks and closed-ended comprehension questions. Most of the narratives of the textbooks are of the closed type as well. We have seen that the overall texture of the textbooks is firm and inflexible because all the lessons have the same layout and proceed in the same way through similar sections. According to Dendrinos, 'the views of language and language learning on which the textbook is based ... reveal ideological meanings and imply different positioning of students as institutionalised subjects' (1992, p149).

In fact the inclusion of closed-ended activities, closed narratives and inflexible texture is ideologically invested: they do not leave space for the students to manoeuvre and show creative participation. Since almost everything is already fixed the students are not invited to make different interpretations, to contribute to the process of text making, to generate new meanings or to present their viewpoints. They find little chance to negotiate with their tutor and classmates or to interact with the tutor and the textbooks. In the textbooks each lesson and each section have pre-specified objectives so that the tutor and students act as the servants of the textbook to achieve its predetermined objectives. Through all of these features of the textbook particular roles and relations are assigned to those involved in the educational discourse, the author as the textbook producer and the tutor and student as the textbook consumers.

Due to the closed readings and activities as well as the predetermined objectives, the student does not have much opportunity to participate in the process of text making, negotiation and interpretation. His/her role is downgraded to an absorber of knowledge and information rather than a negotiator and interpreter. Accordingly, the teacher, as mediator between the textbook and the student, is positioned as a transmitter of knowledge and information and the textbook writer assumes the role of a knower. The pedagogical ideology invested in the textbooks constructs and naturalises asymmetrical power relations, 'coercive relations of power' in Cummins' sense between the educators and the student, rather than coordinate, balanced, harmonious and cooperative relations (Cummins, 2000, p44). The teacher is positioned as a superordinate and the student as subordinate. This hegemonic relation insinuated into the texts is indeed what was observed in the EFL classes: leader-follower or initiator-respondent relations between the tutor and student. Hall (2000) argues that such non-critical literacy has led to learning becoming a passive process of receiving pre-constructed messages and teaching becoming a technical process of implementing the experts' views.

Due to the implicit pedagogical ideology incorporated in the textbooks, an educational hegemony is exercised in that the textbook producers to some extent control the EFL literacy practices taking place in the classroom. 'Hegemony implies a hidden or covert operation of power. It refers to control ... [which] is achieved when arrangements that suit a dominant group's own interests have come to be perceived as simply 'common sense' (Talbot *et al*, 2003, p2). This can happen through the educational theories and pedagogical approaches applied to producing the textbook: what goes on in the classroom, 'the initiation, response and evaluation tradition' observed in the EFL classes is affected by the roles and activities the textbooks assign to the tutor and student through the FL pedagogical ideology (audio-lingualism) insinuated into the exercises and text materials. The textbooks foster classes that are 'teacher-led' in that the teacher controls both the development of the lesson and the process of turn taking to talk (Cazden, 1988). There is an example of this tradition in the observation notes:

> The teacher read out loud the instructions at the top of the next drill on page 25 of the book, 'Listen to your teacher and repeat these sentences after him.' Then, in Farsi (the students' and teacher's first language), he asked the students to listen to him carefully and repeat after him in chorus. He read aloud the first sentence from the book, 'Do you have a loose tooth?' The students repeated after him altogether. The teacher reinforced their response by say-

ing 'that's right' in Farsi. After finishing this drill, the teacher, in Farsi, asked one of the students to pronounce out loud the words containing the /u:/ sound in the next exercise of the book. The student read 'prove, room'. The teacher confirmed the student's answer by nodding his head. Then he, in Farsi, asked another student to pronounce aloud the words containing the /ju:/ sound in that exercise. The student read 'beauty, excuse me'. The teacher, in Farsi, commented 'yes, that's right'.

This hegemony is also due to the reconstructionist ideology invested in the exercises and text materials. Reconstructionism is one of the theories of education which purports that its major function is to bring about changes such as social and behavioural change. In so doing the objectives should be specified and the activities should aim at the attainment of the objectives (Dendrinos, 1992). The EFL course and textbooks in Iranian high schools are objectives-based. Pre-specified objectives are believed to confine students' interaction with educators (Cummins, 2000). In contrast, transformative education which is based on 'a commitment to educate students for full participation' fosters collaborative relations in the classroom by empowering the students to participate further in educational practices, hearing them as subjects with voices and extending their interactions with educators (Cummins, 2000, p.46). Transformative education has received several different names, including 'critical pedagogy', 'pedagogies of resistance' and 'emancipatory literacy' (Santana-Williamson, 2000).

A wealth of research has shown that interaction is essential for acquisition (Swain, 2000; Van Lier, 2000; Gass *et al*, 1998; Swain and Lapkin, 1998; Van Lier, 1996; Seliger, 1983). Further participation by the students in the activities, dialogues and discussions held in the classroom will bring about further interaction which according to Swain (2000) and Van Lier (2000) provides learners with the opportunity to use the target language, make hypotheses about it and test them. Swain also states that collaborative dialogues when teachers and students communicate using the target language are problem-solving, knowledge-building and effective in improving second language learners' communicative abilities. Hall goes one step further and argues that to have truly effective literacy, our practices should be critical in that decisions on materials, contents and lessons should be open to exploration, negotiation and discussion by all participants within the lesson (Hall, 2000, p15). There is a mass of research illustrating that cooperation, interaction and negotiation are essential to improve learners' foreign language abilities.

In addition to the above descriptions, interpretations and explanations the gender relations and social class constructed and naturalised in the textbooks are ideologically invested.

Textbooks, gender relations and social class

One of the issues regarding the ideologies invested in textbooks deals with gender-constructed roles and social class representation in the passages of textbooks. These textbooks attempt to naturalise such roles and classes through specific narratives. According to Harris the linguistic features used in language textbooks can 'feed into, reinforce and serve to legitimise ... forms of discrimination' (Harris, 1992, p29). Looking at the content of the narratives in the textbooks may reveal ideological inscriptions. For instance, the cloze text at the outset of *Textbook I* (pp5-6) is telling:

Complete the passage with the words given:

> good   carefully do   go

My name is Bahram. I'm a student. I'm 15 years old. I ...... to school in the morning. I'm a ...... student. I usually ...... my homework in the afternoon. I study my books very ......

> sometimes   doesn't like   has
>
> wakes up   reading his
>
> am watching   fast   him

Today is Friday. It's seven o'clock in the evening. We don't go to school on Fridays. I .... TV now. I like cartoons very much, but my father ...... cartoons. You can see .... in the picture. He .... a newspaper in .... hands. He's .... it. He usually reads the newspaper carefully, but ...... he reads some pages very ...... He usually .... early in the morning. He says his prayers, eats his breakfast at about 6 and then goes to work. He comes back home in the evening.

> was cleaning   arrived   ate   left
>
> didn't have   was   had

My father didn't go to work this morning. He .... his breakfast at about 8. But my mother .... very busy this morning. We .... some guests. My mother .... the kitchen when they .... They ...... before noon. They ...... lunch with us.

> will do   watch   leave   be

Tomorrow morning I'll .... in my high school. I'll ...... there at about 12:30. I'll have lunch with my mother and sister. In the afternoon I ...... my homework. I'll ......TV in the evening.

143

This passage depicts and introduces a four member, middle-class Iranian family. The elements of the passage contribute to the construction and presentation of an ideological view of a specific social reality about the institution of the family, gender and class. The father is portrayed as a man who wakes up *early* in the mornings, *goes to work*, comes back home in the evenings and reads newspapers in his leisure time *carefully* and sometimes *very fast*. The son of the family is a *good* student who *goes to school* in the mornings, does his homework in the afternoons, studies his books *very carefully* and likes watching television. The mother of the family is a woman *busy with cleaning the kitchen and providing food for the family and guests*. The reader is told almost nothing about the daughter of the family except that the son has lunch with his mother and sister. The choice of activities, roles, adjectival and adverbial modifiers attributed to the male and female characters of the family are meaning-making elements that attempt to transmit and naturalise certain social relations in the middle-class families of the society. Such a choice introduces these families as institutions without any problems, the males of the family as more outgoing and careful personalities and the females of the family as less outgoing and tending to deal with housekeeping affairs. In effect, with regard to social class, not only has the middle-class been mainly introduced and referred to at the cost of all other classes, but ethnic varieties common in different parts of the country are also excluded from the text materials (Sajjadi, 2004, p143).

The frequency count of the sexist features of the EFL textbooks might be indicative of a sexist ideology constructed and naturalised through the content of the books. A postgraduate dissertation on sex discrimination in EFL school textbooks written in Iran in 1998 has produced the following results:

- A greater variety of jobs is attributed to males (80 per cent to males and 20 per cent to females)

- More adjectives describe males (78 per cent describe males and 22 per cent describe females)

- More socially positive adjectives are used for males (93 per cent for males and 7 per cent for females)

- The number of males in the 'subject' position of sentences is more than the number of females

- The number of females in the 'object' position of sentences is more than the number of males

■ Nearly 95 per cent of the reading texts of the textbooks are about males (Feizmohammadpoor, 1998).

In effect, through linguistic devices, a sexist ideology is invested in these EFL school textbooks (Ansary and Babaii, 2003) in which 'females have been significantly under-represented, with a ratio of 6:1' (Sajjadi, 2004, p143). Hartman and Judd (1978) and Gilbert and Rowe (1989), analysing a considerable number of EFL/ESL textbooks used around the world, found similar 'gender stereotypes in which women were generally given subordinate status' (Dominguez, 2003, p5). However, there are EFL/ESL textbooks which present a balanced view of genders. *New Interchange Intro*, written by Jack C Richards (2000), is an EFL/ESL textbook used in various parts of the world which is 'a sex-fair ESL/EFL textbook' (Dominguez, 2003, p16).

Conclusion

This chapter is an attempt to unpack how Iranian high school EFL textbooks affect the construction of identities through naturalising certain ideological views of realities. It was argued that the textbooks pedagogised students as recipients of knowledge rather than negotiators and meaning makers. The power relations insinuated into the textbooks also seemed to frame the classroom practices so that students' participation was impoverished. It was also found that certain gender and social class ideologies were constructed and naturalised in the textbooks. More roles and higher positions were attributed to males, and the middle social class was over-represented.

The significance of this chapter is fourfold. It demonstrates how the educational and social ideologies invested in EFL textbooks contribute to the construction of identities of and power relations between those involved in EFL literacy practices. It also practically depicts how Critical Discourse Analysis could be applied to the analysis of EFL textbooks. As Cots (2006) puts it, revealing connections between language, power and ideology is one of the characteristics of Critical Discourse Analysis which is all too often absent from foreign language programmes. This chapter can be considered a modest contribution to fill this gap. In addition, the insights gained into the nature of the EFL textbooks of Iranian high schools could also be useful in analysing other nationally produced EFL textbooks (Pickering, 1999). The results of this critical analysis could be used to improve subsequent editions of the EFL textbooks used in Iranian high schools.

This chapter suggests three avenues for further research. First, given the descriptions, interpretations and explanations presented here, the following hypothesis might emerge. If the EFL textbooks used in Iranian high schools become less authoritative in their form and structure by incorporating open-ended activities and narratives, there may be less unequal relations in educational institutes and a more coordinate and cooperative climate may be established between those involved in EFL literacy practices. Students would be empowered and more likely to enter the process of meaning production, communication and negotiation. They might find further space to negotiate their viewpoints and interact with the tutor and the textbook. Testing this hypothesis is one of the avenues which deserves further research. Second, as there was no access to the process of textbook production and distribution, what is written about these two processes is general. An exploration of these two processes can also be considered for further research for those researchers who have access to textbook producers and publishers (Rowsell, 2001). Last but not least the effect of sex discrimination in EFL school textbooks on the learning of schoolgirls is also a research topic which may lead to interesting and noteworthy results.

References

Ansary, H and Babaii, E (2003) Subliminal sexism in current ESL/EFL textbooks in *Asian English as a Foreign Language Journal* 5(1), 1-11

Bygate, M, Skehan, P and Swain, M (eds) (2001) *Researching Pedagogic Tasks: Second Language Learning, Teaching and Testing.* Harlow, England: Longman

Cazden, C B (1988) *Classroom Discourse.* Portsmouth, NH: Heinemann

Cots, J M (2006) Teaching with an attitude: critical discourse analysis in EFL teaching in *English Language Teaching Journal* 60(4), 336-345

Cummins, J (2000) *Language, Power and Pedagogy: Bilingual Children in the Crossfire.* Clevedon: Multilingual Matters

Dendrinos, B (1992) *The EFL Textbook And Ideology.* Athens: N. C. Grivas Publications

Dominguez, L M (2003) Gender textbook evaluation on www.cels.bham.ac.uk/ resources/ essays, retrieved 2 Oct 2006

Fairclough, N (1995) *Critical Discourse Analysis.* London and New York: Longman

Feizmohammadpoor, A (1998) Sex Discrimination in High and Intermediate School EFL Textbooks. Unpublished MA Dissertation Tehran: Tarbiat Modares University

Gass, S, Mackey, A and Pica, T (1998) The role of input and interaction in second language acquisition in *Modern Language Journal* 82, 299-305

Gilbert, P and Rowe, K (1989) *Gender, Literacy and the Classroom.* Victoria: Australian Reading Association

Hall, G (2000) Local approaches to critical pedagogy: an investigation into the dilemmas raised by critical approaches to ELT on www.ling.lancs.ac.uk/groups/crile/workingpapers, retrieved 2 Oct 2006

Harris, V (1992) *Fair Enough? Equal Opportunities and Modern Languages.* London: CiLT

Hartman, P L and Judd, E L (1978) Sexism and TESOL materials in *TESOL Quarterly* 12(4), 383-393

Lantolf, J P (ed) (2000) *Sociocultural Theory and Second Language Learning.* Oxford: Oxford University Press

Lave, J and Wenger, E (1991) *Situated Learning: Legitimate Peripheral Participation.* Cambridge: Cambridge University Press

Luke, A (1988) *Literacy, Textbooks and Ideology.* London, New York: Falmer Press

Pickering, A (1999) Headwayland: An Interpretation of the Etiquettes and Ideologies of an EFL Course Book Genre Unpublished EdD Thesis King's College London: School of Education

Richards, J C (2000) *New Interchange Intro, English for International Communication.* Cambridge: Cambridge University Press

Rowsell, J (2001) Publishing Practices in Printed Education: British and Canadian Perspectives on Educational Publishing. Unpublished PhD Thesis King's College London: School of Education

Sajjadi, S (2004) The representation of social actors in the EFL high school textbooks in Iran, *37th Annual BAAL Meeting Abstracts.* London: King's College, p143

Santa-Williamson, E (2000) Critical pedagogy in TESOL: a review of the literature on http:// eric.ed.gov/ERICWebPortal/Hom.portal, retrieved 2 Oct 2006

Seliger, H W (1983) Learner interaction in the classroom and its effects on language acquisition. In Seliger, H W and Long, M H (eds), pp246-267

Seliger, H W and Long, M H (eds) (1983) *Classroom Oriented Research in Second Language Acquisition.* Rowley, MA: Newbury House

Swain, M (2000) The output hypothesis and beyond: mediating acquisition through collaborative dialogue. In Lantolf, J P (ed), pp97-115

Swain, M and Lapkin, S (2001) Focus on form through collaborative dialogue: exploring task effects in Bygate, M *et al* (eds), pp99-119

Swain, M and Lapkin, S (1998) Interaction and second language learning: two adolescent French immersion students working together in *Modern Language Journal* 82, 320-337

Talbot, M, Atkinson, K and Atkinson, D (2003) *Language and Power in the Modern World.* Edinburgh: Edinburgh University Press

Temple, C (2005) Critical thinking and critical literacy on www.criticalthinkinginternational. org, retrieved 2 Oct 2006

Van Lier, L (2000) From input to affordance: social-interactive learning from an ecological perspective. In Lantolf, J P (ed), pp245-261

Van Lier, L (1996) *Interaction in the Language Curriculum: Awareness, Autonomy and Authenticity.* London: Longman

Wiltshire, K (2006) In defence of the true values of learning in *The Weekend Australian* on www.theaustralian.news.com.au/story, retrieved 2 Oct 2006

PART THREE
Culture and subculture within and beyond education

11

Respect: representation and difference in Scotland and Nunavut

Takano Takako

Introduction

Sustainable living is now broadly accepted as important and many authors attribute unsustainability and human induced environmental destruction to a perception of people who are separated from the natural environment and disengaged from the land. Some argue that the separation places human as superior and plants and animals as human resources to be controlled and exploited. Others consider that the perceived separation makes people ignorant of the role of their natural surroundings and nature becomes something trivial. Subsequently people are less likely to have an interest in and to care for the environment.

In this context educational researchers increasingly pay attention to people's relationships with the natural environment (Brookes, 2002; Martin, 1999; Nicol and Higgins, 1998; Orr, 1992; Smith and Williams, 1999). Western advocates of education for sustainable living generally present the traditional approaches of indigenous peoples as models (O'Sullivan, 1999; Smith and Williams, 1999). While the terms indigenous and traditional are contested (Agrawal, 1995; Hirtz, 2003; Schmink, Redford and Padoch, 1992) and the diversity among indigenous peoples must be recognised, these terms are used here in contrast to mainstream western culture which has a Judeo-Christian background and a highly industrialised society. There is a growing trend in traditional societies in North America, who are said to be in close relationships with nature already, to restore the connection with the land by establishing the outdoors as a learning environment (Kushman and Barnhardt, 1999; Rediscovery International Foundation, n.d.). Empirical work is lacking about these attempts not only among indigenous peoples but also in the UK.

This study attempts to understand the people's relationships with their natural environment by exploring educational programmes in Scotland and Nunavut, Canada. The discussion highlights that a notion of respect represents the expressed relationships with the landscape in both case studies but that its meanings and implications within the notion were found to be distinctly different.

Research design and methodology

This study is a part of a larger scale investigation of seven cases, all centred around educational programmes selected through networking and based on a theoretical framework under common criteria (Maykut and Morehouse, 1994). As the research purpose was to explore the complexity of issues around people's relationships with their environment, an ethnographical perspective was adopted with a mixed research design. This was based primarily on participant observation, supported by semi-structured interviews and written surveys as well as conversation and secondary sources. Interviews were conducted with programme organisers, participants, their parents and other involved community members. The participants were interviewed either at the end of the programmes or some time after the completion depending on the logistics. All interviews were recorded digitally and transcribed. In both Scotland and Igloolik the analysis of accounts was based on themes which emerged from the transcripts themselves and other field data. With their agreement programme organisers and key informants were identified in the text which contributed to determining their credibility. The author is shown as TT in quotes and disguised initials are used for the participants.

Overview of the study groups
Scotland
Despite the concern among environmental and outdoor education researchers in the UK about the significance of people's relationships with the environment, the group selection procedures indicated that actual

programmes which aim to build such relationships among young participants in the UK are either rare or too small in scale to be noticed. Four separate groups were selected, all in Scotland, all of which emphasised the building of relationships with the environment as underpinning their endeavours. Their forms of operation represented the diversity of environmental educational attempts in the UK.

The four groups were either voluntary local groups or had charitable status and their stated purposes were to raise environmental awareness and personal social development through engagement in mainly conservation work. The programmes were conducted in areas local to some and remote to other participants. The participants' ages were between 12 years and early 20s (the interviewees were between 12 and 18 years old) and they all lived in a built environment rather than rural villages or the countryside. Some participants lived in England and travelled to Scotland to participate in the programmes.

The Scottish study groups were:

> The John Muir Award Gullane Group
> The John Muir Award Tranent Group
> The Green Team
> A Trailblazer Camp of the National Trust for Scotland (NTS)

The Green Team and the NTS headquarters were based in Edinburgh City, and Gullane and Tranent are towns east of Edinburgh. The John Muir Award scheme is an educational initiative of the John Muir Trust, an environmental conservation organisation, and both the Gullane and Tranent groups conducted their activities within the scheme's framework. The Green Team is a non-profit environmental education organisation. The NTS is a conservation organisation that aims to protect and promote Scotland's natural and cultural heritage. A Trailblazer Camp was their new educational initiative primarily aimed at those aged 16 and 17.

The total number of semi-structured interviews was 38 (19 participants, 13 parents, 5 instructors/organisers, and 1 organiser), and most data was collected between April 2001 and October 2002.

The UK has a history of rapid urbanisation induced by economic growth since the 18th century (Devine, 2000). Consequently the country attracted streams of immigrants from overseas and 90 percent of its population lives in urban areas as of 1991 (Denham and White, 1998). In the face of the destruction of the natural environment the UK has one of the oldest environmental conservation movements in the world, dating back to the1870s, due to 'the enthusiasm for the taming of the wilderness into man's preferred artificial landscapes' (Evans, 1992, p18). The history and the size of contemporary environmental organisations' membership are impressive. For example, founded in 1895, the National Trust for Wales, England and Northern Ireland now has over three million members and owns 248,000 hectares of land (National Trust, 2003). Every year hundreds of thousands of volunteers are reported to be involved in conservation tasks through various schemes all over the UK. As discussed later, this signifies one aspect of what their environment represents.

Since the 1990s environmental issues have been explicitly put on political agendas worldwide and environmental issues are now a major part of the media output (Beckerman, 1995). Nonetheless, many authors claim that general environmental awareness in both the British and Scottish context is not substantial (Evans, 1992; McCormick and McDowell, 1999; System Three, 2000) and that environmental education is not a significantly integral part of the school curriculum (Condie, 2003; Palmer, 1998). The results of a recent environmental attitude survey showed that while 77 per cent of respondents agreed that most people in Scotland today need to change their way of life so that future generations can continue to enjoy a good quality of life and environment, just 46 per cent believed that they personally needed to change their way of life (Hinds, Carmichael and Snowling, 2002). This is the context in which the four study groups in Scotland operated their environment and sustainability education programmes for young people.

Nunavut

The study programme in Nunavut was organised by an elders' charity, the Inullariit Society in Igloolik, as part of their land skills course to 'preserve and promote Inuit culture, language, heritage and traditional values' (Inullariit Society file 1993-1998) by teaching young people traditional knowledge and skills.

Nunavut became the latest Canadian self-governing territory in 1999, occupying the Central and Eastern Canadian Arctic. While it is nearly half the size of Europe, excluding Russia, it has fewer than 30,000 residents, of whom more than 80 per cent are estimated to be Inuit (Statistics Canada, 2001) in 28 communities spread across the region. The Igloolik Island is located about 300 kilometres north of the Arctic Circle, just off the Melville Peninsula in Nunavut. The town of Igloolik has a population of about 1300, of whom about 95 per cent are Inuit. Inuit in the area called Iglulingmiut traditionally lived in camps, moving seasonally in well-defined territories to hunt and harvest wildlife. In the late 1950s the settlement started to grow with government housing and health programmes. Canada's mainstream education system was imposed, together with foreign values, on the Inuit. Schools and missionaries facilitated this assimilation process and contributed to the alienation of indigenous cultures among Inuit communities. Drastic changes in their society have influenced every aspect of their lives and the Iglulingmiut still live in a society in transition.

Despite this, Igloolik is still considered a traditional community by general public in Nunavut. Virtually all Inuit in Igloolik spoke the language fluently in 2002, whereas in Nunavut only 70 per cent of residents speak the Inuktitut language as their first language (Office of the Languages Commissioner of Nunavut, 2002). Most Igloolik households (84 per cent) regularly participate in harvesting wildlife (RT and Associates, 2002). Evidence about the involvement of young people in these subsistence activities is mixed and requires further research.

While the Inullariit Society had organised land skill courses throughout the year for more than 10 years, the study programme, Paariaqtuqtut, was exceptional for the group in the sense that it involved the other communities for the first time in tracing the historical travel route between the two communities. The Paariaqtuqtut involved a 400 kilometre snow machine journey on frozen lakes, rivers and tundra and more than 60 people joined, including twelve registered participants as learning students aged between 17 and 31 and six official elder instructors.

The fieldwork was carried out in April and May 2002. Apart from the numerous people who were talked to and informally interviewed, sixteen semi-structured interviews were conducted (five students, one parent, three instructors/elders/organisers, six involved community members, one organiser). Most interviews were done in English and translators were used for two instructors and two community members.

Identified relationships with the environment
Case studies in Scotland
In the Scottish case studies, analysis of interviews and conversations suggested that those who were involved in the study demonstrated a 'visitor's' attitude rather than a 'dweller's' (Tuan, 1974). The environment is where people take a break to have a recreational nature ex-

perience. The data showed that for young people, including those in their early teens, the environment represents recreation:

> BN: I suppose for people who live in a city, there is an adventure of going out into the countryside, where it is ENDLESS, SPACE, really, which you won't get as much in a town ... I suppose in some ways just how much we, as human beings, have disturbed what was there before we arrived. The country is a place where you can go, and not to have human interference as possible, and still there is enjoyment and everything.

> EG: Because I live in a big city, I never appreciated all the nice landscapes and castles. It is weird to hear English people saying 'oh, wao, it's so nice,' taking lots of photos of the hills. Just by talking with them made me appreciate more ... I began to understand more why people would come to Scotland, and why there are so many pictures of Scotland. I think it's really nice.

The participants in the Scottish case study did not manifest any direct life commitment to the environment and outdoor experiences were clearly outside their daily life. They considered the environment as the place to do conservation work and as separate from their daily life.

The organisers' objective was to be to instil pro-environmental behaviour in the young participants, to encourage them to care for the environment. From their own experiences the organisers believed that environmental behaviour is based on the individual's attachment to and love for the environment which can be nurtured by educational programmes. The following comment illustrates many of these elements:

> ... the basic objective is ... to make people more aware of what's going on, and what difference they can make, and how to improve their environment to make a better place ... I think it comes down to make it a better place for other people to enjoy and to make it a more pleasant experience. Then if they enjoy it, they would want to make a difference, would want to make sure it stays in the condition that is in. (L. Shearer, 24 Feb 2002)

By pro-environmental, the organisers meant an attitude to care, help, protect, conserve and preserve the environment which they also suggested was a natural outcomes of respect. When asked what sort of relationships with nature the organisers wanted to enhance among the young people, they said '... respect ... wanting to look after. Wanting to help preserve' (L. Shearer, 24 Feb 2002) and 'For me, with this work, it is about building a respect ... if they engage with the environment in some way ... they are going to learn a bit about it and learn to respect at the same time' (M. Calder, 20 April 2001).

For the organisers the environment was not necessarily specific but more of a general concept. They wished to nurture a positive attitude among young people to any environment on the planet by building affectionate relationships with the landscape. In this light connection with the environment is a means to the end.

The term respect was also often used by the young people I interviewed.

> ID: We shouldn't abuse it. Nature must be respected. I think we should show more respect, we should try to stop polluting the environment.

> BN: They (the wild animals) have a life just as we have, and we should respect that. We really have to take responsibility for that we can't kill too many of them, or destroy their habitat, because they have an essential role to play.

Early urbanisation history led the environmental movement in the UK in world history (Grove, 1995). Part of the UK culture represents an idea that conservation and protection of the environment are 'a good thing to do' and a high level of participation in conservation activities and charities in the UK demonstrates this.

The study indicated that people who were involved in these educational programmes in Scotland drew a clear line between 'the self' and 'the environment'. Based on an environmental ideology, Scottish organisers designed educational programmes to create an attitude to the other – the environment. Therefore the relationships expressed through the programmes can be described as ideological because they are without a concrete and perceived connection between daily life and the environment.

Igloolik case study

The data analysis from Igloolik led me to an understanding which was different from the Scottish case. The participants in the Igloolik case study had an intimate relationship with their environment physically, intellectually, emotionally, historically and spiritually. For these Inuit, being on the land was 'life' itself and they demonstrated a dweller's attitude. The analysis showed that their environment strongly impacted on, and indeed often defined, their identity. In this respect the environment is interpreted as 'the self' which is in line with Basso's (1996) observation that for the Western Apache people 'selfhood and placehood are completely intertwined' (p86). Therefore building a deep relationship with the land is the goal as this includes happiness and health, unlike the motivations of the Scottish case study. The awareness of the self is interwoven with a connection to the land, to a concept of time, past and future, and to the wider world, including spiritual dimensions. They perceive their life and well-being as inseparable from the land. One of the informants, Iyerak, explained the importance of being on the land as the 'well-being of the person, connection to the land. Connection to wildlife, to everything ... the environment' (23 May 2002). The president of the Inullariit Society, Ivalu, explained:

> You have to be in relation to the land where there are the animals in order to survive ... so that you can have country food. And it's good for your health to be out on the land because you grow up there ... out there. You grow up out there, it's in you to be out there. (15 May 2002)

People in the Igloolik case study spoke of the land as a specific place rather than a concept of the general environment. They recognised 'their land' which they have used over generations and 'their animals' with which they have special relationships based on the principle of generational cycling (Brody, 1987; Fienup-Riordan, 1986). The generational cycle principle, although weakened in general, dictates certain rules: that which is received must be given away; the land that cares for them must be cared for in turn. The core social and cultural value in relation to the environment was expressed as respect. This value was clearly tangible and had practical implications for their daily life.

The following is an example of what young people said about respect.

> EB: I was told that they had respect for animals. If they treat animals bad, sea goddess would command animals not to go this place, those people are bad, so. Respecting animals is another way to keep animals up here

A notion of respect was identified as one of the common key values in relation to the environment in the study groups. All the organisers of the programmes cherished the term respect as an attitude they wanted to see among young people towards the environment. This is illustrated in summary in Figure 1.

Figure 1. Relationships to the land and goals of educational programmes

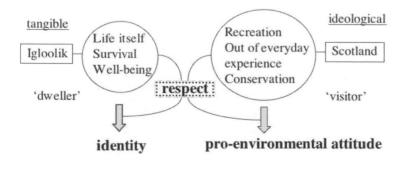

While the two studies, the Scotland and the Igloolik, showed a contrast in many aspects, they both used exactly the same term as important and linked it to relationships with the environment. The participants in both study cases all said that respect naturally entails care and responsibility. However the meaning of care was different between the groups and the following section discusses these kind of differences in the meaning of words which come from different worldviews.

Differences around the notions of respect and care

The programme organisers in Scotland suggested that an attitude of 'care, help, protect, conserve and preserve' in an environmental context was a natural outcome of respect. Like these programme organisers researchers in the UK have stressed that to transform attitudes into the truly environmental, environmental education must encourage respect for nature (Cooper, 1991; Higgins, 1996; Rodger, 1993). In a larger western philosophical framework, Paul Taylor (1989) attempted to establish the grounds for humans respecting nature as a moral principle. In *Respect for Nature*, he distinguishes respect from 'care and concern for living things' and states that care without an understanding of ethical obligation is not genuine respect for nature. Plumwood (1993) holds that respect for others means not treating them as an instrument for the carer's satisfaction (p167). Concerning a notion of care Pálsson (1999) classifies this attitude as 'paternalistic protection' (pp69-70) where humans are masters of nature and adopt a caring mentality. Rodger (1993) provides five categories of human attitude in relation to the environment: humans as users, managers, protectors, admirers and respecters, suggesting that only respecters value the environment in its own right and for its own sake and truly acknowledge its intrinsic value (Rodger, 1993, p13). He accepts but discourages the instrumental and anthropocentric views.

Rodger (1993) asserts that using the environment as a resource for 'the maintenance of life and health', even with prudence, is not 'necessarily wrong' and is 'scarcely avoidable' but is 'insufficient as a basis for a fully responsible treatment of the environment' (p12). Having this position of 'users and managers' at one end of the scale and 'respecters' at the other, he is reluctant to accept the idea of utilising the environment: by respect he means minimum or non-use. Similarly, Taylor (1989) promotes a concept of preservation which entails protecting nature from both present and future consumption. Concerning conservation he writes that if its purpose is for 'future exploitation of wildlife for the enjoyment of outdoor sports and recreation, such conservation activities are not consistent with respect for nature' (Taylor, 1989, p185). He implies that showing respect is about preserving and protecting which means not using or using minimally.

The concept of conservation has been argued to be a social and cultural construction and its contradictory nature has been discussed (Adams 1996/1997; Anderson and Grove, 1987; Brandon and Wells, 1992; Elliot, 1997; Neumann, 1998; Turton, 1987). Elliot (1997) states 'naturalness is a value-adding property', implying an ambiguous demarcation between preservation and creation (p146). Conservation in a modern social context certainly involves controlling and managing of nature to the extent humans decide it should be: how this embodies a notion of 'respect' is not clear. To live in harmony with nature, be at one with nature, and to acknowledge the intrinsic value of every life form are important conceptually but in delineating the meaning of these ideologies in practice within existing western worldviews there are extreme interpretations, countless moral dilemmas and competing claims to consider.

The concept of respect is expressed differently among indigenous peoples compared with the understanding of the term in western societies. In line with Rodger's (1993) perspective, Igloolik study participants match the respecters criteria in that they maintain close relationships with other humans and with the rest of the environment of which they are part (p14). However, the link implied in Rodger's and Taylor's argument between respect and preservation or non-use does not apply equally to them. In the context of Yup'ik people in Alaska, Fienup-Riordan (1990) interprets that respect includes love and fear and that this is a term to describe a relationship with humans, animals and parts of the natural world (p168). Brody (1987) analyses an Inuit's understanding of the world and concludes that 'for them, respect is a system of wildlife management that includes harvesting' (p77). For Inuit, respect for animals as well as all parts of the environment determines the success of a hunt. From this perspective a notion of respect has a direct link with sustainability in their worldview. Nonetheless, animals are their food and the motivation for hunting falls into Rodger's anthropocentric position and this accords more with users and managers than with respecters.

Linked to a concept of respect, the term 'care' was also often used by the Inuit during the fieldwork. The term was used about the proper treatment of the killed animals and their meat and bones. Caring and respect for and protection of animals takes a form that is different from western expectations. The following are interview accounts of the Paariaqtuqtut participants:

TT: Do you respect animals?

MB: Hmhm, I do. I like to go hunting

TT: In what way do you think people have to protect nature?

EB: One of the many ways to protect nature is ... eh ... to keep on hunting and ... keep the animals population in balance, and if there were to be a sudden change, try to respect the change, and if they have to go through a dent, they have to go through ...

EP: If I am to shoot caribou, and I didn't kill it, I would follow the caribou all the way (to kill) so I won't get the caribou sick. Even if I am to go home, I have to kill the caribou first. So I do have respect

From interview accounts in Igloolik with young people and elders it was clear that by 'taking care of animals' they meant to 'keep on hunting'. Being part of the environment did not preclude the fact that humans owe their existence to some other life, no matter how much they respect the natural world. Indeed the deep sense of respect among Inuit for the natural world comes partly from this dependence and indicates a direct connection between their life and the natural world.

This is not to suggest that one way of thinking is better than another but to confirm that a certain concept in a certain culture has limitations in being applied to other worldviews and that people's relationships are expressed differently across cultures.

Working through differences

For the Inuit involved in the study being on the land was life itself and was tied strongly to their identity and well-being. The programme's ultimate goal was to help young Iglulingumiut 'be and become an Inuk' with its core bonded with the land. The relationships with the land, including the knowledge and skills involved in the programme, had practical meanings in their daily life. The groups in Scotland visited 'wild places' primarily for recreational enjoyment. The UK programmes aimed to cultivate a caring attitude towards the environment chiefly through conservation work. However, in contrast to the Igloolik case, the experience was largely divorced from daily life.

From the fieldwork data in the UK and a reading of the relevant literature, it is clear that caring in western societies implies protection and preservation through non-use or minimal use of the wild environment.

161

It also includes the alteration and re-creation of the environment into something some people thought it should be. For the Inuit study group caring was expressed as culturally proper interaction with the natural world, which encompasses spirit and inanimate beings. The Inuit do not construct a hierarchy among all beings in the world. Their ancestors have used the land over generations but have not altered the landscape in the manner of the industrialised nations.

Fienup-Riordan (1986) states that environmental changes set the stage for cultural transformation. A suggestion that the human relationship with the environment is not one-way implies that the landscape represents the people who are concerned and *vice versa*. While a notion of respect represented the individuals' perceptions of their relationships with the land, what emerges in its meanings and implications are demonstrated very differently. The study exposed differences in meanings of respect which lead to further questions, such as 'What are the implications of these differences?' and 'How can we address the common environmental issues given such differences in our relationships with the environment?'. Researchers and educators need to be aware of these questions as we work through different worldviews, addressing a common future on the Earth.

References

Adams, W (1996) *Future Nature: A vision for conservation.* London: Earthscan

Adams, W (1997) Rationalisation and conservation: ecology and the management of nature in the United Kingdom. *Transactions of the Institute of British Geographers* 22, 277-291

Agrawal, A (1995) Dismantling the divide between indigenous and scientific knowledge. *Development and Change* 26, 13-439

Anderson, D and Grove, R (1987) Introduction. The scramble for Eden: past, present and future in African conservation. In Anderson, D and Grove, R (eds) *Conservation in Africa: People, policies and practice.* Cambridge: Cambridge University Press.

Basso, K (1996) Wisdom sits in places: notes on a western Apache landscape. In Feld, S and Basso, K (eds) *Senses of place.* Santa Fe, NM: School of American Research Press

Beckerman, W (1995) *Small is Stupid: Blowing the whistle on the greens.* London: Duckworth

Brandon, K E and Wells, M (1992) Planning for people and parks: Design dilemmas. *World Development* 20(4), 557-570

Brody, H (1987) *Living Arctic: Hunters of the Canadian north.* London: Faber and Faber

Brookes, A (2002) Lost in the Australian bush: Outdoor education as curriculum. *Journal of Curriculum Studies* 34(4), 405-425

Condie, R (2003) Environmental studies. In Bryce, T G K and Humes, W M (eds) *Scottish Education* (2nd ed). Edinburgh: Edinburgh University Press

Cooper, G (1991) The role of outdoor and field study centres in educating for the environment. *Journal of Adventure Education and Outdoor Leadership* 8(2), 10-11

Denham, C and White, I (1998, 19 March 1998) *Difference in Urban and Rural Britain: Sosio-demographic characteristics and distribution of the urban and rural populations based on the 1991 Census.* Retrieved 22 February 2005 from http://www.statistics.gov.uk/CCI/article.asp?ID=632&Pos=&ColRank=2&Rank=224

Devine, T M (2000) *The Scottish Nation: 1700-2000.* London: Penguin Books

Elliot, R (1997) *Faking Nature: The ethics of environmental restoration.* London: Routledge

Evans, D (1992) *A History of Nature Conservation in Britain.* London: Routledge

Fienup-Riordan, A (1986) *When our Bad Season Comes: A cultural account of subsistence harvesting and harvest disruption on the Yukon Delta.* Anchorage, AK: Alaska Anthropological Association

Fienup-Riordan, A (1990) *Eskimo Essays: Yup'ik lives and how we see them.* New Brunswick NJ: Rutgers University Press

Grove, R (1995) *Green Imperialism: Colonial expansion, tropical island Edens and the origins of environmentalism, 1600-1860.* Cambridge: Cambridge University Press

Higgins, P (1996) Connection and consequence in outdoor education. *The Journal of Adventure Education and Outdoor Leadership* 13(2), 34-39.

Hinds, K Carmichael, K and Snowling, H (2002) *Public Attitudes to the Environment in Scotland 2002* (Research Findings No.24): Environment and Rural Affairs Research Programme

Hirtz, F (2003) It takes modern means to be traditional: on recognizing indigenous cultural communities in the Phillipines. *Development and Change* 34(5), 887-914

Inullariit Society file (1993-1998) Files owned and located in Inullariit Society in Igloolik

Kushman, J and Barnhardt, R (1999) *Study of Alaska Rural Systemic Reform.* Fairbanks, AK: Authors

Martin, P. (1999) Critical outdoor education and nature as a friend. In Miles, J and Priest, S (eds) *Adventure Programming.* State College PA: Venture Publishing

Maykut, P and Morehouse, R (1994) *Beginning Qualitative Research: A philosophic and practical guide.* London; Washington DC: Falmer Press

McCormick, J and McDowell, E (1999) Environmental beliefs and behaviour in Scotland. In McDowell, E and McCormick, J (eds) *Environment Scotland: Prospects for sustainability.* Aldershot: Ashgate Publishing Company

National Trust (2003) *The chairman of the finance committee's accounts commentary.* Retrieved 28 August 2003 from http://www.nationaltrust.org.uk/main/nationaltrust/agm/2003/4_Accounts_Commentary.pdf

Neumann, R P (1998) *Imposing Wilderness: Struggles over livelihood and nature preservation in Africa.* Berkeley, CA: University of California Press

Nicol, R and Higgins, P (1998) A sense of place: A context for environmental outdoor education. In Higgins, P and Humberstone, B (eds) *Celebrating Diversity: Learning by sharing cultural differences.* Buckinghamshire: The European Institute for Outdoor Adventure Education and Experiential Learning and the National Association for Outdoor Education

O'Sullivan, E (1999) *Transformative Learning: Educational vision for the 21st century.* London: Zed Books

Office of the Languages Commissioner of Nunavut (nd, 2002) *Inuktitut/Inuinnaqtun.* retrieved 11 April 2003 from http://www.aboriginalcanada.gc.ca/abdt/interface/interface2.

nsf/LaunchFrameSet?OpenAgent&RefDoc=13.9.12.html&URL=http://www.langcom.nu.ca/
english/index.html&altlang=http://www.langcom.nu.ca/francais/index.html&disp=e&end

Orr, D W (1992) *Ecological Literacy: Education and the transition to a postmodern world.*
New York: State University of New York

Palmer, J A (1998) *Environmental Education in the 21st Century: Theory, practice, progress
and promise.* London: Routledge

Plumwood, V (1993) *Feminism and the Mastery of Nature.* London: Routledge

Pálsson, G (1999) Human-environmental relations: Orientalism, paternalism and com-
munalism. In Descola, P and Pálsson, G (eds) *Nature and Society: Anthropological perspectives* (reprinted, originally 1996 ed) London: Routledge.

Rediscovery International Foundation (nd) Rediscovery: Cultural and natural heritage programs for youth [brochure] Vancouver BC Canada

Rodger, A (1993) *Values and relationships towards the environment.* Paper presented at
the values in environmental education conference, Stirling

RT and Associates (2002) *Igloolik community economic development plan* (A draft paper of
community economic development plan for Igloolik by a consultant company) Iqualuit: RT
and Associates

Schmink, M Redford, K and Padoch, C (1992) Traditional peoples and the biosphere: Fram-
ing the issues and defining the terms. In Redford, K and Padoch, C (eds) *Conservation of
Neotropical Forests: Working from traditional resource use.* New York: Columbia University
Press

Smith, G and Williams, D (eds) (1999) *Ecological Education in Action: On weaving education, culture, and the environment.* Albany: State University of New York Press

Statistics Canada (2001) 2001 census retrieved 8 April 2003 from http://www12.statcan.
ca/english/census01/products/standard/popdwell/Table-PR.cfm

System Three (2000) *Survey on Environmental Issues in Scotland* (No SOS 100). Edinburgh: System Three

Taylor, P W (1989) *Respect for nature: A theory of environmental ethics* (2nd, first published
1986 ed). Princeton, NJ: Princeton University Press

Tuan, Y-F (1974) *Topophilia: A study of environmental perception, attitudes, and values.*
London: Englewood Cliffs

Turton, D (1987) The Mursi and national park development in the Lower Omo valley. In
Anderson, D and Grove, R (eds) *Conservation in Africa: People, policies and practice.* Cambridge: Cambridge University Press

12

Urban pedagogy: a challenge for the 21st century

Stephen Dobson

Introduction

I t is not uncommon for educational policy makers to claim legitimacy for their work by connecting it with the desire to enhance literacy through learning basic skills such as reading, writing, numeracy and competence with computers. Could it be argued that to live in an urban environment requires the development of its own fundamental skills? What these urban skills might be and how they might constitute the framework of a future urban pedagogy is the topic of this chapter.[1] The number of people living in cities is continually growing so that urban space has become an important component in the everyday experience of children as a well as adults.

Connected with this goal is the epistemological desire not to propose the establishment of a single, all-encompassing paradigm for urban pedagogy. Instead, in the spirit of Lakatos (1970, pp132-133), the intention is to propose a research programme, one of many possible ones, which is capable of developing skills in urban pedagogy. A research programme entails a hard core of assertions, a protective belt of auxiliary, less strong assertions, a positive heuristic suggesting paths of research to pursue and a negative heuristic telling 'us what paths of research to avoid'. The concept of a research programme originates from a debate about the construction of natural science knowledge but it is used here to refer to what might constitute the knowledge base or curriculum in urban pedagogy. Retaining the term 'research' in the term 'research programme' is intentional and indicates that those participating in urban pedagogy will be invited to research and co-construct their own knowledge of the urban.

Two different research programmes could have been examined instead. First, the exploration of the urban environment as a socio-ecological. This was the approach adopted by Wirth (1964) in his classic study of the 'city as a way of life' and resembles the core assertion for today's Center for Urban Pedagogy in New York, where concerns for the environment are uppermost.

A second research programme for urban pedagogy has been proposed by Jones (1997) in London. The relationship between the school and the community is central to his view. If the latter is dysfunctional the school becomes a surrogate family. If the school is dysfunctional in the sense of discouraging learning, learning in the community becomes central. He drew attention to the experiments in USA in the 1960s and 70s when children learning zoology did it at the zoo, those learning drama did it at the local theatre and so on (Wilson, 2004). Learning in the community can also take place through the religious schools organised by different ethnic groups at weekends. That such schools exist reflects how 'peripheral groups seldom have access to significant institutions in a manner sufficient to bring about a reallocation of power and resources, including those related to education' (Jones, 1992, 210).

Regarding the balance of pedagogy between school and community, Jones (1997) argues that new teachers should remain aware of these options, while concentrating their daily efforts on the state-funded formal school system. In other words, the school as an urban institution remains central.

The research programme proposed here differs from the two mentioned above by making urban experience its key component, rather than the urban environment or schools in the urban community. The core assertion of this chapter is: living and learning to live in an urban context entails an awareness and understanding of urban experience.

Its goal is to explore how a research programme based on this assertion could provide a framework to develop the skills for an urban pedagogy. The subjects participating in such a pedagogy could be youth or adults. While the specific details of the curriculum will be the subject of a subsequent essay inspired by SooHoo *et al* (2004), some indications of how this proposal can be realised are suggested here.

What is the city?

Baumann (2003, 30) focuses on how urban inhabitants are more sceptical and fear face-to-face interaction in an age of what he calls 'liquid modernity'. People possess a preference for cultivating 'islands of similarity and sameness' (p30) among those of a similar socio-economic background: segregated housing patterns therefore emerge.

His proposal is that planners should create spaces where people can have more shared experiences and develop shared horizons based upon face-to-face interaction: 'the ... propagation of open, inviting and hospitable public spaces which all categories of urban residents would be tempted to regularly attend and knowingly/willingly share' (p34).

Taking on board these views, still leaves the question of the relevance of urban experience itself for educationalists. How can the spaces Baumann talks of be created and how can people be schooled into desiring and managing such experiences?

In academic journals such as *Urban Education* and *Education and Urban Society* the kind of topics typically examined are the social segregation of pupils in different schools, social exclusion, cultural diversity and gender. However, while these topics are undoubtedly to do with living in urban areas and attending schools, the focus is not upon urban experience itself. The concern is rather with what happens in urban schools and how the schools might assist in the reduction of different forms of socio-economic inequality.

Experience and pedagogy

In making urban experience the core assertion in a research programme on urban pedagogy, the aim is to stay close to what educationalists have called the experience of 'learning by doing'. A number of points can be made about the character of urban experience in an urban pedagogy:

- Simmel (1950) explained the difference between urban and rural experience. In the latter a person is more likely to meet familiar faces, the pace of life is slower and the number and intensity of stimuli are less.

- To increase one's understanding of urban experience in a 'learning by doing' manner is to embark upon a project of *bildung* (self-formation). It entails a self-overcoming as new urban experiences confront old ones (Dobson *et al*, 2006). For some adolescents this results in fragile identities (Ball *et al*, 2000).

■   Urban experiences can take place in informal arenas. Pedagogy is moved from the formal, institutionalised space of the class-room, with fixed and stable teacher-pupil roles, to the street and the community. The informal life of the street potentially contains many shifting significant others.

When urban experience entails these things we are talking about an *erfaringspedagogikk* (a pedagogy of experience). This is what writers such as Kolb (1984), Wallace (1999) and Schon (1987) have called experiential learning based upon observations, integrated into abstract conceptual schema. Jameson (1988, 353) provides an example with his concept of cognitive mapping and its connection to identity formation (*bildung*).

Cognitive mapping for Jameson (1988, 353), building upon Lynch's (1960) classic book, *The Image of the City*, aims to imagine not only the experience of urban space, but how this is connected with socio-economic, class-based and global experiences of exploitation. His proposal (1984, 92) entails a 'pedagogical political culture which seeks to endow the individual subject with some new heightened sense of its place in the global system'. The goal is therefore clear: to make sure 'we may again begin to grasp our positioning as individual and collective subjects and regain a capacity to act and struggle', but how he will achieve this, other than through cognitive maps, is unclear.

Protective belt assertions

Around the core assertion of urban experience as the subject matter of urban pedagogy a number of protective belt assertions are proposed. They rest upon the core assertion of urban experience but are less strongly held in that they can be modified and even abandoned without meaning that the legitimacy of the core assertion is questioned. The criterion for selection is that they contribute to a heightened understanding of urban experience.

a) The *flâneur*

To saunter, stroll, wander, promenade, to be a *flâneur* – these are the terms describing walkers who have time on their hands. Not the commuter in a rush or the child running for their school bus. For Benjamin, the *flâneur* planted his feet one after the other in order to let the seed of uncharted and unexpected experiences grow in an unhurried fashion: 'The style of the *flâneur* who goes botanising on the asphalt ...' (Benjamin, 1983, p36).

The walker is able to plant and reap experiences from an activity which has become increasingly unnatural to many urban dwellers who are addicted to the intoxicating thrill of motor, train and air travel. The walker can recapture and re-experience space otherwise surrendered to planners, architects and the owners of capital.

This was the intention of the International Situationalists, among them Debord (known for his *Society of the Spectacle*, 1977), who talked of drift (*dérive* in French) – the unplanned walk of locomotion without a goal, where one just followed one's feelings to map the psycho-geography of a place and how it felt, e.g. threatening or the opposite. Situationalist psycho-geography can be defined as the following: 'the specific effects of the geographical environment ... on the emotions and behaviour of individuals' (Anon quoted in Sadler, 1998, p92).

The *flâneuse*? Benjamin with his concept of the *flâneur* has reproduced the male culture of the nineteenth century where the only public role allowed for the sauntering woman was as a prostitute or as an embellishment on the sleeve of their husband's wealth (Wolff, 1989). Through masculine gaze women are consigned to the status of objects and less able to experience being a flâneuse without fear for their own safety.

Fear and urban experience raise the question of how the city is imagined (Westwood and Williams, 1996). Pile, inspired by psychoanalysis, also draws heavily upon Benjamin's concept of phantasmogia to highlight the procession of images passing before the urban dweller. These images can take on the character of a dream experience and be the source of 'wishes and desires, anxieties and fears' (p96). In other words, the images we have of the city can influence how it is experienced both consciously and unconsciously.

b) Educating the senses
Young children have to learn to look and not talk to strangers on public transport. They must be taught how to use their senses and not disclose their inner feelings and emotions and Simmel's advice (1950) was to act in a cold, calculating manner to others. Other senses must be educated, such as the acoustic, olfactory, tactile and gustatory. For example, certain sounds, we learn, are background sounds, such as the muffled sound of London at night or early in the morning (Bull and Back, 2003). McLaren (2000, p243) has talked of the manner in which rap music functions as an experience of the urban: 'Rap unmakes feelings of security and safety in middle-class homes and neighborhoods. It indexes areas of concrete rage and generalised despair'.

For some, rap functions as part of a negative heuristic, something to be disciplined, controlled and avoided where possible. For others it is part of a positive heuristic, something to be desired:'by bursting through the representational space of whiteness and by advancing political solidarity in the from of an imagined community of struggle' (McLaren, 2000, p250).

Educating the senses connects with the romantic tradition of *bildung* proposed by writers such as Schiller in Germany and Rousseau in France.

c) Signifiers, codes and commodity culture

Access to urban experience and its codes is important. But what is a code? Signs, composed of signifiers, signifieds and referents are organised into sets of codes or grammars that must be learned if we wish to communicate (Gundersen and Dobson, 1996).

Bernstein sought to understand the code-based character of the pedagogic process. He coined the term elaborated codes and their opposite, restricted codes. For Bernstein (1986, p474) the former referred to a form of communication that used a range of 'syntactic alternatives, which speakers take up in the organisation of speech'. The latter restricted codes were more contextual and fixed. Bourdieu (2004, p17) was also interested in the coded character of interaction, specifically cultural capital as a code governing pedagogic activity, societal recognition and access to power. But they both underplayed or perhaps even lacked Benjamin's insight into the fact that codes in urban space can change with each new generation. This is a dialectical process of opposition where the breaking of one code and the imposition of its successor can be a violent and turbulent affair (Dobson, 2002, p4). This means that if pedagogy is to have more than a descriptive task limited to exposing and confirming existing codes in society it must also have a political and emancipatory project: the breaking and making of new codes in an urban environment that reaches beyond the bounds of the classroom. For example, racial codes are visible in urban space and have been changing so that mixed-race relationships are more openly expressed.

Benjamin was sensitive to both the code and aura of commodities:

> The crowd is not only the newest asylum of outlaws; someone abandoned in the crowd. In this he [the *flâneur*] shares the situation of the commodity. He is not aware of this special situation, but this does not diminish its effect on him and it permeates him blissfully like a narcotic that can compensate him for many humiliations. The intoxication to which the *flâneur* surrenders is the

intoxication of the commodity around which surges the stream of customers. (Benjamin, 1983, p55)

In this way Benjamin found a way of describing and experiencing the secular opium of the people and the intoxication they had learnt to enjoy. My point is simple: in the urban space a person must learn to interpret the codes encountered. On this basis shared understanding and communication with others is possible. The diagram below sums up the points made above.

Core and protective assertions in urban pedagogy

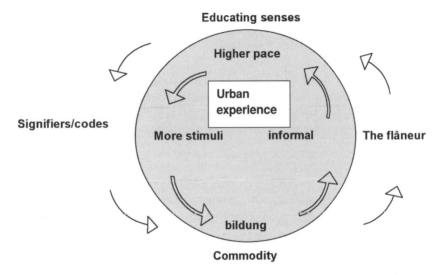

An example: the urban pedagogy of Iain Sinclair

Sinclair has undertaken several walking projects. One walk around the M25 London orbital produced this account:

> The harder the rain comes down, the faster we stride. We're erasing every-thing we investigated on the original walk. The smoke from the burning stack at the London Waste facility in Edmonton is distinguished from river mist, spray from the elevated carriageway. The sky has dropped. (Sinclair, 2002, p452)

His writing style has been noted for its stinging acerbity as he struggles to find signifiers to express his politicised interpretations:

> The A13 shuffle through East London is like the credits sequence of the Mafia soap, The Sopranos; side-of-the-eye perspective, bridges, illegitimate businesses about to be overwhelmed by the big combos. Black smoke and blue smoke. Waste disposal. A well-chewed cigar...To drift through low cloud, through the harp strings of the suspension bridge, is to become a quotation; to see yourself from outside. (Sinclair, 2002, p40)

Sinclair's books, a mixture of text and photographic image, are carefully crafted and edited reflections of his experience as a *flâneur*. In his celebrated *Lights out for the Territory* (1997) his goal was to provide a record and understanding of the hidden mythical, psychic geography of London. Rather than public survey cartography he sought to create maps that connected people to mythical places and events. He defined the walking plan as follows:

> The notion was to cut a crude V into the sprawl of the city, to vandalise dormant energies by an act of ambulant sign making. To walk out from Hackney to Greenwich Hill, and back along the River Lea to Chingford Mount, recoding and retrieving the message on walls, lampposts, door-jambs: the spites and spasms of an increasingly deranged populace. (Sinclair, 1997, p1)

The signifiers he mapped included graffiti, shop signs and pub signs. Graffiti parodies the codes of capitalism by advertising meanings for consumption and also on occasions includes us in the parody. Thus, 'we're behaving like insects' (p15) found in Dalston indicates how we are all mass consumers following each other in our purchases and not the least in our walking habits.

Sinclair uses the term *flâneur* on several occasions, along with the term psycho-geography (p85) and its clear reference to the International Situationalists. For him to walk always represents an opportunity to experience *bildung*. His definition of the *flâneur* is 'a stubborn creature, less interested in texture and fabric, eavesdropping on philosophical conversation pieces, than in noticing everything' (p4). On occasions Sinclair regards the *flâneur* as a stalker (p75).

As an illustration of his method consider how on one walk he stumbled across the funeral of one of the Kray brothers. The local support for these London gangsters, notorious in the 1960s, was evident in the tributes and the length of the funeral procession: the East End had its 'reputation to uphold' (p69). Sinclair identified a connection between the pit bull dog traditions of the East End and the dog breeding dreams of Ronnie Kray. He closes this account of the funeral by noting how even drug pushers in BMWs make the journey to touch the Kray gravestone. The connection between living/mortal and dead/immortal is made.

In Sinclair's urban pedagogy, the core assertion of urban experience is understood in terms of the life of the streets and the community. It is beyond the formal sphere of the school, experiencing the pace and stimuli of urban life. Protective assertions are also present: Sinclair, the *flâneur*, stopping to eat local food, usually a full English breakfast, early on all the walks is an indication of the education of the senses (taste). In Sinclair's work it is the reading of signs, looking for their political and mythical meanings, which remains upper-most in his interests. There is an open critique of governments and commodity capitalism: his view of codes and signifiers is always political. Put simply, it is a politics of representation.

Realising urban pedagogy – how?

In debates on informal pedagogy it is not unusual to encounter the view (Phoenix, 2004) that youth identities are constructed in an informal manner. But the setting is the school and what takes place there. What is ignored is the informal pedagogy taking place outside of the formal school institution. The argument in this chapter for urban pedagogy has focused on precisely this.

Jones (1997) considered the community as an experience outside of the school. But continued to regard the school as the most important site for education. In opposition to him, the community, as expressed and experienced in the life of the street, remains central to my conception of urban pedagogy. It is here that the educational efforts for such a pedagogy might be concentrated.

In moving to such an arena, identity formation – *bildung* – is less fixed and controlled by the formal teacher-pupil relation of the school. The role of peer groups, respected community elders and the media-mediated views of style and consumption occupy a key role. The answer to the question 'who does the educating in an urban pedagogy?' is that it is not necessarily the teacher in the classroom. Likewise, the answer to the question 'who are the pupils in such a pedagogy?' is not necessarily those of normal school age. It can be adults. However, some caution must be taken with respect to the age of younger participants. The activity of the *flâneur* should not be allowed for those too young to wander the city on their own. This means that young people in their mid to late teens would represent the younger age bracket for participation and they would walk in pairs or small groups, rather than alone. If they were accompanied by adults the age of participants could be younger.

Following the lead of Ball *et al* (2000) urban pedagogy might emphasise the role of the family as it exerts an influence on the socialised frames of perception and thought of adolescents (p23). This would make the family an important source of educational influence so that family members could become teachers about the urban experience.

Flemming Røgilds in his series of books on youth in an urban environment and particularly *Det Utsatte* (*The Marginalised*, 2004) describes and accounts for the way in which peer group interaction is fundamental to identity formation. For him urban pedagogy is more to do with peer group influences than with the family. For many of the immigrant youths he follows in Copenhagen, adults such as teachers, parents or community elders are not considered to be prime models for identity formation. Whether we call these peer groups forms of subgroups or even gangs is not relevant to the key point that peers can be a primary focus for identity formation in the kind of urban pedagogy proposed above. This is the case for many youths who would not claim an immigrant background. For Røgilds the immigrant youths take part in what he calls border pedagogy, a term taken from the USA educationalist Giroux (1994), as they build identities in the border region between Danish and immigrant identities.

Many classroom educationalists will be skeptical about letting their pupils wander the streets and this will be one of the main criticisms of this proposal. But to back off from increasing pupil awareness of different forms of urban experience is to neglect the everyday context and challenges that many pupils face. As a prelude to actively seeking urban experiences teachers could run workshop sessions in the school classroom where pupils tell of their experiences, of the senses they use and of memorable stories. They could use different elements of the diagram to focused on.

Not all urban experiences should be sought: in the workshops the less desirable and dangerous ones can be discussed and ruled out. The journeys into urban arenas outside the school can be limited and directed so that they do not become a form of random and unplanned drift (*dérive*) in the spirit of the International Situationalists. Such experiences can be reserved for students who are older and approaching adulthood.

One way of documenting urban experience is to let students work on their own joint projects. To reflect the different senses the projects can be multi-modal, composed of text, images, sounds, tastes and surfaces that can be touched. This might entail everything from images taken on mobiles to the re-creation of small tasters of food sampled on journeys into the urban environment.

Participants in urban pedagogy should be encouraged to organise and reflect upon their urban experiences. Much of this reflection can be cross-disciplinary, drawing together knowledge from different fields and subjects such as the history of construction, literacy defined widely in terms of how different cultural signs are made and understood, the sociology and psychology of urban inhabitants, living conditions and personal health and safety. Participants can be given the opportunity to work upon their soft skills, in particular those connected with working in groups, and to select urban issues and problems according to their interests.

Concluding remarks

In the resultant cross-disciplinary research programme proposed above, with the goal of developing skills in an urban pedagogy, the core assertion of urban experience has been based upon four elements: the faster pace of life in the urban sphere, more stimuli, the informal and *bildung*. Around this core four less crucial assertions were added as a protective ring: signifiers/codes, involvement with commodities, the *flâneur* and an education of the senses. These assertions can be researched and practiced through a negative heuristic, suggesting what not to pursue, and a positive heuristic, suggesting what to pursue.

However, a difficulty arises – in Lakatos' conception the protective belt assertions could be modified or abandoned if found to be deficient. It is also possible to argue that some of those proposed should be included in the list of core assertions. For example, should the *flâneur* be part of this core? Not necessarily, the urban can be experienced from the car or the tram. So, the *flâneur* does not have to be part of the core. Similarly, the experience of commodities is not necessarily a core assertion because non-commodity experiences are possible in the urban arena. It is harder to argue that signifiers, codes and an education of the senses should not be part of the core, especially when *bildung* involves some form of educating the senses and learning to understand and interpret the codes.

It might be argued that socio-economic class is a protective belt assertion since the experience of the urban changes according to class. This would concur with the work of Ball *et al* (2000), who highlight the differential, divisive and unequal manner in which the urban is experienced. For some social groups the city is experienced as a place of danger rather than of security. The importance of social class for experience was also identified by Benjamin (1983, p117): *erlebnis* (repetitive experience, 'passed through and lost') is typical of the working-class as they work and are less likely to be *erfahrung* (collectively shared, historical experience that is recalled as meaningful).

175

Irrespective of whether new elements are added to the protective belt or moved into the core assertion, a focus upon urban experience would still stands as the key defining element of a research programme, and content for the urban pedagogy proposed in this chapter.

This does not preclude others constructing different research programmes and curricula for an urban pedagogy. Instead of drawing upon experience, the focus might be on the urban as an ecological site. The point is not therefore that different research programmes should fight for hegemony but that a tolerance for differences could be encouraged.

Note

1 An earlier version of this essay was published in *London Review of Education* (2006), 4, 99-114.

References

Ball, S, Maguire, M and Macrae, S (2000) *Choice, Pathways and Transitions Post-16. New Youth, New Economies in the Global City*. London: Routledge

Bauman, Z (2003) *City of Fears, City of Hopes*. London: Goldsmiths' College

Benjamin, W (1983): *Charles Baudelaire. A Lyric Poet in the Era of High Capitalism*. London: Verso Books

Bernstein, B (1986) A Sociolinguistic Approach to Socialization; with some Reference to Educability. In *Directions in Sociolinguistics. The Ethnography of Communication*. Edited by Gumperz, J and Hymes, D. Oxford: Basil Blackwell

Bourdieu, P (2004) The Forms of Capital. In *The Sociology of Education Reader*. Edited by Ball, S. London: Routledge-Falmer, pp15-29

Bull, M and Back, L (eds) (2003) *The Auditory Culture Reader*. Oxford: Berg

Debord, G (1977) *The Society of the Spectacle*. Detroit: Black and Red (in French 1967)

Dobson, S (2002) *The Urban Pedagogy of Walter Benjamin. Part I, II, III*. London: Goldsmiths Press

Dobson, S, Brodalen, R and Tobaissen, H (2006): Courting risk – the attempt to understand youth cultures. *Young, Nordic Journal of Youth Studies* 14, 49-59

Giroux, H (1994) Insurgent Multiculturalism and the Promise of Pedagogy. In *Multiculturalism: A Critical Reader*. Edited by Goldberg, D. Oxford: Blackwell

Gundersen, R and Dobson, S (1996): *Baudriallard's Journey to America*. London: Minerva Press

Jameson, F (1984) Postmodernism, or the cultural logic of late capitalism. *New Left Review* 146, 35-64

Jameson, F (1988) Cognitive Mapping. In *Marxism and the Interpretation of Culture*, Nelson, C and Grossberg, L (eds). Houndmills: Macmillan

Jones, C (1992) Cities, diversity and education. In *World Yearbook of Education 1992. Urban Education*. London: Kogan Page

Jones, C (1997) The school in the city. In Heilbroun, R and Jones, C (eds), *New Teachers in an Urban Comprehensive School. Learning in Partnership*. Oakhill: Trenham Books

Kolb, D (1984) *Experiential Learning*. London: Prentice Hall

Lakatos, I (1970) Falsification and the methodology of scientific research programmes. In *Criticism and the Growth of Knowledge*, Lakatos, I and Musgrave, A (eds). Cambridge: Cambridge University Press

Lynch, K (1960) *The Image of the City*. Cambridge, Mass: MIT Press

McClafferty, K, Torres, C and Mitchell, T (eds) (2000) *Challenges of Urban Education: Sociological Perspectives for the Next Century*. New York: State University

McLaren, P, Gansta Pedagogy and Ghettocentricity (2000) The hip-hop nation as a counter-public sphere. In McClafferty *et al* (eds). *Challenges of Urban Education: Sociological Perspectives for the Next Century.*

Phoenix, A (2004) Using informal pedagogy to oppress themselves and each other. *Nordisk Pedagogikk* 1, 15-28

Pile, S (2005) *Real Cities, Modernity, Space and the Phantasmagorias of City Life*. London: Sage

Røgilds, F (2004) *De Utsatte* (The Marginalised). Copenhagen: Forlaget Politisk Revy

Sadler, S (1998) *The Situationalist City*. Cambridge, Massachusetts: MIT Press

Schon, D (1987) *Educating the Reflective Practitioner*. London: Jossey-Bass

Simmel, G (1950) The metropolis and mental life. In *The Sociology of Georg Simmel*. Edited by Wolff, K. Glencoe: Free Press

Sinclair, I (1997) *Lights Out for the Territory*. London: Granta Books

Sinclair, I (2002) *London Orbital. A Walk Around the M25*. London: Granta Books

SooHoo, S (ed) (2004) *Essays on Urban Education. Critical Consciousness, Collaboration and the Self*. Orange, CA, Chapman University Press: Hampton Press

Wallace, M (1999) When is experiential learning not experiential learning? In *Learners, Learning and Assessment*. Edited by Murphy, P, London: Sage

Westwood, S and Williams, J (eds) (1996) *Imagining Cities. Scripts, Signs, Memory*. London: Routledge

Wilson, T (2004) Community matters. In SooHoo, S. (ed) *Essays on Urban Education. Critical Consciousness, Collaboration and the Self*. Orange, CA, Chapman University: Hampton Press

Wirth, L (1964) *On Cities and Social Life: Selected Papers*. Edited by Reiss, A. Chicago: Chicago University Press.

Wolff, J (1989) The invisible flâneuse: women and the literature of modernity. In *The Problems of Modernity*. Edited by Benjamin, A. London: Routledge.

13

Discourse, subjectivity and the margins: students' constitutions of Shazas, Bazas and Dir'y 'ippies

Deborah Youdell

Introduction

How children and young people come to be variously and hierarchically located in and beyond education is an enduring concern for educators. One recent set of responses to this concern has been to use notions of difference and marginality to help to make sense of these positionings, using, adapting and deploying conceptual tools developed by key post-structural theorists such as Michel Foucault, Jacques Derrida and Judith Butler. The specific ideas that have been engaged and used in this work include ideas of discourses as regulative and productive, of identity, or more precisely subjectivity, as being constituted through discourses, of these productions being partial and incomplete but always implicated in relations of power, and of the fundamental need to be recognisable in a given context in order to 'be'.

Educators have begun to use these conceptual tools to interrogate how the students we teach come to be who they are, how these becomings are entangled with the practices that take place everyday in classrooms, corridors and canteens and how these processes are connected with long-recognised class, race, gender and (dis)ability inequalities in experiences and outcomes in schooling and beyond (Hey, 2006; Rasmussen, 2005, 2006; Renold, 2006; Talbert and Steinberg, 2004; Youdell, 2006a, 2006b).

This chapter identifies my own interpretation of the notions of difference and marginality and demonstrates my use of the post-structural tools identified here to understand practices inside schools, including those that are implicated in producing inequalities. As the chapter focuses on an episode of data that was generated through an in-depth ethnographic study in a London secondary school it explores how discourses that constitute difference as neutral or equal but different are deployed in ways that obscure discursive axes of hierarchical differentiation such as race and class and contest insider/outsider, Same/Other locations in ways that lay claim to the margins. Specifically, this analysis shows how a group of London secondary school students deploys a discourse of sub-cultural difference. As the group deploys this discourse there seems to be an intention, perhaps tacit, of deflecting pro-school, middle-class identifications as well as the privilege of Whiteness and instead constituting sub-cultural, marginal cool. These discursive moves simultaneously and perhaps unintentionally mask and constitute class, race and learner privilege. The extract below illustrates the ordinariness of these practices and suggests that their effects may be neither ordinary nor benign.

Dir'y 'ippies/Shazas and Bazas

Taylor Comprehensive, London, UK Sitting in a group around a table in the Year Base, an infrequently used classroom that is designated as the social space of the year group. DY (researcher, woman, White, late 20s) is with Vici (girl, White), Pipa (girl, White), Suzi (girl, White) and Tom (boy, White) all students aged 15-16. The rest of the tutor group are in a lesson. The group begin to talk about how they believe they are perceived in the school.

Vici: We are seen as very, very, uncool because we are seen as (laughing and imitating a south east London accent) dirty hippies

[...]

DY: Dirty hippies, who thinks you're dirty hippies?

(simultaneously) Tom: Everyone

(simultaneously) Pipa: It's actually (changing pronunciation to imitate a south east London accent) dirty hippies

Suzi: (imitating east London accent) Dirty hippies

All: (laugh)

DY: (trying to repeat and write as pronounced) Dirty hippies?

Vici: Spelt: D, I, R, apostrophe, Y ...

Pipa: Apostrophe, I, double P, I, E, S

All: (laugh)

DY: (pronouncing as instructed) Dir'y 'ippies

[...]

Vici: The opposite end of the scale to (repeating imitated accent) Dir'y
'ippies are Shazas and Bazas

(fieldnotes)

These data were generated during 1998, before the name 'Chav' was popularised in the UK. The names Shaza and Baza clearly resonate with Chav, so much so that the now common usage of this name risks leaving Shaza and Baza feeling out of date. Yet Shaza and Baza, as I recalled with discomfort as the discussion took place, and the more recently popularised Chav also resonate with the names used by myself and my friends to identify (and constitute) other students and ourselves in our East Midlands secondary school during the early 1980s. Our Shazas were 'Sharons and Tracys' whose male equivalents were 'Garys'. We believed that we were referred to or constituted ourselves as 'Grebs' and 'Trampy Punks'. Greb was mostly considered inaccurate, perhaps injurious?, Trampy Punk was embraced. These are names that echo in the later 'Indie Kids' and 'Alternatives' and most recently the 'Skaters' and 'Emos' (Emotionals). The names used shift over time but they remain connected to the names that precede and replace them and, as I will show, to the meanings that they cite and inscribe.

The exchange represented in the episode might be seen simply as students who, having been called a name (Dir'y 'ippie), retaliate by insisting that the name is not after all an injury and then by retorting with other names (Shazas and Bazas). It is not clear that a student named here as Shaza or Baza has actually ever addressed one of these students as Dir'y 'ippie. Vici, Suzi, Pipa and Tom and their friends are almost always absent from the talk of the students they name Shazas and Bazas. Where Vici, Suzi and the others do appear (usually at my instigation) they are named as 'Bods' or 'Boffins' and quickly disregarded. Some or all of these names: Bods and Boffins, Swots, Geeks, Try Hards, Teachers' Pets, Creeps and Keenos may be familiar.

In the analysis that follows I argue that these names, while temporally and contextually shifting, endure. Far from being the benign markers of pop/sub-cultures, they intersect with and are deeply implicated in the reproduction of class, race, gender, sexuality, and (dis)ability inclusions and exclusions.

Tools for understanding subjects

Sticks and stones will break my bones, but names will never hurt me
(children's rhyme, source unknown)

> Being called a name is ... one of the conditions by which a subject is con-
> stituted in language [...] One comes to 'exist' by virtue of this fundamental
> dependency on the address of the Other
> (Judith Butler, 1997, *Excitable Speech* p2 and 5)

While the children's rhyme insists that what I am called has no effect, Judith Butler's work in *Excitable Speech* argues the centrality of the name – *of being named* – to subject-hood, to being a person, even if this is not a name that I have chosen, or would choose, for myself and/or if it brings with it the threat of injury, marginalisation, containment or another effect that I do not desire and may not even recognise.

Butler's claim rests on two ideas from the work of Michel Foucault. First, his understanding of discourses as bodies of meaning that are at once regulatory and productive, that create the knowledges, or 'regimes of truths', through which we come to know ourselves and the world (Foucault, 1991). Second, his understanding of subjectivation which builds on Louis Althusser's (1971) ideas about subjection through a turn to a call – 'hey you!' – or interpellation. Foucault's subjectivation suggests that through the ongoing repetition and revision of discourses, I become a subject who can act at the same time as I am subjected to discursive relations of power (Foucault, 1990, 1991). Judith Butler's (1990, 1993, 1997) take-up of the notion of performativity is also important here. The performative is understood as an utterance, practice or even a silence that brings into effect the thing that it appears to simply refer to, describe or enact. While the performative is constitutive of the person that it names, by being named the named person comes to appear to pre-exist this or any other naming. With these theoretical tools subjects, including the subjects of schooling, are understood to be constituted and constrained again and again by ongoing practices that are made meaningful by the discourses that frame and mediate them.

In this framework the notion of difference might be taken as calling up pluralist diversity or a politics of difference in which the axes of difference along which pluralism or politics might organise, such as race, ethnicity, culture, religion, gender, sexuality or disability, are understood as citations of discourses that carry with them abiding histories and meanings and which are themselves productive of subjects within these terms (Youdell, 2006a). After the work of Jacques Derrida (1978, 1988) notions of difference and marginalisation also highlight the relationship between the Same and the Other, where inextricably entangled but hierarchically organised binaries define the inside and the outside, the we and the they. And, in Derrida's notion of differance (spelt with an a), this entanglement leaves meaning constantly deferred and the subordinate

term an insistent absent presence. With this understanding of difference, categories of race, class, gender, sexuality, disability and the discourses through which they are constituted come to mark what is
outside a normative centre and so reproduce the privilege of what is
taken for granted, as normal, as ideal, as the Same. Similarly, while policy
discourses increasingly recognise marginalisation and seek ways to
ameliorate this, this very recognition is simultaneously a moment in
which individualised, self-reflexive and responsible consuming subjects
are constituted at the centre and Other subjects are constituted at the
margins. Indeed, these policy frames produce the margins as a place one
does not or should not want to be and never as a site of possibility. They
also obscure how positions of difference and marginality are themselves
mobile, contested and potentially redeployed into the constitution of
privilege.

This theoretical framework has a number of methodological implications (Youdell, 2006a). It insists on the importance of understanding
contextual specificity and mobility of practice. It insists that data are
generated, not collected, by a researcher who is wholly implicated in
the constitutions that s/he studies. And it suggests that those data
generated should be interrogated to identify the discursive practices
embedded in them and the potentially constitutive force of these.

Queer practices of the Other or policing the privilege of the Same?

Exploring the constitution of, relationship between, and performative
force of 'Shazas and Bazas' and 'Dir'y 'ippies' offers insight into the
intersections, collisions, and silences in and between school, student
and wider discourses. It also allows us to see how these discourses are
implicated in constituting biographical, sub-cultural and learner
subjectivities in particular constellations, and how these are entangled
with education's insiders and outsiders. The data do not simply represent an account of student and pop- or sub-cultures: the data are significant because they demonstrate how privilege and hierarchy are reproduced even as they are denied and obscured, and the data show how
the margins can become desirable or sought after (but only by those
who do not have to be there?). The episode of data introduced earlier is
taken up again now.

Dir'y 'ippies/Shazas and Bazas

[...]

Vici: We are seen as very, very un-cool because we are seen as (laughing
and imitating a south east London accent) dirty hippies.

[...]

DY: Dirty hippies, who thinks you're dirty hippies?

(simultaneously) Tom: Everyone

(simultaneously) Pipa: It's actually (changing pronunciation to imitate a south east London accent) dirty hippies

Suzi: (imitating east London accent) Dirty hippies

All: (laugh)

DY: (trying to repeat and write as pronounced) Dirty hippies?

Vici: Spelt: D, I, R, apostrophe, Y ...

Pipa: Apostrophe, I, double P, I, E, S

All: (laugh)

DY: (pronouncing as instructed) Dir'y 'ippies

[...]

Vici: The opposite end of the scale to (repeating imitated accent) dir'y 'ippies are Shazas and Bazas

Suzi: Have you heard of them?

DY: No, I don't think they self-identify in the way that you do.

Vici: No they don't, cos they just sit here and go (whining) 'Ner ner'. No, they don't know that they're referred to as Shazas and Bazas but we know that we're refereed to as Dir'y 'ippies cos we are (with slight laugh in voice) on the ball.

[...]

The group goes on to engage in an extended discussion of the different styles of clothing, hair, jewellery, shoes, bags that distinguish Dir'y 'ippies and Shazas and Bazas. Hair wax or hair gel, and in what quantity; record bag or sports bag; silver or gold jewellery. When I offer Mridula, an Indian girl in the tutor group, for classification she doesn't fit: she is not a Dir'y 'ippie but, says Vici, 'she's not a true Shaza (laughing), her hair is not solid and she doesn't wear quite enough gold jewellery either!'. Music is also crucial. While Dir'y 'ippies listen to alternative rock and brit-pop, Shazas are imagined nursing broken hearts to R&B love songs. And while homophobic Bazas use 'gay' as a catch-all insult and term of derision, Dir'y 'ippies celebrate queer. Vici summarises: 'You could almost write out a set of definitive rules for Shazas and Bazas and Dir'y 'ippies' and Tom elaborates: 'The point is, Shazas and Bazas keep to those rules'.

[...]

Suzi: Another thing is speech. You see, we all speak quite clearly so you can understand what we're saying

Pipa: (squeals)

DY: Is there a social class thing about being a Dir'y 'ippie or a Shaza or Baza?

Pipa: Erm ...

Vici: If we're honest, sort of, not strictly but it does tend to be

(simultaneously) Suzi: A trend

Vici: It's not a definite decision but, a trend. Probably anyway

Pipa: Sort of

(simultaneously) Suzi: If you take a case study in Taylor, that is

Tom: And the people who are more inclined to work in school. The people that are more inclined to work and come from slightly more middle-class backgrounds tend to be, don't you think?

Suzi: Erm, not exactly. I'm not sure that I'd quite agree with that. I wouldn't say Dir'y 'ippies tend to work

(fieldnotes)

In the context of the (absent) relations between the Dir'y 'ippies and the Shazas and Bazas, the names the Shazas and Bazas *do* call the Dir'y 'ippies, that is, Bod and Boffin, and the recognisable quality of the names under discussion, it seems plausible and even likely that the Dir'y 'ippies were never actually called this. Rather, it seems that these students are citing names that circulate in discourses reaching far beyond the specific context of this school and whose historicity (Butler, 1990), their temporal connection to names and meanings that have preceded them, lends them their performative force. The names at stake here have the potential to constitute the student population in particular ways.

As the Dir'y 'ippies extrapolate the minutiae of the differences between these two sub-cultural styles it is almost possible to imagine that this is all that is going on. On the surface these names might appear to reference nothing more than a nebulous array of teenage choices concerning clothing, hair styles, musical genres, effort in school work and so on. But Bourdieu's (1984) analysis of distinction insists that these apparent 'tastes' have differential values in differentiated markets and that it is these relative values that are at stake. The class and race privilege that is cited and inscribed through these students' discursive practices, while implicit, is unavoidable. This is because these apparent choices at once mask and cite an array of discourses that constitute subjects along intersecting lines of social class, gender, race, sexuality and intelligence/ability. They are the very discursive practices that cite and inscribe these discourses and the subjects that are constituted through them. As Mike Apple (2001) has argued in relation to race, the insistent absent presence of white professional middle-classness and, by extension, the privilege of Whiteness (Ladsen-Billings, 2004; Leonardo, 2004; Gillborn, 2005), are inescapable here.

The specific pronunciation of Dir'y 'ippie is central to both Dir'y 'ippie and Shaza and Baza. Dir'y 'ippie as an injurious name is pronounced with an (imagined) 'real' east London accent. As a recuperated and re-inscribed self-identity it is pronounced with a self-conscious parody of this 'real' east London accent. Distinct modes of speech are also positioned as crucial markers of difference: Dir'y 'ippies 'speak quite clearly so you can understand' and implicitly the reverse is true for Shazas and Bazas. In the UK context where regional dialect and accent are prominent markers of social class, these assertions of differential modes of speech expose how the categorisations are infused by and inscribe a discourse of distinct and hierarchically organised social classes. The Dir'y 'ippies suggest that they 'know' how they are referred to while the Shazas and Bazas' 'failure' to know is indicated by their (imagined) whining 'ner ner', a non-linguistic utterance that constitutes their childishness or idiocy. As the group moves to this distinction between the two asserted sub-cultures, a discourse of differential intelligence is deployed. That this intelligence is constituted as classed – through silently cited discourses of predetermination, eugenics and merito-cracy – remains implicit. As the group turns to discuss modes of speech the discourse of classed intelligence that runs through these subjec-tivating discourses becomes overt. The assertion of distinct educational orientations, albeit an assertion that is internally disputed, also draws on and inscribes discourses of social class. When asked explicitly the group hesitantly confirms the social class distinctions between the categories.

These assertions of differential modes of speech expose how the cate-gorisations are infused by and inscribe a discourse of distinct and hier-archically organised social classes. That the opposition Dir'y 'ippie/ Shaza and Baza is synonymous with the opposition middle class/ work-ing class is inescapable. The assertion of distinct educational orienta-tions, albeit internally disputed, also draws on and inscribes discourses of social class. The intertwining of these multiple discourses is such that these discursive markers of difference are exposed as being commen-surate: 'middle-class-intelligent-positive educational orientation but not pro-school' (Dir'y 'ippies) comes to be understood in opposition to 'working-class-unintelligent-negative educational orientation and possibly anti-school' (Shazas and Bazas).

Dir'y 'ippie/Shaza and Baza is also marked by and simultaneously inscribes race. The group does not explicitly state that these apparent sub-cultures are in any way raced but this does not mean that race discourses are absent in the students' practices nor that their practices do not have raced effects. That the opposition is synonymous with middle-class/working-class infers that in some way the opposition is already raced: the disproportionate poverty of the non-White population in Britain implies that middle-class Dir'y 'ippies are predominantly but not exclusively White. The racialised nature of the opposition becomes more explicit when the group discusses named individuals: named Dir'y 'ippies are all White students, named Shazas are White and Mixed-race, named Bazas are White, Mixed-race and Black. The most notable absences are Black girls and Asian students. When I name Mridula, an Indian girl, the binary momentarily becomes a 'spectrum'. Nevertheless, in discussing (constituting) this spectrum, the opposition persists: Mridula is more of a Shaza than a Dir'y 'ippie. As such, the apparently Same/Other binary of Dir'y 'ippie/Shaza and Baza also functions as a totality of intelligibility in which there is no place for students from certain minority ethnic backgrounds. Students who fit neither category become the other-Other who are impossible subjects in the terms of this student milieu.

The silence around race combined with the normative status of White and the enduring privilege of Whiteness does not mean that the fashion and musical preferences that the group enlist to Dir'y ippie and allocate to Shaza and Baza are either race-neutral or simply White. Instead, the group identifies a Dir'y 'ippie eclecticism that is on the surface racially-inclusive (a pop-sub-cultural multicultural pluralism?). Yet this also appears to be the sort of expropriation of minority ethnic cultural forms that has been and remains constitutive and indicative of the operations of Whiteness. Simultaneously, the group rejects for themselves and allocates to Shazas and Bazas a particular, narrow set of mainstreamed 'Black' fashion and musical styles. While this might seem to allow Shaza and Baza a degree of racial diversity, it is a version of diversity that denies counter-cultural forms that have not been incorporated into the mainstream. It is once again a practice of Whiteness.

Dir'y 'ippie/Shaza and Baza is also constituted through and inscribes particular modes of intelligible masculinity, femininity and sexuality. Dir'y 'ippie incorporates both female and male students whereas the female and male parts of Shaza and Baza are distinct. The group's discussion of Shazas and Bazas cites discourses of compulsory heterosexuality and traditional modes of passive femininity and active masculinity, whereas their account of themselves cites liberal discourses of gender and sexuality equality/alternaeity. Indeed, a key feature of Dir'y 'ippie is that it embraces non-heterosexual identities and the additional value of these within the Dir'y 'ippie discourse and milieu.

Within institutional discourse of the ideal learner this ideal is a-sexual (Epstein and Johnson, 1998) and heteronormativity suggests that the good student is proto- (but not actively) heterosexual within institutional discourse. Yet the class, race and educational privilege of D'iry 'ippie appears to mediate this queer self-identification and render it institutionally acceptable (Youdell, 2004, 2005). Indeed, in a discursive frame of liberal-progressive education, the sub-cultural alternaeity of the Dir'y 'ippies and the claim to queerness that intersects this may even become evidence of their social, cultural and intellectual creativity. It is possible that they approximate the ideal learner not in spite of identifying as queer but because they are constituted through a constellation of discourses and subject positions that at once compensate for and valorise queerness.

Vici, Suzi, Tom and company believe that they are and constitute themselves as excluded ('outcast') from the mainstream of the student population on the basis that they are 'un-cool' Dir'y 'ippies. In this sub-cultural discursive frame it is the Dir'y 'ippies who are constituted or who constitute themselves as Other. They 'respond' to this Othering by constituting their marginalisation as a radical alternative and thereby recuperate it through an ironic/parodic/radical reinscription of the injurious name through which their marginality has been constituted. As such, the marginal Other is constituted as a radical and therefore desirable identity: it is constituted as *über* cool, but only to the marginalised elite that is 'in the know'.

Dir'y 'ippie contrasts with the other position apparently available to these students: Bod or Boffin. Acknowledging a positive educational orientation which might also be pro-school and confirming middle-class status threatens to undermine the radical Other location of D'iry 'ippie and recast it as the sub-cultural minority and the privileged Same (middle-class, high attaining). That is, it might be exposed as being Bod or Boffin. If this discursive shift occurs, then the conservative Same (sub-cultural majority) appears as the marginalised (working-class) Other, particularly within those discursive frames that exceed the limits of the school's student sub-cultures.

Middle-class-white-queer-high ability-alternative youth-culture/ Working-class-white-black-hetero-low ability-mainstream youth-culture

At a superficial level Dir'y 'ippies and Shazas and Bazas are readily recognisable and the distinctions between the two groups draw upon established social 'truths'. Yet while the Dir'y 'ippies report and offer a commentary on these 'truths' they also participate in a citational chain of classed and raced practices that constitutes these. These students constitute themselves and others as particular subjects. In so doing they inscribe those discourses of embedded, distinct, hierarchically organised, and classed and raced identities that are both necessary for the success of these performatives and entwined with educational inclusions and exclusions.

As noted, the particular performative names deployed by young people vary temporally and contextually: Sharons and Tracys become Shazas become Chavs. What remains constant is the way that pop/sub-cultural discourses and the performatives they cite obscure how they are marked by and constitutive of classed and raced subjectivities as well as class and race privileges and exclusions even in their silences about and denials of class and race.

Yet these silences, erasures and denials cannot undo these sedimented meanings. The intertwining of the discourses that are deployed explicitly and implicitly by the Dir'y 'ippies is such that particular discursive markers of difference do come to appear synonymous. middle-class, White, intelligent, liberal (radical? queer?), positive educational orientation (but not pro-school), good student, ideal learner (Dir'y 'ippies) becomes opposed to working-class, White or Black (but perhaps not other minority ethnicities), unintelligent, conservative (reactionary? traditional? homophobic?), negative educational orientation (and possibly anti-school), bad student, undesirable learner (Shazas and Bazas).

Helene Cixous and Catherine Clement's (1986) question *Where is she?* offers a series of pairs such as sun/moon, passive/active, whose privileged/subordinated and masculine/feminine relation are very clear. Taking the categorical subject positions through which the young people in this episode are made as recognisable subjects and recognisable subjects of schooling, the question can be asked, *Where is the ideal learner?*

Middle-class/working-class
White/Black

Hetero/homo (queer?)
Mainstream/alternative
High ability/low ability

When these hierarchical pairs are taken individually enduring discourses suggest that it is the leading term that will be synonymous with the ideal learner. When these are drawn into constellations and when the question is applied to the pair 'Dir'y 'ippie/Shaza Baza' this normative construction of 'who' might approximate the 'ideal' is troubled only by a highly contingent valorisation of queerness.

The turn to sub-cultural difference and marginality cannot erase the classed and raced nature of the constituting names deployed in this episode or their oblique but enduring intersection with school cultures. By extension this turn to sub-culture cannot overwrite the respective privilege and disadvantage embedded in them: in the classroom, the GCSE examination, the further and higher education market places and ultimately in the employment market, it is the Dir'y 'ippies – the White, middle-class, high attaining, and positively educationally orientated students – who score highly for Bourdieu's social, cultural, symbolic and linguistic capital (Bourdieu, 1990, 1991). It is how the students are recognised within these broader, official contexts that is likely to have the most bearing on educational experiences, outcomes, and futures.

Pipa, Suzi, Tom and Vici constitute themselves as marginal, as Other, in the student *milieu*. And yet as the group extrapolates *what they are not*, they inadvertently expose the institutional and social privilege, a privilege that rests upon middle-class Whiteness, that their practices eschew. These students are themselves implicated in the discursive production of the privilege of middle- classness and Whiteness through their apparently benign practices of youth sub-culture. And these practices are implicated even as they are produced as a site of imagined injury, of being called a name – Dir'y 'ippie – by a Shaza or a Baza.

References

Althusser, L (1971) Ideology and ideological state apparatuses. In L. Althusser, *Lenin and Philosophy*. London: Monthly Review Press, pp170-186

Apple, M W (2001) *Educating the 'Right' Way: Markets, standards, God, and inequality*. London: RoutledgeFalmer

Bourdieu, P (1984) *Distinction: A social critique of the judgement of taste*. Cambridge, Mass: Harvard UP

Bourdieu, P (1990) *The Logic of Practice*. Stanford: Stanford University Press

Bourdieu, P (1991) *Language and Symbolic Power*. Cambridge, Mass: Harvard University Press

Butler, J (1990) *Gender Trouble: Feminism and the subversion of identity.* London: Routledge

Butler, J (1993) *Bodies That Matter: On the Discursive Limits of 'Sex'.* London: Routledge

Butler, J (1997) *Excitable Speech: A politics of the performative.* London: Routledge

Cixous, H and Clement, C (1986) Sorties: out and out: attacks/ways out/forays. In H. Cixous and C. Clement, *The Newly Born Woman.* Minneapolis: University of Minnesota Press pp63-134

Derrida, J (1978) *On Writing and Difference.* London: Routledge

Derrida, J (1988) Signature event context. In *Limited Inc.* Elvanston: Northwestern University Press

Epstein, D and Johnson, R (1998) *Schooling Sexualities.* Buckingham: Open University Press

Foucault, M (1990) *The History of Sexuality: An introduction.* London: Penguin

Foucault, M (1991) *Discipline and Punish: The birth of the prison.* London: Penguin

Gillborn, D (2005) Education policy as an act of White supremacy: whiteness, critical race theory and education reform. *Journal of Education Policy* 20(4), 485-505

Hey. V (2006) The politics of performative resignification. *British Journal of Sociology of Education Special Issue, Troubling Identities: reflections on Judith Butler's philosophy for the sociology of education* 27(4), 439-459

Ladsen-Billings, G. (2004) Just what is Critical Race Theory and what's it doing in an nice field like education? In G. Ladsen-Billings and D. Gillborn (eds) *The RoutledgeFlamer Reader in Multicultural Education.* London: RoutledgeFalmer pp49-68.

Leonardo, Z (2004) The souls of White folk: critical pedagogy, whiteness studies, and globalization discourse. In G. Ladsen-Billings and D. Gillborn (eds) *The RoutledgeFlamer Reader in Multicultural Education.* London: RoutledgeFalmer pp117-136

Rasmussen, M L (2005) *Becoming Subjects.* London: Routledge

Rasmussen, M L (2006) Play School, melancholia, and the politics of recognition. *British Journal of Sociology of Education Special Issue, Troubling Identities: reflections on Judith Butler's philosophy for the sociology of education* 27(4), 473-488

Renold, E (2006) 'They won't let us play ... unless you're going out with one of them': girls, boys and Butler's heterosexual matrix in the primary years. *British Journal of Sociology of Education Special Issue, Troubling Identities: reflections on Judith Butler's philosophy for the sociology of education* 27(4), 489-510

Talburt, S and Steinberg S (eds) (2004) *Thinking Queer.* NY: Peter Lang

Youdell, D (2004) Wounds and reinscriptions: schools, sexualities and performative subjects, *Discourse* 25(4), 477-494

Youdell, D (2005) Bent as a ballet dancer: the possibilities and limits for a legitimate homosexuality in school. In M L Rasmussen, E Rofes and S Talburt (eds) *Youth and Sexualities: Pleasure, subversion and insubordination in and out of schools.* Basingstoke: Palgrave Macmillan pp201-222

Youdell, D (2006a) *Impossible Bodies, Impossible Selves: Exclusions and student subjectivities.* London: Springer

Youdell, D (2006b) Subjectivation and performative politics. *British Journal of Sociology of Education Special Issue, Troubling Identities: reflections on Judith Butler's philosophy for the sociology of education* 27(4), 511-529

14

Private lives: middle-class practices, class insulations and four-wheel drives

Stephen J Ball

An account of class, rank or social hierarchy must be thin indeed unless accompanied by an account of the passions and sentiments that sustain it (Miller, 1997, p245)

This chapter attempts to give a little thickness to the account of social class, specifically the middle class via an analysis of the sentiments of one social class fraction in one location. The financial middle class, what Bernstein calls agents of control in the economic field, who are 'likely to share common interests and common ideology' (Bernstein, 1990, p135) or what Savage, Barlow, Dickens and Fielding (1992) identify as post-moderns: private sector professionals in financial services, advertising or property, living in Battersea, South London. I draw obliquely and in speculative fashion on a set of data from an ESRC-funded study of middle-class (Vincent and Ball, 2006) or, more precisely, service-class (Goldthorpe, 1995) families in London[1]. The study focused on these families choosing childcare, but here I am not so much interested in this per se as in some aspects of the distinctions, symbolic and practical, which inform and organise their choices and some of the everyday class practices which are illuminated by their choices.

Class here means an identity and a lifestyle and a set of perspectives on the social world and relationships in it, marked by varying degrees of reflexivity. Class is also a trajectory, a path through space and time, a 'history of transactions' (Walzer, 1984) and some specific parts of a class trajectory are sketched in here. Class positions and perspectives are produced from and invested with the traces of earlier choices, improvisations and opportunities as well as being inflected by chance. Transactions are cumulative; 'aspects of action and interaction are constantly being negotiated, reformulated, modified and so on as a result of experience' (Devine, 1997, p9).

And why is the middle class interesting in relation to all this? As Savage (2000, p159) argues pertinently:

> If there is still a role for class analysis it is to continue to emphasise the brute realities of social inequality and the extent to which these are constantly effaced by a middle class, individualized culture that fails to register the social implications of its routine actions.

The specific concerns of this chapter focus on the organisation, sculpting and planning of the lives of young children or the logics and arts of social reproduction within the family. Here are some speculative possibilities for making sense of current aspects of class relations and practices: some of the ways in which middle-class families 'insert' their children into the social world through 'consumption practices' (Baudrillard, 1998, p60). The data are used as a set of starting points from which some indications of what may be more general developments in social life and spatial practices in world cities, around a particular set of themes, will emerge: privatised and defended social lives, cocooning, insular morality, social enclaves, homology and class advantage.

The distinctions and sentiments of this fraction and the logic of practice in which they are embedded constitute a particular local habitus. Robson and Butler (2001) argue that you cannot simply read off the values, attitudes and lifestyles of different class fractions from their occupational position. Middle-class formation is better understood as emerging from the interplay of capitals and habitus and the specific opportunities offered by particular market places. 'Our model of middle class diversity [is] as the outcome of social, occupational and spatial factors' (Robson and Butler, 2001, p2146).

The nub of Butler and Robson's argument is the importance of locality. They write about the way that middle-class individuals and groups, particularly those in dual income households with children, have 'reacted to the effect of globalisation on their careers and lives' (p2145). And argue that 'As they have increasingly lost a sense of place-based rootedness in the occupational hierarchy and services economy, they have struggled to replace these in their domestic and residential lives' (p2145), they claim that such middle-class groups 'desire to build a local community within the global city that maps onto their particular set of values, backgrounds, aspirations and resources' (p2150). As a result distinctive areas have been created with particular styles or characteristics, which reflect the lifestyle differences within the middle-class: 'different areas appeal to and attract different sections of the middle class' (p2149).

The result of all this is not a set of neat patterns but rather a concatenation of factors which have effects and consequences in terms of the realisation of class and class identities in particular settings. Savage, Bagnall *et al* (2004, p29) point out that localities are different 'sites for performing identities. Individuals attach their own biography to their 'chosen' residential location'. The processes of gentrification are 'localised' and involve 'differing relations to forms of capital' (Butler and Robson, 2001, p2160) enacted by different fractions of the middle class. Distinctive areas are thus created with particular styles or characteristics and represented by different narratives.

The place here is Battersea, or more precisely an area known as 'between the commons' (Wandsworth and Clapham) and also referred to as 'Nappy Valley' because of the high concentration of families with young children. Coincidentally it is where I live – in a sense I can claim to be a participant observer of the realisation of identities explored here. However, the area was chosen for other reasons, mainly because it had featured in the work of Butler and Robson, which gave us some sense of the sorts of middle-class families to be found there and a research base on which an analysis could be built.

A high proportion of the men and women in Battersea are employed in the financial sector. One of Butler and Robson's (2001, p2161) respondents commented that 'the Northcote Road [in Battersea] is like a branch of the City now'. Many of the world's largest financial companies are represented[2]. It is described by Butler and Robson (2001, p2153) as 'an area whose 'suitability' and 'habitability' have been assiduously contrived, primarily through manipulation of markets (in education, housing and leisure)'. 'Between the commons' 'has become a carefully cultivated 'urban village' in which young professionals can conveniently educate their children, work in the metropolitan economy and enjoy the pleasures of central London before moving on to still more desirable parts of Wandsworth or the southern home counties' (Butler with Robson *et al*, 2003, p17). The local middle-class, most of them at least, feel at ease here among others of their ilk.

> There are quite a lot of like-minded people in the area, well it's locally known as Nappy Valley, so there's lots of children's facilities, the Commons are an attraction ... I know quite a lot of people in the area, so I feel quite comfortable here (Cheryl)

> ... it has changed, and obviously an awful lot of estate agents where there used to be shoe menders and things ... you can't buy proper food now really in the market so much as you used to, it's all olive stalls and basket making and things like that (Lindsay)

In the central area of 'between the commons', the houses are mainly three or four bedroom Victorian terraces, extremely well-maintained and often extended: lofts, basements and side-extensions to kitchens. Currently even the smaller terraced houses go for £700,000 plus. Thus the residents are strong in economic capital and this can be seen in the type of shops and restaurants that flourish on the main thoroughfares and the proliferation of private schools in the area. The respondents in our study who lived in Battersea, when asked what attracted them to the area, mentioned the presence of many other families with young children, the array of child-friendly activities that have developed to cater for families and the 'good' private schools. As respondents described it:

> We moved from a childless area to 'Buggy Jams.' (Margot)

> ... perfect for children, it's not called Nappy Valley for nothing. (Lynn)

> Both people we shared [our nannies] with were accountants, they're all accountants round here. (Linda)

> Both of us are very committed to state education which is very unusual in this area. (Linda)

Family life 'between the commons'

Outlined here is part of a temporal-spatial grid within which a particular kind of childhood is constructed. It is a grid with tight boundaries and fixed temporal sequences. It is a grid of local space and spaces: homes (and nannies), nurseries, activities, and private schools which are joined up by cars, of a particular kind, and linked over time through the project of the production of children as particular kinds of educational subjects. It is a project driven by 'futurity', based upon careful planning for and investment in the educational futures of children, typically long-term. It is a grid of insulations, of homogamy (literally self-fertilisation), 'marked and ordered' by 'implicit cognitive and social messages' (Bernstein, 1990, p80). It rests on a 'collectively orchestrated' selection of spaces and places within which, in Bernstein's (1990) terms, 'pollution is necessarily visible' and the fundamental rule is that 'things must be kept apart' (p81).

By commenting briefly on each of the components of the grid – nannies, nurseries, activities, schools and cars – I hope to convince readers that there is some kind of articulated cultural unity here, at the centre of which is what Bourdieu calls 'homogamy'. Bourdieu (1987, p6) argues that 'The homogenising effect of homogenous conditionings is at the basis of those dispositions which favour the development of relationships, formal or informal (like homogamy), which tend to increase this very homogeneity'. There are certainly plenty of indications in the data of the ways in which childcare and educational settings are sought and used by these families to maintain and ensure social homogamy. Homogamy rests upon and is demonstrated within the power of allusions, asides, avoidances and aversion, the work of loose-fitting but practical classifications, senses 'of place' and of 'being out of place'. In other words, a sense of social structure, 'a structure of affinity and aversion' (Bourdieu, 1987, p7).

Some of these nuances of aversion and attraction can be best glimpsed through the eyes of Battersea 'dissidents', those families who find their sentiments askew in relation to their neighbours, who are themselves a little 'out of place' and discomfited by their social and cultural surroundings, whose habitus is slightly misaligned with the 'local'. These discomforts and misalignments make some of what is implicit and embedded in habitus momentarily visible. Whereas normally, as Bourdieu (1990, p61) suggests, through the 'systematic 'choices' it makes among the places, events and people that might be frequented, the habitus tends to protect itself from crises and critical challenges by providing itself with a milieu to which it is as pre-adapted as possible'. Accounts of some of these dissidents follow.

Take Sally for instance. Although intending to send her children to a private school, she contrasts herself and her family with the sorts of middle-class parents to be found in some of the private schools in the locality she has visited. They are 'sort of very City men and sort of flowery women, and we didn't feel comfortable with that either for the children or for ourselves'. She spoke about the relative social mix in the school she eventually chose whereas 'some of the other schools we started to call Christian master race schools'. Sally also pointed to some subtle differences between her child and what she described as the 'very well-dressed class' that attend her daughter's nursery; dress (flowery women) is a subtle but effective signifier of difference here.

Alice wanted the locally-preferred middle-class state primary school (Goldwater) for her son: 'I'm very keen that he should go state. I think it's a really good start rather than imagining that the whole world consists of Volvos and four-wheel drives'. Again, by allusion, Alice points to and wants to avoid for her child the possibility of a life-world view constructed within and limited to a particular sort of and different middle-class social environment from her own. She wants to evade for her child some of the social messages embedded in the local habitus.

Juliet is thinking of nursery schooling, in part at least, in relation to where her daughter will go to primary school and whether she can get her into Goldwater, where:

> there's lots of well-heeled middle class parents but there's also a council estate on the doorstep so there's a kind of mixture which is nice. It's not all people driving four-wheel drives like the school across the road [a private school] where you see the kind of procession of armoured cars to collect these children. It's a fantastic school, they are interviewing children at three ... my [daughter'd] probably do really well but I don't like the whole deal really, plus you have to cough up a large amount of money not just for the school but for the uniform.

Once more there is a visibility of distinctions, through the rejection of middle-class 'others', the middle class who are 'not us', the carriers of values into which these 'dissident' parents do not want their child socialised. Nonetheless, Julia also points up the tension between normative differences and structural advantage, and the imperative to 'do the best' for your child – 'putting the family first' (Ball, 2003). Because, 'then again, if we got into Goldwater [the local state school], she'd be thrown into a class of thirty kids so I don't know, we are tending toward private at the moment'.

Home and nanny

In Battersea qualified nannies are widely used, especially for younger children, in about equal numbers to private nurseries. There is a growing number of nanny agencies in the locality. In 2004 the average rate for a central London full-time live-out nanny was £27,000 gross. In their study of six London localities Butler with Robson *et al* (2003, p114) found nannies to be the most popular choice of child care in only two areas, Battersea and Barnsbury, and they make the point that this 'kept control by ensuring that all socialisation occurred within the home'[3]. More precisely, employing a nanny allows parents to retain a degree of control over such issues as food, television watching and play activities.

In practice children move around with nannies, who congregate in local cafes and again meet other children like themselves. Nonetheless, for the most part, the use of nannies and the local private day nurseries both provided for secure, closed and carefully crafted social relations and social networks around childcare:

> We're massively lucky because we can afford to do it this way because its incredibly expensive. We do pay tax, we employ her full-time to give me flexibility and all the other activities that he [son] does on top of that I reckon it would come to £35-40,000 a year. (Philippa)

Nurseries

The nurseries used by most of this sample were expensive and exclusive, socially segregated and linked to local circuits of private schooling:

> It's children like our children, so children of middle-class parents who can afford to spend nearly nine hundred pounds a month sending their kid to childcare (Cheryl)

They also evinced a pedagogic style which tends towards the 'visible'. At Goldfinch staff members talked about their good relationship with private prep schools in the area:

> Yes, and we're very fortunate here, and I'm sure people hear this, that the children do manage to get into schools of their first choice. Usually that's the case. And that's bound to, sort of, get around as well. And that might help [recruitment] ... (Owner)

This nursery is aware of its place in the local private care and education systems. This awareness means that it seeks to some extent to tailor its provision to the pedagogies in operation at the private prep schools. It is a Montessori-influenced setting but does not operate in strict Montessori style, because:

> Montessori is all about free choice ... And you do not sit them down and say, 'right, we're all going to have a work session now.' If they spent their entire time doing exactly what they chose to do, when they went, as you said, on to Eton House, Broomwood, Thomas', they would struggle so badly, because they're made to sit there. And that's why you really – we couldn't do it, could we? It would be awful for them. (Staff member)

> So, even at two and a half they are encouraged to come and work with the teacher, come and sit at the table. It might last for thirty seconds, and if that's all then that's fine. Just to get used to working with the teacher, listening to her instructions and then carrying them out. But it really is alright if they just, you know, stay for a minute or so, and then go off and choose their own work. But that's what they'll be doing in the next setting. (Owner)

There appeared to be significant differences in the pedagogies employed at nurseries in Battersea and our other research setting Stoke Newington. As far as we can tell from our data, the private elite Battersea nurseries were more formal, with a stronger classification of activities and clear boundaries between work and play (Vincent and Ball, 2006). The headteacher of the local state infant school talked of 'converting' parents whose children attend the local private nurseries away from more formal approaches to learning which she associates with private schools:

> And if they want their child to be learning in a vertical way, where they're just being taught the skills for reading, writing, learning another language, then perhaps our way isn't the right way, isn't the best place for their child to be. [...] Parents who want something a little bit more formal very often will go to a private school that will teach their children in that way. And that's their decision; that's their decision.

For the children of the local middle class, nursery schooling provides the first glimpse of the sort of 'pressured academic environment' (Lacey, 1974) that will be part of their educational experience for many years to come. They are beginning to learn to become the applied, productive and successful educational subjects that the social reproduction of their class requires:

> We're not a pushy – I wouldn't say we're a pushy school at all. But then, if we know a child is able to achieve a certain amount of work, we won't take, sort of, their sloppiness, we'll say, 'oh come on', you know, 'we can do better than that. Let's have another go and see if we can do it even better than that'. But just, sort of, you know, being fun about it, but pushing them onto that next step all the time ... (Manager, Sparrow nursery)

The stretching and preparing of the child also goes on at home as cultural capital is transmitted within the family. It also occurs through paying for extra-curricular activities.

Activities
Another enclave of social and cultural reproduction is provided by 'enrichment activities' – private, paid-for classes and activities.

The 'making up' of the child in terms of particular 'talents' or 'abilities' is 'the product of an investment of time and cultural capital' (Bourdieu, 2004, p17) and also money. Increasingly this 'making up' involves drawing upon a whole range of commercial activities and entertainments. The buying-in of experiences and advice and support also extends to tutoring and parenting classes.

Table 1. Number of families mentioning environment activities for their children in our two research settings

	Music	Ballet/Dance	Gym	French	Drama	Sport
Battersea (26)	23	6	6	7	2	7
Stoke Newington (28)	15	8	1	5	4	5

> You [to son] used to enjoy music, didn't you? ... And [son] did a French course in the summer. Again, [carer] took him, I took him if I was at home, [carer] took him if I wasn't. And it has worked very well. It is expensive, that's the drawback, it is very expensive ... (Margaret)

> [The nanny] used to take her to Tin Pan Annie, which is a, sort of, a music class around here ... all these other things which cost an arm and a leg? (Kathryn)

All of this must be scheduled and serviced by carers as children are escorted or driven from one activity to the next. These activities take the place of an unsupervised public life for the child:

> Yes, we have an eldest child who has got an enormous amount of energy ... and has wanted to get into everything. Last year he was doing tennis, swimming, he was in the school play ... and that took up early evening and lots of the days. So, that's, sort of, singing, drama. Art he did, they've all done French club. They both started piano and didn't want to continue, which is a real pity; still, I think he might come back to that. And now [one son] wants to learn the saxophone, but we'll have to see about that. (Judy)

The other role and perceived benefit of these activities is to prepare the child for success at school. They are evidence of the planning ahead, the concern with the future that defines the approach of the middle classes to education (Ball, 2003). As well as being fun for toddlers, enrichment activities have a second practical purpose for the future, apart from ensuring that the child is in a state of 'learning readiness'. This is to formulate the beginnings of a CV for the child. A proven track record in music, drama, art or sport can increase a child's attractiveness in a competitive private school market it serves as symbolic capital and profits of distinction.

The enrichment activities and classes suggest an accumulation of 'gratuitous knowledge' through 'unintended learning made possible by a disposition acquired through domestic or scholarly inculcation of legitimate culture' (Bourdieu, 2004, pp26-30). This is 'the work of the bourgeois family' and their agents. It involves the development of 'the capacity for inspired encounters with works of art and high culture in general' or an introduction to 'the principles of specific aesthetic legitimacy' in particular artistic fields. Through activities and visits to galleries and museums and confrontations with conventions and institutions the child is inducted into the 'caste' of 'those who understand'.

Private schooling

> The local state schools here have got 40 per cent of children who come from homes where English is not the first language, it seems to me a little unfair on Ben if he's going into the classroom and there's gonna be time spent with 'hair', 'coat', 'shoes', 'drink' which he is almost doing now. I think it's likely that the children are going to end up in a fee-paying school. (Diane)

For many of the Battersea parents, private schools offer a cultural milieu, 'a communicative order of self-recognition' (Teese, 1981, pp103-4), which is coherent and undiluted, and constitutes a 'protected enclave for class formation' (Sedden, 2001, p134). As Teese (2000) concludes, private schools are fortified sites within diverse school systems which represent class projects and 'renew middle-class culture and collectivity in predictable ways across generations'. The lives of these children are carefully sculpted within carefully chosen locations of play and learning, separated and shielded from 'dangerous' others:

> ...then again, if we got into Goldwater [the local state school], she'd be thrown into a class of thirty kids so I don't know, we are tending toward private at the moment. (Andrea)

> I think morally I'd quite like for them to go to state school but in fact both of us realised that it would take a lot to persuade us that it was not a benefit to send them private given that we could just about afford it, we thought it would be better. (Diane)

These schools are forms of escape from the risky business of state schooling and its social mixing and concomitant distributions and redistributions of teachers' time and attention. Private schools 'sell themselves' both in terms of the advantages they offer and the particular values they seek to transmit: 'they're very academically focused, they also do really good sport, but it's still really high pressure' (Monica).

The schools represent and embody traditional forms of education, as signified in the peculiarities of their uniforms which are very much forms of reinvented tradition: straw hats for girls and caps and blazers for boys, knickerbockers, pinafores and gym-slips, the games played (rugby, cricket, lacrosse), church attendance and the familiar curriculum structures and contents. As with the children's activities, uniforms and team games are part of the inculcation of gender-appropriate 'embodied dispositions', making the child's body readable in a particular way and subject to visible classification. In both these sites there is learning about gender, self-control, social graces, and skills of interaction. Bourdieu asserts that 'Taste, a class culture turned into nature, that is, embodied, helps shape the class body' (Bourdieu, 1986, p190).

Defensive automobilities

The four-wheel drive (Lexus, BMW, Volvo, Mercedes, Range Rover and Chrysler) is one of the recurring markers of fractional distinction in the Battersea area. The 'deviations and dissidences' (Butler with Robson *et al*, 2003, p49) in these data point up the 4WD as a tactical demarcator in the definition of class fractions and who and what they are and are not. What does this signify and communicate? How does it represent the predominant values and lifestyle, the habitus of the Battersea middle class? I suggest, not with great originality, that the 4WD as part of an ensemble of social practices indicates and enacts, to use Faith Popcorn's term, the social 'cocooning' of this class fraction. Cocooning is the act of insulating or hiding oneself from the normal social environment or what Popcorn defines as 'the need to protect oneself from the harsh, unpredictable realities of the outside world' (Popcorn and Marigold, 1997, p7).

The 4WD is a defensive/aggressive choice of car. It enacts both style and substance. It fits with local norms of display and presentation, inscribing distinction 'in the hard durable reality of things' (Bourdieu, 1990, p139). Its size and construction provide a highly protected environment, a form of what Williams (1983, p188) called 'mobile privatisation', 'an ugly phrase for an unprecedented condition', in which 'people are living as private small-family units' in a time of unprecedented mobility. This also articulates more generally with the residents' descriptions of the 'between the commons' area and their reasons for choosing it as somewhere to live. 'Safety' is referred to repeatedly (Butler with Robson *et al*, 2003, p85-90). In relation to this, the 4WD makes its particular contribution to the 'visual landscape of fear' (Low, 2004, p56).

Many of us drive cars of some kind, and too many people drive their children to school. But the 4WD in this context carries connotations of a whole 'stylisation of life' and a particular values set. It is associated here in particular with the school run and the schools of choice for these families are private social enclaves themselves. However, the distaste or disgust expressed by some of the Battersea 'dissidents' for the 4WD is perhaps indicative of other 'fractional' class differences located within matters of lifestyle. Lawler (2005, p438) suggests that 'disgust is an immensely powerful indicator of the interaction between the personal and the social', and here may indicate some kind of adherence by the 'dissents' to what Savage, Barlow *et al* (1992) call the 'liberal professional/ascetic' fragment of the middle class and its avoidance of conspicuous consumption.

Discussion

What exists here, following Butler and Robson (2001), is the realisation of a particular and distinct, localised middle-class habitus in Battersea, which is rooted in a specific combination of capitals and forms of social relationships. 'This *spatialization of class* binds populations together in imaginary ways according to the micro-territories they inhabit ...' (Burrows and Gane, 2006, p808). Battersea, as Butler and Robson put it, has a 'one-dimensional and rather stifling atmosphere of conformity' (2001, p2153) and a 'very strong sense of 'people like us' gathering together' (p2153). This commonality and the concomitant sense of safety and convenience of schools and services are important to many of the inhabitants. Social capital and mutuality are horizontal and primarily instrumental. Social capital is 'present but latent and masked by a culture in which 'eating out' is preferred over 'joining in' (Butler with Robson *et al*, 2003, p12) and 'the common good in Battersea is established through market-based commonalities of interest based on households acting atomistically' (Butler and Robson *et al*, 2001, p2159). Although the local Natural Childbirth Trust was very active and a number of our respondents were members and some participated in a local Residents Association, of the six localities studied by Butler with Robson (2003, p123), Battersea had the lowest proportion of respondents who were members of trade unions (24 per cent) and the lowest reporting social, political or religious activity membership (12 per cent).

There is little evidence of what Sharon Zukin calls 'mingling with strangers' (Zukin, 1995) as a basis for 'shaped citizenship'. Indeed, the social lives and relations of the Battersea families are tightly bounded and well-insulated from the frissons and ambiguities of the theatre of the city with its class, gender, ethnic and sexual mixes. Nor is there much indication of the development of an everyday social confidence or tolerance of difference, which Zukin sees as coming from sharing public spaces with others. The majority of the Battersea families, except the 'dissents', seem concerned to establish firm boundaries and relative social exclusivity from the earliest stages of their children's care and education. The Battersea children move from nannies at home to private nurseries to private school, all of which are privileged and 'secure sites' insulated from the social mix and social diversity (Teese, 2000).

The 'good life' is located firmly within the family. These families are sure of themselves and their values, they are confident and convey a sense of entitlement but also seem wary of the risks and insecurities of social life in London. This area is being socially constituted as a kind of 'privatopia' (McKenzie, 1994) made up of homogenous social settings – private nurseries and schools, private activities and leisure, and private health insurance. Battersea is increasingly becoming an exclusionary class enclave where personal rather than public values predominate and 'sameness, status and security' (Low, 2004, p46) are realised[4].

Notes

1 The research (Nov 2001-April 2004) explores how middle-class parents choose childcare for their young children in two London settings. The project as a whole addresses a set of issues embedded in the operation of 'lived' pre-school, child care markets. The study is a qualitative one, which will when completed involve some 114 semi-structured interviews with parents (57 mothers and 14 fathers) and providers as well as others closely involved in local childcare provision. It builds upon a pilot study (see Vincent and Ball, 2001). The sample was elicited in a variety of ways; by advertising in local magazines and NCT newsletters; putting up posters in local shops, libraries and child care facilities; by attending child care events and facilities and approaching parents or carers directly; and by word-of-mouth 'snowballing'.

2 In contrast, in our other research area, Stoke Newington, a high proportion are employed in the arts, media, law and higher education. A specific combination of social, cultural and economic factors make Stoke Newington and Battersea inhabitable in different ways by middle-class families (see Ball, S. J., C. Vincent, *et al* (2004) Middle class fractions, childcare and the 'relational' and 'normative' aspects of class practices, *the Sociological Review* 52, 478-502).

3 Battersea parents were also the most reluctant to allow their children to play outside unsupervised (Butler and Robson 2003 p129).

4 This chapter relies heavily on research analysis and writing done with Carol Vincent and has benefited from long-standing arguments with her about what can and cannot be said about our sample and about different class strategies. I am grateful.

References

Ball, S J (2003) *Class Strategies and the Education Market: The middle class and social advantage.* London: RoutledgeFalmer

Baudrillard, J (1998) *The Consumer Society.* London, Sage

Bernstein, B (1990) *The Structuring of Pedagogic Discourse.* London: Routledge

Bourdieu, P (1986) *Distinction: A social critique of the judgement of taste.* London: Routledge.

Bourdieu, P (1987) What makes a social class? On the theoretical and practical existence of groups. *Berkeley Journal of Sociology* 23(1), 1-17

Bourdieu, P (1990) *The Logic of Practice.* Cambridge: Polity Press

Bourdieu, P (2004) Forms of capital. In Ball, S J, *The RoutledgeFalmer Reader in the Sociology of Education.* London: RoutledgeFalmer

Burrows, R and Gaine, N (2006) Geodeographics, software and class. *Sociology* 40(5), 793-812

Butler, T and Robson, G (2001) Social capital, gentrification and neighbourhood change in London: a comparison of three South London neighbourhoods. *Urban Studies* 38(12), 2145-2162

Butler, T and Robson, G (2003) Negotiating their way in: the middle classes, gentrification and the deployment of capital in a global metropolis. *Urban Studies* 40(9), 1791-1809

Butler, T and Robson, G (2003) Plotting the middle classes in London: gentrification and circuits of education in London. *Housing Studies* 18(1), 5-28

Butler, T. with Robson, G *et al* (2003) *London Calling: The Middle Classes and the Remaking of Inner London.* Oxford: Berg

Devine, F (1997) *Privilege, Power and the Reproduction of Advantage.* British Sociological Association Annual Conference, University of York 7-10 April

Goldthorpe, J (1995) The service class revisited. In Butler, T and Savage, M. (eds) *Social Change and the Middle Classes.* London: UCL Press

Lacey, C (1974) Destreaming in a 'pressured' academic environment. In Eggleston, J. (ed) *Contemporary Research in the Sociology of Education.* London: Methuen

Lawler, S (2005) Disgusted subjects: the making of middle class identities. *The Sociological Review* 53(3), 429-446

Low, S (2004) *Behind the Gates: Life, Security and the Pursuit of Happiness in Fortress America.* New York: Routledge

McKenzie, E (1994) *Privatopia: Homeowner Associations and the rise of residential private government.* New Haven: Yale University Press

Miller, W (1997) *An Anatomy of Disgust.* Cambridge MA: Harvard University Press

Popcorn, F and Marigold, L (1997) *Clicking: 17 Trends That Drive Your Business – And Your Life.* New York: Harper Collins

Robson, G and Butler, T (2001) Coming to terms with London: middle class communities in a global city. *International Journal of Urban and Regional Research* 25(1), 70-86

Savage, M (2000) *Class Analysis and Social Transformation.* Buckingham: Open University Press

Savage, M and Bagnall, G (2004) *Globalization and Belonging.* London: Sage

Savage, M, Barlow, J *et al* (1992) *Property, Bureaucracy and Culture: Middle class formation in contemporary Britain.* London: Routledge

Sedden, T (2001) Revisiting Inequality and education; a reminder of class; a retrieval of politics; a rethinking of governance. *Melbourne Studies in Education* 42(2), 131-144

Teese, R (1981) The social function of private schools. *Melbourne Working Papers.* University of Melbourne: Sociology Research Group

Teese, R (2000) *Academic Success and Social Power: Examinations and Inequality.* Melbourne: Melbourne University Press

Vincent, C and Ball, S J (2001) A market in love? Choosing pre-school child care. *British Educational Research Journal* 27(5), 633-651

Vincent, C and Ball, S J (2006) *Childcare, Choice and Class Practices: Middle-class Parents and their children.* London: Routledge

Vincent, C, Ball, S J, *et al* (2004) The social geography of childcare: making up a middle class child. *British Journal of Sociology of Education* 25(2), 229-244

Walzer, M (1984) *Spheres of Justice: A defence of pluralism and equality.* Oxford: Martin Robertson

Williams, R (1983) *Towards 2000.* London: Chatto and Windus

Zukin, S (1995) *The Culture of Cities.* Oxford: Blackwell

Notes on contributors

Elizabeth Atkinson is a Reader in Social and Educational Inquiry in the School of Education and Lifelong Learning, University of Sunderland. She has published widely on educational research, policy and practice, particularly in relation to the need for radical uncertainty in the over-certain audit culture of contemporary education. Her recent and current research focuses on equality and social justice, with a specific focus on lesbian, gay, bisexual and transgender equality in primary school settings. Elizabeth is the Director of the ESRC-funded *No Outsiders* project, which supports primary teachers in exploring strategies to challenge heteronormativity and address sexualities equality in their own professional settings. For more information about the project, go to http://www.nooutsiders. sunderland.ac.uk.

Stephen J Ball is Karl Mannhein Professor of Sociology of Education at the Institute of Education, University of London. His work is in 'policy sociology' – the use of sociological theories, concepts and methods to critically interrogate policy processes and policy effects. His substantive interests are in the 'market form' and social class. His most recent books are *Education plc: private sector participation in public sector education* (Routledge, 2007) and *Education Policy and Social Class* (Routledge, 2006). Stephen is an Academician of Social Science and a Fellow of the British Academy.

Renée DePalma received her PhD in 2003 from the University of Delaware (USA), where she developed and taught modules on equality and diversity for trainee teachers. Her research and teaching has focused on social justice in terms of ethnicity, language, race, gender and sexuality. She has been working at the University of Sunderland in sexualities equality research since 2004, and is currently working as Research Fellow for the *No Outsiders* project.

Stephen Dobson is professor in education at Lillehammer University College, Norway. He is joint leader of the Norwegian national network for pupil assessment and his research interests include refugees, youth cultures, assessment and educational philosophy. He has also published a collection of poems in Norwegian.

David Gough is Professor of Evidence Informed Policy and Practice and Director of the Social Science Research Unit (SSRU) and its Evidence for Policy and Practice Information and Coordinating (EPPI) Centre, Institute of Education, University of London. Previously he worked at the University of Glasgow and Japan Women's University. He directs the Methods for Research Synthesis node of the ESRC National Centre for Research Methods and research projects for the Department for Education and Skills, the Teacher Training and Development Agency, the Social Care Institute of Excellence, and the Department for Work and Pensions. He is editor of the journal *Child Abuse Review* and associate editor of the journal *Evidence and Policy.*

Dr Ruby Greene is a lecturer in the Centre for Health Planning and Management at Keele University and programme director for the MSc course in Reproductive Health Management. She is the course director for the Reproductive Health and the Health Information Education and Communication Strategies and is responsible for short courses in Programme Management in HIV/AIDS for Developing Countries, and the Planning and Management of Maternal and Child Health. She is module director for the Key Skills module for all of the Centre's postgraduate programmes. Her areas of speciality include adolescent fertility, reproductive health including HIV/AIDS and sex education. She is a member of the Royal Society for Health and a book review editor for the *International Journal of Health Planning and Management*. Her research interests are in transactional sex, sexual and reproductive health issues affecting BME populations and sex education. For further information please contact r.greene@keele.ac.uk.

Jennifer Lavia is a Lecturer at the School of Education, University of Sheffield and Director of its Caribbean Programme. She is coordinator of the School's Discussion Group on Postcolonial Theories, Education and Development. Jennifer's main research and teaching areas include: Caribbean Studies in Education; Gender and Education; Teacher Professionalism; Educational Research for Social Justice; Narrative Research; Postcolonial Theories; and Educational Leadership.

Ahmad Nazari has a PhD in Applied Linguistics from King's College London. He has taught at the University of Hertfordshire and the University of Sunderland in the UK. He is currently the MA TESOL Programme leader at the University of Sunderland where he teaches Theories of L2 Learning, Language and Power and Research Methods to MA TESOL students. He is also a reviewer of the ELT journal. His key area of interest lies in processes of L2 learning and teaching.

Carrie Paechter is Professor of Education and Dean of the Graduate School at Goldsmiths College, London. Her research interests, which have been developed out of her experience as a mathematics teacher in London secondary schools, include the intersection of gender, power and knowledge, the construction of identity, especially with regard to gender, space and embodiment in and outside schooling, and the processes of curriculum negotiation. She regards herself as a Foucaultian poststructuralist feminist in orientation and writes regularly on issues of research methodology in this context. Her most recent books are *Educating the*

Other: gender, power and schooling (1998, Falmer Press), *Changing School Subjects: power, gender and curriculum* (2000, Open University Press) and *Being Boys, Being Girls: learning masculinities and femininities* (2007, Open University Press).

Michael Reiss is Professor of Science Education at the Institute of Education, University of London and Head of its School of Mathematics, Science and Technology. He is Director of Education at the Royal Society, Chief Executive of Science Learning Centre London, Honorary Visiting Professor at the University of York, Docent at the University of Helsinki, Director of the Salters-Nuffield Advanced Biology Project, a member of the Farm Animal Welfare Council and editor of the journal *Sex Education*. His research and consultancy interests are in science education, bioethics and sex education. For further information see www.reiss.tc.

John Storey is Professor of Cultural Studies and Director of the Centre for Research in Media and Cultural Studies, University of Sunderland, He has published widely in cultural studies, including six books. His work has been translated into Chinese, German, Japanese, Korean, Persian, Polish, Serbian, Spanish, Swedish, and Ukrainian. He is a Visiting Professor at the universities of Henan and Wuhan, China.

Takano Takako works as an independent researcher and lecturer, a visiting professor at WASEDA University in Tokyo, and a chair of an educational charity called ECOPLUS based in Japan. She is a board member of Japan Environmental Education Forum, Outward Bound School Japan and National Myoko Outdoor Learning Center, international committee member of Japan Camp Association. Her research and consultancy involves community enhancement, place-based education and sustainability education.

Maddalena Taras is senior lecturer in the School of Education and Lifelong Learning at the University of Sunderland. Her research expertise and interests focus on assessment theory and practice, particularly self-assessment, and metaphoric constraints of language in academic contexts.

Deborah Youdell is a Senior Lecturer in the Sociology of Education at the Institute of Education, University of London. Her work is concerned with understanding subjectivities, including race, ethnicity, gender, sexuality, social class and ability and disability, and their connections to social injustices and educational inequalities. She is co-author, with David Gillborn, of *Rationing Education: policy, practice, reform and equity*. Her recent book, *Impossible Bodies, Impossible Selves: exclusions and student subjectivities*, was published in 2006 by Springer.

Index

Citation index